Jack The Ripper:

Straight for the Jugular

by
Prash Ganendran

Copyright © 2021 by Prash Ganendran
All rights reserved. No part of this book may be reproduced or used in any manner without written permission of the copyright owner except for the use of quotations in a book review.

Why *this* Jack the Ripper book?

Out of all the books out there on Jack the Ripper, why should you choose this one? Some authors write purely about their own favoured suspect and present new theories, while others specialize in the history and geography of the Whitechapel area. What I offer you is a detailed yet concise account of the Jack the Ripper murders, with sufficient depth to provide a thorough understanding of the case, but without unnecessary prevarication or idle speculation. In short, I go 'straight for the jugular!'

I've added colour to the story with an omnium-gatherum of snippets about the denizens of Whitechapel and the social context in which they lived, and along the way we'll be checking in with what the police and press were up to during the Autumn of Terror. We'll learn about the lives of the victims, and we'll also tackle some important questions, such as:

- Did detectives really dress up as women?
- Why did The Ripper stop killing (or did he?)
- How can we apply our modern knowledge of crime to shed light on the Whitechapel Murders?
- Could criminal profiling help to solve the case?
- What misconceptions and fallacies have crept in over the last century?

This book assumes no prior knowledge and is accessible for those who are new to studying Jack the Ripper, but also provides a substantial refresher for those who already have some familiarity. I won't try to sell you my favourite suspect (although I do have one, of course), but I will impartially examine the candidacy of the most well-known suspects. By the end of the book, you will be able to hold your own in any conversation about the Whitechapel murders. The case will soon draw you into its dimly lit, foggy depths and refuse to let you go, as you venture into a story of horror and depravity which left behind no conclusion, only pages full of unanswered questions.

How this book came about

I have been fascinated by the case for more than 25 years, after discovering and promptly devouring a book in my local library at the age of eight. I kept on asking the question, who *was* Jack the Ripper? Countless others have wondered the same thing, and countless more will do so as future generations discover the mystery for the first time.

I forgot about true crime for many years as the day-to-day demands of adult life took over, but when I found myself forced to spend hours lying down each day due to the onset of a degenerative spinal condition in 2017, I rediscovered my passion for being an armchair detective and began reading more on the subject and listening to podcasts and audiobooks.

In 2020 I started my own successful true crime podcast, *Prash's Murder Map*, covering crimes from across the globe, both solved and unsolved, including the cryptic, baffling case of the Zodiac Killer. But I couldn't be entirely satisfied until I had tackled Jack the Ripper. The material could not be dealt with in one 45-minute episode, so I dedicated a whole series to it, brought to life with voiceovers, sound effects, and music. Some of the characters' voices were lent by well-known Ripper historians Philip Hutchinson and Karl Coppack, along with former Scotland Yard Detective Peter Bleksley.

Due to my spinal condition, I stopped the show as it was becoming too physically demanding. Instead, I decided to turn the material I had painstakingly gathered into a collection, which is now a book called *I Just Wanted To Kill: 15 True Crime Cases*. I wanted my Jack the Ripper series to bloom into a book too, so I continued my research and added further details to transform it into the volume you now hold in your hands. If you would like to explore my podcast, all the episodes remain in the public domain on all major podcast platforms, for old and new listeners to enjoy.

I have been careful to check every detail to separate fact from fiction; not an easy task as the waters have been muddied over the years, but everything I've stated can be verified and I've tried to make it clear when something is just a theory or my own speculation. All the sources are listed at the back of the book.

Any dialogue included has been taken from the inquest documentation or police records from the time. Finally, as I am from the UK, please note that spellings are British English. I hope you enjoy the book. Please consider leaving me a rating and a review as I love to read constructive feedback.

Contents

WHY *THIS* JACK THE RIPPER BOOK? 2

HOW THIS BOOK CAME ABOUT 3

LONDON'S EAST END AND THE EARLY WHITECHAPEL MURDERS 6

MARY ANN "POLLY" NICHOLS 30

ANNIE CHAPMAN 52

ELIZABETH "LIZ" STRIDE 83

CATHERINE EDDOWES 107

MARY JANE KELLY 145

AFTERMATH 179

THE SUSPECTS 193

Chapter One
London's East End and the early Whitechapel Murders

Whitechapel 1888. Murky streets lit only by a flickering gaslight casting malevolent shadows in every corner. A looming, faceless figure leaning over a mutilated body, then disappearing like a phantom into the maze of narrow streets. Letters written in blood-red ink.

This is the case everyone has heard of, one of the original unsolved mysteries that not only haunted the streets of London's East End, but still haunts researchers and true crime enthusiasts today, over a century later. It is the most memorable case where an unforgettable nickname was bestowed upon the killer, conjuring up images of a demon dressed as a doctor, clutching a bag full of implements of death - although we'll soon see that this symbolic portrayal was far from the truth.

This is the story of Jack the Ripper. It is also the story of the victims. The canonical five: Mary Ann Nichols, Annie Chapman, Elizabeth Stride, Catherine Eddowes, and Mary Jane Kelly, as well as two women who were killed shortly before the Autumn of Terror: Emma Smith and Martha Tabram. Were they also victims of the bloodthirsty apparition we know only as The Ripper? Just like all the other unanswered questions this case inspires, we may never know.

Let's imagine ourselves as time travellers newly arrived in the late 19th Century, standing on a street corner in Whitechapel. By this time, London was the biggest capital city in the world and the centre of the British Empire, ruled by Queen Victoria. The West End was affluent and enjoyed plenty of new restaurants, hotels, and concert halls, whereas the East End had only pollution, overcrowding and poverty. In 1887, Sir Arthur Conan Doyle published the first Sherlock Holmes novel, but books and entertainment were a world away for the inhabitants of Whitechapel, an area which stretched between Aldgate and Spitalfields in the West, to Mile End in the East. It was the worst district in the city, avoided like the plague by everyone except those who had no choice, but this was a world where there were no guarantees and no safety nets.

There would have been a mélange of sounds all around; horses' hooves, the cries of market traders, dogs and cats, hurdy-gurdy music, people talking, shouting, and laughing. It was a labyrinth of narrow streets, home to slums and tenement buildings, with 800 people crammed into every acre. Of the 900,000 people living in the East End, around 80,000 were concentrated in Whitechapel. Almost half of them were living in poverty. Streets were only wide enough for a hansom cab to pass, which was a horse-drawn carriage and the main method of transport around the city for those who could afford it. For everyone else, walking was the only option. You would hear the clip-clopping of horses' hooves almost continually, as there were around 11,000 hansom cabs in London and over 50,000 horses. But it wasn't just the sound that would hit you, it was the smell. A few years later the city would experience the Great Horse Manure crisis, as streets became so full of the stuff that authorities could not see a way to solve the problem. The answer was as dramatic as it was unanticipated. Henry Ford's motor cars had replaced horse-drawn travel almost entirely by 1912. But back in 1888, this was nothing but a distant dream.

The stench of dung and horse urine would not be the only scents to have filled your nose as you walked the cobbled streets, although technically, they were not made from cobbles, but setts, which were squarer and more regular. Your nostrils would have been assailed by thick black smog drifting over from the West End factories, the pungent smell of fish from the docks, rotting fruit, roasting chestnuts, and the fetid stench of cesspools and drains under the houses, in the days before more sophisticated plumbing solutions arrived. The sewer system was built by civil engineer Bazalgette in the 1860s which reduced outbreaks of cholera and typhoid, but hygiene for people living in the East End remained poor, as they had to queue for hours to access parish water pumps to wash themselves. It is unsurprising that the inhabitants were frequently dirty and rarely changed their clothes or bedding. Illnesses transmitted through dirty water were not their only problem. The smog that filled the streets caused a marked increase in respiratory conditions, leading to the deaths of more people in the second half of the 19th century than any other illness. Other common causes of death were tuberculosis, measles, dysentery, venereal disease, epilepsy, and premature birth.

It was a place of dilapidation, decay and want, but one of the few things in good supply were public houses, full of weary souls trying to drown their sorrows, occasionally bursting into song or a brawl, depending on their mood.

Although not quite the melting pot of ethnicities and cultures that London is today, some streets in the area were predominantly Jewish, while others were an eclectic mix of Jewish, Irish, English and Germans. Tens of thousands of Jews had found their way to London following the Russian pogroms in Eastern Europe, and they clustered together in areas of Spitalfields such as Middlesex Street. They came to escape persecution and poverty, and while many of them escaped the latter and set up successful businesses, working as butchers, boot finishers, tailors, cigar makers and many other trades, they still found themselves the victims of anti-Jewish sentiment from many of the native Londoners.

Their arrival put pressure on housing in an already overcrowded area, and in 1886 and 1887 there was fierce rioting by the unemployed, who rampaged across the West End, causing damage to shops and houses as they went. London was not the only city to see violent uprisings. In Chicago, an 1886 demonstration calling for workers' rights resulted in the Haymarket massacre, for which the blame was pinned squarely on socialism and anarchism.

Lolesworth Buildings, Thrawl Street – an example of tenement buildings built in 1885 to house the large number of immigrants. Families with as many as 10 children would live in just two or three rooms (Photo by Derek Voller, 1973)

It was not only riots that a time traveller to Whitechapel would need to watch out for. Gangs roamed the streets, alcoholism, sexually transmitted diseases, and domestic violence were rife. Whilst it would be wrong to imagine that every street in the area was a den of iniquity, there were some parts of Whitechapel to which even the police were reluctant to go, notably Thrawl Street, Dorset Street, and Flower and Dean Street. The latter was described by social commentator James Greenwood as *"perhaps the foulest and most dangerous street in the whole metropolis."* Another writer, Watts Phillips, used rather colourful prose to describe the Petticoat Lane Market, saying it was *"a Modern Babel…a perfect sea of greasy bargainers, blocking up the thoroughfare."*

"What of those who were not criminals?" the time traveller to 1888 might ask. "How did they make a living?" There were few opportunities for single women, whether widowed or unmarried, particularly if they had children. In Victorian England, women were raised to be housewives and received very little education. Those from more advantaged backgrounds might secure jobs as nurses or teachers, while others worked as domestic servants, shop assistants, laundresses, or in factories.

Thousands of people eked out just enough to survive, toiling in the factories for anywhere between 10 and 18 hours a day in hazardous conditions. Any mistakes or rule breaking were punished by fines, so an unfortunate worker who arrived late, kept their workbench untidy, or was found to have dirty feet, might be docked half a day's pay, leaving them in an even more precarious position, barely able to feed themselves and pay for a bed for the night.

The 1,400 female workers employed by match manufacturer Bryant & May were among those working for poverty wages in inhumane conditions. As if the poor pay and long hours were not enough, many of the girls suffered from "Phossy Jaw", a condition caused by inhaling noxious phosphorous fumes which led to the jaw literally rotting away, and in many cases, the surgical removal of the jawbone. Those who fell ill would not only lose their health and many years from their life expectancy, but they would also lose their job, leaving them with no income. Social reformer Annie Besant brought the plight of the Bryant & May match girls into the public eye, and the subsequent outcry forced employers to improve conditions. Even after this, life in the factories remained harsh, hazardous, and unjust. But they had very little choice. If they did not, or could not work, their only options would be to take their chances on the street, or enter the workhouse, which many considered to be a fate worse than death.

People queuing outside S. Marylebone Workhouse c1900 (Wellcome Images)

Piece workers had the advantage of working from their own homes, so they avoided some of the worst dangers of factory life and were able to work together as a family to increase their productivity. Despite this, these jobs were far from comfortable. For example, fur pickers developed respiratory illnesses from inhaling the fine fibres all day and night, and children were often kept at home to help with the work, in defiance of the 1870 Education Act which had made school attendance compulsory. Garment workers could earn as much as one shilling a day if they worked quickly enough, and a shirt finisher, who had to sew on linings, create buttonholes, and attach buttons, was paid about 3d (3 pence) per dozen shirts.

There were 12 pennies (d) to the shilling and 20 shillings (s) to the pound (£). Wages ranged from about 4s a week for a young factory worker, to £3 a week for a skilled labourer, which would have been considered a good salary. Lodgings in a poor neighbourhood would have cost less than 5s a week, but commonly, people paid as little as 4d a night for a simple bed in a hostel. The downside was that they had to share the room with as many as 60 other people! The more you could afford, the more security and comfort you could have, with 8d a night offering more privacy. A pint of milk was 2d, an egg was 1d and a pound of bacon was 8d.

Not everyone agreed that Whitechapel and its surrounding areas were hell on earth. Reverend Samuel Barnett, vicar of St Jude's and longtime resident, reminded people that *"the greater part of Whitechapel is as orderly as any part of London and the life of most of its inhabitants is more moral than that of many whose vices are hidden by greater wealth."*

There were many who understood that the root of any criminality amongst the inhabitants lay in their abject poverty, and they sought to alleviate this with charitable work. As well as efforts towards slum clearance, a community college called Toynbee Hall was set up by Reverend Barnett, there was a Jewish Ladies' Association for Preventive and Rescue Work in Spitalfields, and there was a soup kitchen in impoverished Fashion Street catering for Jewish people.

Wood engraving (The Illustrated London News)

It was against this backdrop of overcrowding, disease, and poverty that the Whitechapel murders took place. There were 15,000 homeless and many more hopeless. Many women whose husbands had either left them or died, had no option but to turn to prostitution. These days, it is considered more appropriate to use the terms "sex work" or "escorting", but I will use the word prostitution for the purposes of this book, to represent the historical language of the time. In 1888, there were estimated to be 1,200 full time prostitutes and around 50 brothels in Whitechapel; fewer than there had been in 1887, as Police Commissioner Sir Charles Warren had ordered the closure of 200 brothels in response to the campaigning of social reformers. Many prostitutes did not operate in brothels, but down dark alleyways, backyards, or dimly lit doorways, to hide their illegal profession from the constabulary. Unfortunately, this made them an ideal target for Jack the Ripper.

Prior to the passing of the Peel Act in 1829, law and order was maintained by night watchmen, so by the time Jack the Ripper began terrorizing the streets of Whitechapel, the police force was only about 60 years old. Sir Robert Peel, who was Home Secretary at the time, but later became Prime Minister, passed his famous act to make the country safer. Policemen colloquially became known as "Bobbies" or "Peelers".

Police constables were commonly recruited from the military or the agricultural industry. They were expected to have an excellent record, so anyone with a history of drunkenness or other misdemeanours would not have been accepted into the force. Ex-Navy men or former firemen were particularly welcomed as they would be physically fit and used to heights. New recruits had to be aged between 21 and 27 years old, in good health, able to read and write, and have letters of recommendation from prominent members of society, such as a doctor or civil servant. They had previously been forbidden from growing facial hair, but by the 1880s this regulation had been removed. They had to meet a strict height requirement and if they didn't measure up to at least 5'9", they wouldn't get the job, although this was relaxed to 5'6 ½" when the force was in desperate need of men. Height was particularly useful given the limited resources they had to fight crime; they did not carry guns and only had a truncheon and a pair of handcuffs to rely on, so the taller and broader they were, the better. This helped them to intimidate criminals and have a better view of what was going on in a crowd.

Most new recruits came from outside London and had grown up in the countryside, as the belief was that these men were stronger and in better health than their city counterparts, who were more likely to have spent their lives in poverty, breathing in the smog and foul air.

Officers of the law worked eight hour shifts and only had one day off every two weeks. Their duty times were usually from 6:00 a.m. to 2:00 p.m., 2:00 p.m. to 10:00 p.m. or 10:00 p.m. to 6:00 a.m. Before each shift began, the sergeant would rally them round and tell them about anything they should be aware of that day. Officers were expected to stick to their specific beats (routes) and sergeants regularly went out to check that constables were where they should have been. It was very unusual for a PC to be found in a pub or having a cup of tea with a nightwatchman en route, and repeated infractions would not have been tolerated. Variation was built into the beats to avoid criminals becoming familiar with prescribed routes, and plainclothes Detective Constables, or DCs, also walked the streets.

They had significant powers, as they could arrest anyone and hold them for questioning with very little reason. Being promoted was a serious business, and they had to pass exams to progress through the ranks. Being an officer of the law was a lonely job and could lose them the respect of their friends and neighbours, so they tended to stick together and created their own clubs and social groups. They were encouraged to be practicing Christians.

A fascinating book, Victorian Murders by Jan Bondeson, offers many lurid examples of other crimes that had taken place around this time, providing a context which is often forgotten. Whilst none of these murders were as heavily publicized as those of the homicides in Whitechapel, some of them were nearly as gruesome.

For example, in 1879, 60-year-old Julia Thomas employed 30-year-old Irish woman Kate Webster to work in her Richmond home. Kate had a good reference, but this later transpired to have been forged by a friend. Mrs. Thomas soon began criticizing Kate's work, and the two were habitually at loggerheads. One day, when Mrs. Thomas arrived home from church, Kate threw her employer down the stairs, slit her throat, then strangled her (in that order). She then cut her into pieces with the help of a saw, a chopper, and a knife, before placing the parts in the kitchen copper boiler to remove the flesh. While she waited for the body to disintegrate, Kate visited the local pub for refreshments. She then calmly cleaned up, hid the remaining bones and skin in a wooden box and a Gladstone bag, and continued to live in the house as if nothing had happened. She threw the box and bag into the River Thames, but they washed up the following day. Police began to find other parts including a human foot and an ankle, and eventually arrested Kate Webster. Legend has it that before her arrest, she had been offering two tubs of lard for sale in the neighbourhood...which came from residue left behind in the copper boiler. Mrs. Thomas's head was not found. Many years later, famous naturalist David Attenborough bought a house in Richmond just between the local pub and the cottage where Mrs. Thomas had lived. The old pub closed in 2007 but Attenborough bought it with the intention of redeveloping it. In October 2010, workmen excavating the site discovered a skull, which was later confirmed by a coroner to belong to the murdered woman.

For a killer to chop their victim into pieces was not uncommon in those days. Just a few years earlier, Henry Wainwright, a successful businessman, had done exactly that. His factory was located at 84 Whitechapel Road, coincidentally less than half a mile from the Ripper murder sites. He got tired of his mistress, Harriet Lane, so he shot and dismembered her, packing her remains into two parcels. He carried these along the road, hoping to dispose of them, but was caught in the act by the police, who must have been horrified to see the severed body parts tumbling out onto the pavement when they insisted on inspecting the contents of the parcels.

It is commonly believed that there were five Ripper victims, known as the canonical victims, or C-5. However, some historians question whether they were all the work of the same killer, while others believe that more murders should be added to the list.

Before we examine the five canonical murders, we will look at the cases of two women killed just before what is known as the Autumn of Terror, included in the looser grouping called The Whitechapel Murders.

Emma Elizabeth Smith was born in 1843, so in 1888 she was 45 years old. She sometimes claimed to be a widow, but at other times said that she had left her husband years before. She had a habit of getting into fights and frequently sported a black eye or a collection of cuts and bruises as a result. Like many people living in the area, she was a heavy drinker. She was 5'2" with a fair complexion, light brown hair, and a scar on her right temple. She lodged at 18 George Street in Spitalfields and normally left at around 6:00 to 7:00 p.m. to look for customers, as she had turned to prostitution to earn what money she could. Emma had been lodging in the same place for years, but many people had to take a bed anywhere they could find one, which they paid for each night, usually at a cost of fourpence.

Artist's impression of Emma Smith, 1888

If they did not have fourpence, they did not have a roof over their head; it was as simple as that. If they had only tuppence, they could drape themselves over a washing line strung up across a room, along with lots of other people, which was not much better than sleeping on the floor. There was no need to worry about oversleeping, as in the morning the landlord would untie the washing line, so everyone would be rudely awoken as they tumbled to the ground. People commonly referred to their fourpence fee as their "doss" money, which meant the money they needed to pay for a bed for the night.

Emma Smith left her lodging house at around 6:00 p.m. as usual on Easter Monday, 3 April 1888. At around 1:30 a.m. she was passing St Mary's Church when she noticed three men approaching her, one younger than the others and under 20 years old. She felt uneasy and crossed the street to avoid them, but they followed her. She began to run, but the three men chased her. They caught her at the junction of Wentworth Street and Old Montague Street, and Osborne Street and Brick Lane, near Taylor's cocoa factory. She was beaten, robbed, and subjected to a horrific sexual assault, just a minute's walk from the safety of home. Mary Russell, deputy manager of the George Street lodging house, was appalled when she saw Emma staggering home sometime later, her face bloodied and her ears cut. Mary insisted on taking her to the London Hospital. She and another lodger who was there at the time, Annie Lee, were astonished that Emma had managed to walk home in the state she was in. At the hospital, house surgeon George Haslip treated her as best he could. As she drifted in and out of consciousness, Emma tried her best to describe her attackers and the details of her assault. Sadly, she died of peritonitis just a few days later, although some sources state she succumbed to her injuries within hours.

Detective Inspector Edmund Reid headed the investigation for the Metropolitan Police, a name which might sound familiar as he was played by Matthew Macfadyen in the BBC series Ripper Street, whose storylines were fictional but woven within an accurate historical context. Reid was a fascinating character, having started off life as a delivery boy and ship's steward, before joining the Met Police in 1872 and being promoted to Detective just two years later. He was the shortest man in the force at 5'6" as at the time he joined, the height requirement had only just been lowered from 5'9" because they were badly in need of men. In 1877 he made the first descent from a parachute from 1000 feet and was awarded a medal in 1883 from the Balloon Association of Great Britain in celebration of his record-breaking ascent from Crystal Palace. As well as ballooning, he enjoyed acting and singing.

D.I. Reid discovered that at 12:15 a.m. on the day of the murder, Margaret Hames, a fellow George Street lodger, had seen Emma Smith near Commercial Road and the East India Dock Road, talking to a man in a dark coat and a white scarf, but it was thought that he had nothing to do with the attack.

It seemed clear from Emma's story that the assault had been perpetrated by three men, who were likely members of a gang. Prostitutes were particularly at risk from the gangs which infested many streets in the area, as they used violent tactics to extort money from them, sometimes on the pretense of offering protection. Although gang violence was not uncommon in Whitechapel, the sickening attack on Emma Smith was particularly brutal and shocked the city. There were no witnesses, and nobody was ever brought to justice. Whichever group was responsible, or even if the three men were not affiliated with an organized gang, it was almost certainly nothing to do with Jack the Ripper. But because the murder of Emma Smith occurred in the Whitechapel area just a few months before the canonical five, it has become viewed as the first in the series of unsolved murders of prostitutes.

Around four months later, there was another frightful incident. At around 4:45 a.m. on Tuesday 7 August 1888, dock labourer John Reeves was getting ready for work. The sun was just rising, and he yawned as he left his room at the George Yard Buildings and made his way towards the stairs. What he saw there shot him into immediate wakefulness. A woman was lying on her back in a pool of blood, her hands clenched at her sides. Reeves ran to fetch a Bobby, and PC Thomas Barrett, badge number 226H, hurried to the scene. The report described the victim as follows:

Age: 35 to 40
Profession or calling: Prostitute
Height: 5'3"
Hair: Dark
Complexion: Dark
Dress: Green skirt, brown petticoat, long black jacket, black bonnet, sidespring boots, all old.

Cab driver Alfred Crow who also lived in the George Yard Buildings, had returned home at approximately 3:30 a.m. and noticed a shape on the first-floor landing, but as it was still dark, he could not tell that it was a body and assumed it was a homeless person sheltering from the wet weather outside. This was a frequent occurrence, as the door was usually kept unlocked. Residents Joseph and Elizabeth Mahoney had seen nobody on the landing when they passed at 1:40 a.m.

George Yard Buildings

Police photographed the body, and it was removed to the Whitechapel mortuary, also known as the Dead Shed, as it was just a brick shed in Old Montague Street, which no longer exists.

Dr Timothy Killeen conducted the postmortem and estimated the time of death at around 2:30 a.m. He found 39 stab wounds, including five to the left lung, two to the right lung, one to the heart, five to the liver, two to the spleen and six to the stomach, but the focus of the attack had been on the breast, belly, and groin. Killeen believed that all but one of the wounds were inflicted by a right-hander, probably with a penknife. He surmised that the final wound was made with a dagger or bayonet to the heart. Although doctors and surgeons were well versed in knife wounds at this time, modern forensics now show that it was unlikely a bayonet was used because of the way the skin yields to stab wounds, and they now believe that all 39 came from the same weapon. It could be that the same area was stabbed more than once, affecting the depth and size of the injury. The postmortem report no longer exists so we only have newspaper accounts to go on.

The problem was that nobody knew the victim's name. Three people gave three different identifications of the corpse, so on Thursday 9 August, the inquest was adjourned for two weeks while attempts were made to discover the woman's identity. That same afternoon, prostitute Mary Ann Connelly, alias Pearly Poll, came forward with a name. The victim was 39-year-old Martha Tabram. Shortly afterwards, Martha's estranged husband confirmed the identification.

She was born as Martha White in 1849, and her parents had died when she was just 16. On Christmas Day 1869, she

The Illustrated Police News, 18 August 1888

married foreman furniture packer Henry Tabram in St Mary's Parish, Newington and they had two sons. By 1875, their marriage had deteriorated, not helped by Martha's heavy drinking, but even after they separated, Tabram continued to support his ex-wife with 12s a week. Even with this relatively generous payment, Martha harassed him in the street, pestering him for more money, most of which was spent on alcohol. In response, he reduced her allowance to 2s 6d a week.

Excessive drinking was a problem all over the country, but the media tended to focus more on the blight of alcohol on the East End. Magistrate Montagu Williams said, "*There is no mistake about what is the cause of nearly all the crime in the East End of London. The curse of all is drink, and I must say that the wives are often worse than the husbands.*"

It can be difficult for us to understand why people in such dire straits chose to spend their last pennies on alcohol, rather than a good meal and a safe bed for the night. It could be that living in such desperate situations with little hope of future security, and at risk of violence every day, made people lean upon alcohol to forget their daily troubles for a while. It is easy for us in our comparatively comfortable modern lives to say that their little money should have been spent more wisely, but we must remember that their world was very different from our own. In addition, drinking water in many areas was unsanitary and carried disease.

After Martha's breakup with Tabram, she began living with carpenter Henry Turner. She had a habit of not returning home until 11:30 p.m., having been taken to the police station to sober up after suffering from hysterical fits or seizures brought on by excessive drinking. Turner did not have a regular job in 1888 and made ends meet by selling cheap trinkets like needles and pins, and the two of them lodged at a house in Commercial Road. Their landlady Mrs Boulsfield had once said, *"Martha was a person who would rather have a glass of ale than a cup of tea."*

Around July 1888, Martha and Henry left their lodgings without giving notice as they were struggling to pay the rent. Shortly after this, the couple broke up. Martha went to live at Satchell's Lodging House at 19 George Street, Spitalfields, but despite continuing to sell trinkets, she could not afford the doss money, so she resorted to selling her body like so many other women were forced to. She had no idea that finding enough rent money would soon be the least of her concerns.

John Reeves, the man who found her body, said he had seen no footprints on the stairs and no sign of any weapons. Detective Inspector Edmund Reid took on the case.

Detective Inspector Edmund Reid

Pearly Poll, who had made the identification, professed that she and Martha had been with two soldiers on the night of the murder, one a Corporal and the other a Private of the Guards, between 10:00 p.m. and 11:45 p.m. They had allegedly walked about Whitechapel going from pub to pub before separating, Poll going with the Corporal and Martha with the Private, with obvious intentions.

Police Constable Barrett had also seen a Private of the Guards at around 2:00 a.m. on the night of the murder, while on patrol in George Yard. He reported that the soldier said he was waiting for a friend who had "gone off with a girl".

D.I. Reid arranged for all the Corporals and Privates from the Grenadier Guards who had been on leave on the night of the murder, to take part in an identity parade. The military were very willing to assist. Pearly Poll was asked to attend the next morning to see if she could recognize any of the men, but she failed to appear. Police finally found her on Sunday 12 August, and she agreed to go to the tower for the identification the following morning. Regrettably she was unable to see the two men that she and Martha had spent the evening with. PC Barrett also attended but he too was unable to identify the soldier to whom he had spoken.

Two days later, Detective Inspector Reid took Pearly Poll and PC Barrett to view the Coldstream Guards at the Wellington Barracks. This time, Poll pointed out two men, a Corporal and a Private, but they had strong alibis. The investigation was thorough, and the men's bayonets were inspected, but no evidence was found.

In spite of Poll's certainty that she would be able to recognize the two men if she saw them again, it seemed that the case was going nowhere. No other witnesses came forward to corroborate Poll's story, which is strange as according to Poll, the two women and the two soldiers had walked around the area together for at least an hour and 45 minutes. Many researchers now believe that her story was a lie, fabricated to receive attention. This was supported by Edmund Reid's reports of Pearly Poll's mental state, as she threatened to drown herself but then claimed, *"I only said it for a lark."* In one of Reid's final reports on the case, he said:

"Enquiries were made to find some other person who saw the deceased and Pearly Poll with the Privates on the night of the 6th *but without success. Pearly Poll and the PC having both picked out the wrong men, could not be trusted again as their evidence would be worthless."*

The inquest resumed on 23 August. Martha's sister-in-law, Ann Morris, came forward to say she had last seen Martha around 11:00 p.m. on Monday 6 August in Whitechapel Road as she was entering the White Swan pub. Nobody had seen anything of her after that.

The verdict was that the deceased had been murdered by some person or persons unknown. It seemed that one of the most brutal killings London had yet seen was to go unpunished. One of the questions that remained was why nobody had reported hearing any screams. Surely Martha would have cried out or struggled while being stabbed 39 times? Although forensic experts still disagree today about which was the killing blow and in which order the wounds came, she would not have died instantly. One explanation for the lack of screams is that she was passed out drunk at the time of the murder, having entered the George Yard Buildings to shelter from the elements for the night if she had been unable to make her doss money.

Superintendent of the building, Francis Fisher Hewitt, and his wife might have been able to shed some light on this, as their bedroom was just 12 feet away from where the body was found. Mrs. Hewitt admitted to hearing a cry of

"Murder!" but was sure it came from outside in the street. She said, "*The district round here is rather rough and cries of 'Murder!' are a frequent, if not nightly occurrence.*"

It strains credulity that she heard a shout from outside the building, but not from just outside her own bedroom door. Those who are keen to believe Martha Tabram was a Ripper victim use this point in their favour, arguing that only the infamous Whitechapel Murderer could have killed with such stealth, disappearing into the night like a shadow, without a trace. A simpler explanation is that Mr. and Mrs. Hewitt did hear something but were too scared to investigate. They could not admit this, as it would not have been good publicity if it became known that the superintendent of the building had heard a vicious attack in progress and ignored it. Instead, when questioned by the press, he came up with this suggestion: "*It is my belief that the poor creature crept up the staircase and she was accompanied by a man, but a quarrel took place and that he then stabbed her.*"

If he believed a quarrel had taken place, surely this would have been audible from his bedroom just feet away? This could in fact be an accurate account of what really happened, which the Hewitts heard but refused to admit out of fear. They had good reason to be fearful, as unbelievably, newspapers in those days printed the names and addresses of all witnesses. The police must have agreed that Hewitt's statement was questionable, as they chose not to call him to the inquest.

It is my view that Martha Tabram was not a victim of Jack the Ripper as the Modus Operandi (MO) was very different, but to allow you to decide for yourself, we need to learn more about the mysterious, elusive figure known as the Whitechapel Fiend and the barbaric way he slaughtered women at their most vulnerable. What was the driving force behind such a bloodthirsty monster who sunk to the depths of depravity? Although the East End was no stranger to violence, the murder rate in London was not as high as one would expect, with no murders at all in Whitechapel in 1886 or 1887. In 1888, there were just 28 homicides in the whole of the city, out of a population of six million. But five of these murders would stand out forever, living on in history for generations of researchers and criminologists to puzzle over.

In the next chapter, we will examine the first of the canonical murders officially attributed to Jack the Ripper, so pack your doss money and a change of clothes because we'll be staying in London's gloomy, labyrinthine streets for a while. Leave those top hats, capes, and Gladstone bags behind though, because we're going to cut through the myths and study only the facts as we progress through the Autumn of Terror and see if we can put a name to arguably the most infamous serial killer of all time.

Chapter Two
Mary Ann "Polly" Nichols
Bucks Row, 31 August 1888

Bucks Row ran parallel to Whitechapel Road and it was extremely dark as there was only one streetlamp at the end of the road. The shadows made it feel even more threatening and oppressive as it was just 24 feet across at its widest end, although this was not the narrowest street in the area by far. The road was lined with warehouses, factories, and terraced cottages, as well as the five-storey high Board School, which educated children between 5 and 12 years old and had a distinctive rooftop playground. This building still exists, although it has long since been turned into apartments.

Bucks Row as it was c1920s (Hulton Archive)

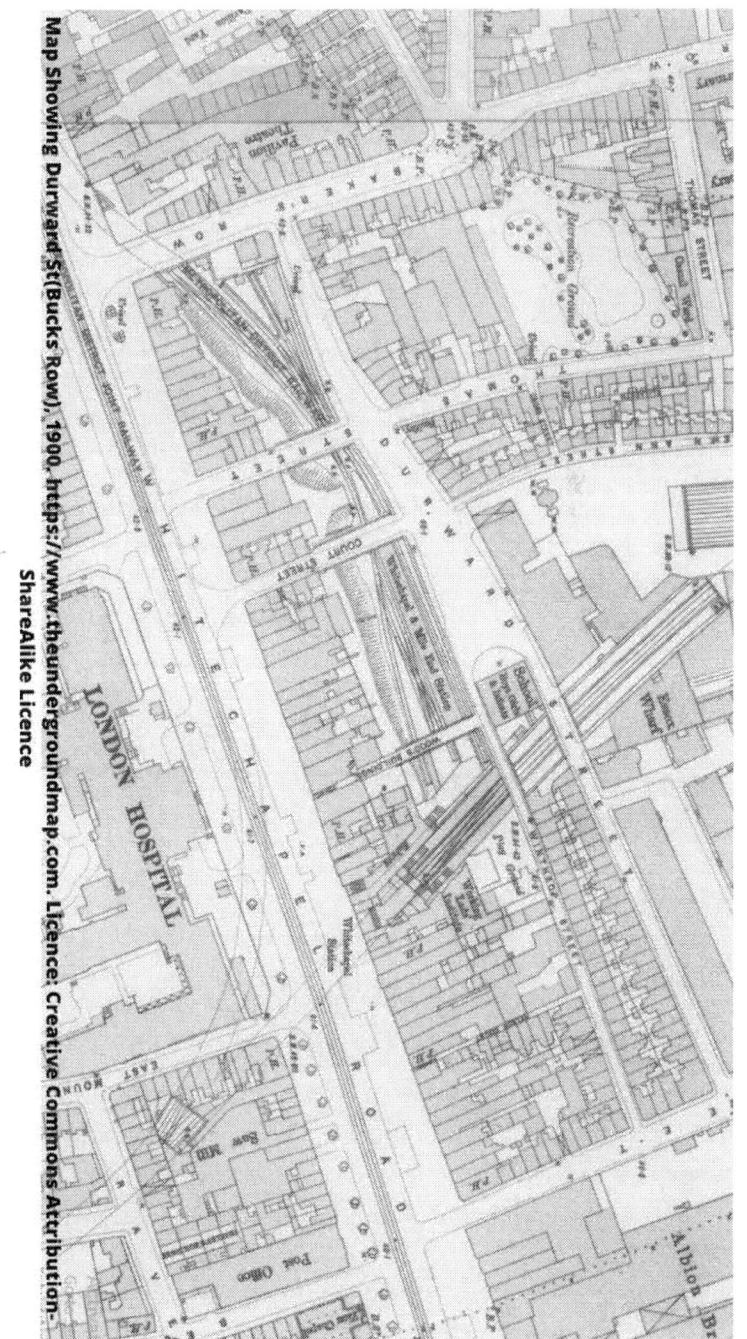

Map Showing Durward St (Bucks Row), 1900. https://www.theundergroundmap.com. Licence: Creative Commons Attribution-ShareAlike Licence

Brown's Stable Yard sat between the Board School and a row of cottages. It was in front of the dark gateway belonging to the Stable Yard that an unwitting man on his way to work first stumbled across a body at about 3:40 a.m. on Friday 31 August 1888.

The man, whose name was Charles Lechmere, thought at first that someone had left a tarpaulin lying there, but when he looked more closely, he realized the ghastly truth. As he was wondering what to do, another man, Robert Paul, entered Bucks Row. Paul lived in Foster Street and was on his way to work in Corbett's Place, just off Hanbury Street. Paul was on his guard when he saw someone standing in the road, as many people had been beaten and robbed here by one of the numerous gangs in the area. When Lechmere called out to him, *"Come and have a look at this woman,"* he was relieved that he was not about to be attacked.

Paul walked over to where Lechmere stood, touched the woman, and found that her hands were cold and limp. Her bonnet lay on the ground next to her. Lechmere said, *"I think she's dead,"* to which Paul replied, *"I think she's breathing, but very little if she is."* He asked Lechmere to help him move her, but Lechmere did not want to and suggested they fetch a Bobby.

Constable Mizen was on his beat in Hanbury Street; a name worth remembering as it soon became the scene of the next murder in the sequence. As we learned in the previous chapter, a beat was the term for the territory that each officer patrolled. Every policeman had his own beat, which would take roughly 15 to 30 minutes to walk. They would continue traversing this route for their entire shift, checking that everything was normal, acting on anything suspicious, and generally making their presence known – both for reassurance and deterrence, depending on whether you were an innocent citizen or a criminal. Sometime during each shift, all officers on duty would meet up at a fixed point, called a "joining beat". The Metropolitan Police was split into 20 divisions covering different areas of the city.

The spot where the body was found

Another part of Constable Mizen's role was as a "knocker-upper", which required him to knock on doors to wake up the household. It was common for people to start work as early as 4:00 a.m.

As Constable Mizen continued his beat, looking for anything out of the ordinary and knocking up as he went, he was approached by Robert Paul and Charles Lechmere. Paul told him, *"There's a woman lying in Bucks Row,"* to which Lechmere added, *"She looks to me either dead or drunk."* Paul said, *"I think she's dead."*

Constable Mizen replied, *"Alright,"* but it was not immediately apparent to the two men whether the policeman intended to go to the scene or not, which Paul said was a shame and had surprised him, when he spoke to the Lloyds Weekly Newspaper about the incident later. No more than four minutes had passed between the discovery of the body and the two men notifying Mizen, according to Paul's account.

When Mizen arrived in Bucks Row, he found Constable Neil of J division, who had already stumbled across the body on *his* beat. With the light from his bullseye lantern, he saw the woman's eyes were wide open, and blood was oozing from her throat. Neil signalled with his lamp to his colleague, PC Thain, who was just passing the end of Bucks Row, and told him, *"Here's a woman has her throat cut. Run at once for Dr Llewellyn."* Meanwhile, PC Mizen went to fetch the ambulance cart.

Dr Llewellyn, who lived just 300 yards away, came immediately and pronounced life extinct. He gave the order for the body to be moved to the "Dead Shed" (the Whitechapel Mortuary) although it was not his legal right to do so, and he should have waited until an inspector had arrived. After the body was removed from the scene, a bucket of water was thrown over the street to wash away the blood.

It was not yet completely light, so the full nature of the crime only became apparent after the body had arrived at the Dead Shed, as neither Dr Llewellyn, nor the two men who found the woman, had noticed the extent of her wounds. On examining the corpse, Inspector Spratling found that the victim had been horribly mutilated, the intestines bulging from a deep abdominal wound, and he called the Welsh doctor back to conduct a full postmortem. Here's how one newspaper reported the murder:

"*The affair is enveloped in complete mystery, and the police have as yet no evidence to trace the perpetrators of the horrible deed. As Constable John Neil was walking down Bucks Row, Whitechapel, about a quarter to four o'clock this morning, he discovered a woman, between 35 and 40 years of age, lying at the side of the street with her throat cut right open from ear to ear. The wound was about two inches wide and blood was flowing profusely. She was conveyed to the Whitechapel Mortuary, where it was found that, besides the wound in her throat, the lower part of her person was completely ripped open. The wound extends nearly to her breast and must have been effected with a large knife. As the corpse of the woman lies in the mortuary it presents a ghastly sight. The hands are bruised and bear evidence of a severe struggle. Some of the front teeth have been knocked out, and the face is bruised on both cheeks and very much discoloured.*"

Dr Llewellyn's postmortem report offered even more detail:

"*The body was that of a female of 40 or 45. Five of the teeth were missing, and there was a slight laceration of the tongue. There was a bruise on the lower part of the jaw on the right side of the face, which might have been caused by a fist or pressure from a thumb. There was a circular bruise on the left side of the face, which also might have been inflicted by the pressure of the fingers. On the left side of the neck, one inch below the jaw, was an incision about four inches in length, running from a point immediately below the ear. An inch below was a circular incision, terminating* at a point three inches below the right jaw and completely severing all the tissues down to the vertebrae. The large vessels of the neck on both sides were severed. The incision was about eight inches in length. The cuts must have been caused by a long-bladed knife used with great violence. On the left side of the lower abdomen was a very deep, jagged wound. There were several incisions running across the abdomen with three or four similar cuts, running downwards, on the right side, all caused by a knife. The injuries were from left to right and might have been done by a left-handed person. All were caused by the same instrument."

Dr Llewellyn's assertion that the killer might have been left-handed was later questioned and contradicted. His description notably failed to mention that the victim's intestines were hanging out of the abdominal wound, probably because this was not the full postmortem report, as those records have not survived, and we only have police and newspaper reports to refer to. It is possible that the intestines were not protruding originally, and rough handling of the body and the bumpy journey on the cart to the mortuary caused them to erupt from the deep wound.

There was to be further confusion around the circumstances of the body's discovery, when Robert Paul explained in the Lloyds Weekly News on Sunday 2 September how he had found the body and notified PC Mizen, giving himself the starring role and downplaying Lechmere's involvement. Until this time, everyone had believed that PC Neil was the first to stumble upon the scene. At the inquest on 4 September, PC Mizen declared that the men who approached him had said, *"You are wanted in Bucks Row by a policeman, there is a woman lying there,"* and insisted that he was not informed that the woman was dead. When Lechmere was asked by the jury whether he had said this, he replied *"No, because I did not see a policeman in Bucks Row."*

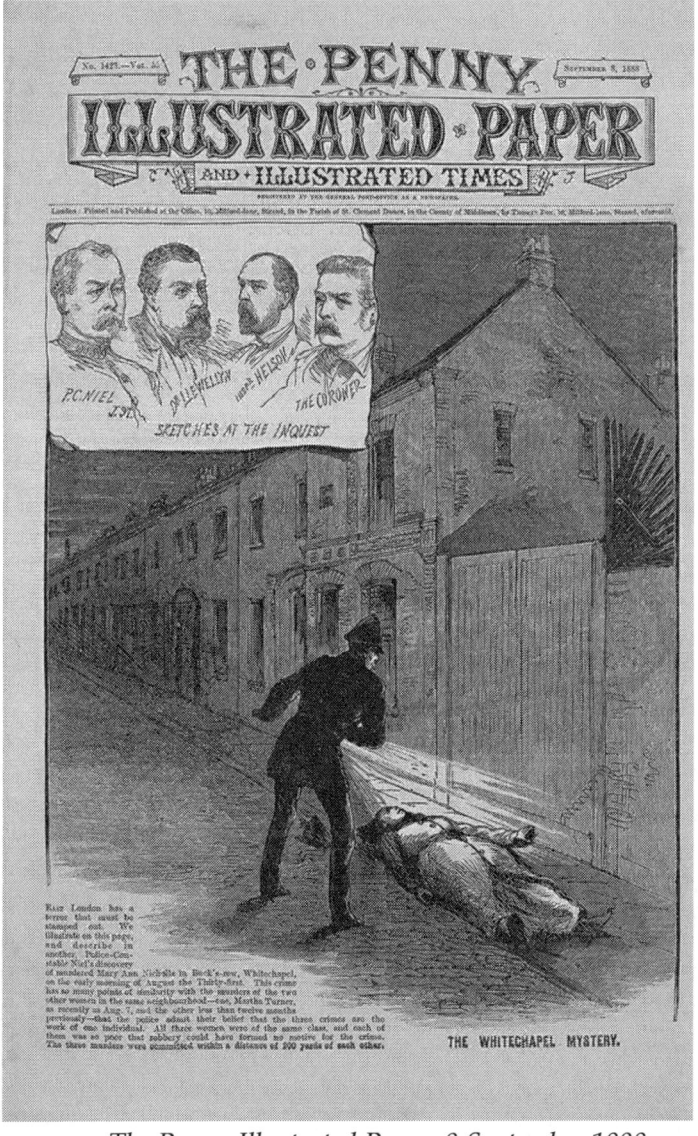

The Penny Illustrated Paper, 8 September 1888

This discrepancy could have arisen due to a failing on PC Mizen's part to take the men's details. I speculate that he did not take the report seriously and was reluctant to investigate, possibly expecting to find a drunk vagrant lying in the street. After all, this was very early in the sequence of murders, so he would have had no reason to be on high alert. When he arrived in Bucks Row to see that PC Neil had discovered a body, it occurred to him that the situation was graver than he had first thought, and he then realised his negligence in not writing down the witnesses' details. He could have twisted their words to make it sound as though the men had come to fetch him on behalf of another policeman, which would have exonerated him from this dereliction of duty, as he could reasonably have expected that this other policeman had already taken down the name and address of Charles Lechmere and Robert Paul.

So who was the victim, and what were her movements in her final hours on earth?

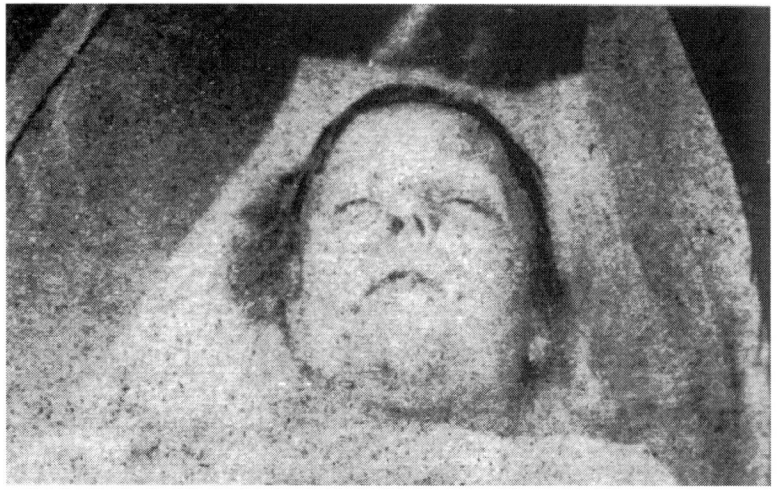

Mortuary photo of Mary Ann "Polly" Nichols

Mary Ann Walker, known as Polly, was born in 1845 in the City of London and had celebrated her 43rd birthday just five days before her death. She was 5'2" with brown hair turning grey, several missing teeth, high cheekbones, and either brown or grey eyes depending on the source you read. A friend from her lodging house, Emily Holland, described her as, *"a very clean woman who always seemed to keep to herself"*.

Polly married a printer's machinist called William Nichols in 1864 and the pair were among the first tenants of social housing owned by Peabody, a housing association which still exists today. Polly earned 30 shillings a week working in a printer's shop, and the couple had three sons and two daughters.

Her marriage fell apart when she discovered that her husband was having an affair and by 1881 they had split for good. Polly turned to prostitution, moving from lodging house to lodging house, and even sometimes the workhouse, occasionally sleeping rough in Trafalgar Square.

Workhouses were the last resort for people living in poverty and many would rather have died than enter one. If you were unfortunate enough to go there, any clothing and possessions you still owned would be taken away from you, men and women would be separated, and you would be forced to take a bath in a tub of water which had been used by up to 20 people before you. You would be given a uniform and shown to your bed, which was nothing more than a hammock just a few inches above the ground. The nightmare would continue the next morning when you would be woken at 5:00 a.m. for a meagre breakfast, before spending the whole day working, which could entail scrubbing, cleaning, breaking stones, chopping wood, or many other back-breaking tasks. Women were also assigned needlework or oakum picking, which was unravelling the fibres from old ropes to be sold to shipbuilders, who mixed them with tar to seal the lining of wooden boats. This was far tougher work than it sounds, and long days of doing this would make the fingers bleed and even cause tendonitis and nerve damage. But there was no choice. Workhouse inmates had to labour for long hours to earn their bed and food. The menu would have featured pea soup, barley soup, rice pudding, or if they were lucky, meat and potato pie. Workhouses were an all too familiar part of life for people living in poverty. Silent film actor Charlie Chaplin spent time in a workhouse when he was just seven years old, and American author Jack London visited England in 1902 and spent time in workhouses and doss houses just so he could experience what life was like for those inside them. His visit must have left a strong impression on him, as he later referred to Whitechapel as *"the abyss"*.

Fortunately for Polly Nichols, when she entered Lambeth workhouse on 16 April 1888, she did not remain there long. It was common for workhouses to find jobs for female inmates, and they secured her a position as a domestic servant for a wealthy couple. A letter exists that she wrote to her father about her new role.

"I just write to say you will be glad to know that I am settled in my new place and going all right up to now. My people went out yesterday and have not returned, so I am left in charge. It is a grand place inside, with trees and gardens back and front. All has been newly done up. They are teetotallers and religious, so I ought to get on. They are very nice people, and I have not too much to do. I hope you are all right and the boy has work. So goodbye for the present.
From yours truly

Polly
Answer soon, please, and let me know how you are."

By "the boy", she was referring to her eldest son Edward, who was living with Polly's father; the other four children had stayed with her ex-husband William Nichols. The last time she had seen her father had been two years before in June 1886 at her brother's funeral. His name was Edward too, and he had died after accidentally setting his hair alight with a paraffin lamp. This letter about her new job was the last time she ever had contact with her father.

Inexplicably, even though she'd had a taste of a more comfortable life, Polly ran away from her job in July 1888, stealing clothes and money from her employers and ending up in a lodging house once again.

On the night of Thursday 30 August 1888, Polly tried to get a bed at 18 Thrawl Street, Spitalfields, but was turned away as she did not have enough money. She said, *"I'll soon have my doss money, see what a jolly bonnet I have!"*, referring to how easy she thought it would be to attract a client with her new hat, to earn her fourpence to pay for a bed for the night.

Just after midnight, on Friday 31 August, she was seen leaving the Frying Pan Public House at the corner of Brick Lane and Thrawl Street. At 2:30 a.m. she bumped into friend and fellow lodger Emily Holland on the corner of Osborn Street and Whitechapel Road, which was where Emma Smith had been attacked several months before. Back then, this was near a grocer's shop, which today is a fish and chip shop named Jack the Chipper. Emily asked Polly to go back to the lodging house with her, but Polly told her she still had to find her doss money; she had earned it three times over that day but spent it on alcohol. She told Emily it would not be long before she returned.

Emily went back to the lodging house while Polly went in search of a client, visibly drunk. She staggered east down Whitechapel Road, and this was the last time she was seen alive. A little over an hour later, she was found dead in Bucks Row. The Autumn of Terror had just begun.

At this time there were no suspects and the name Jack the Ripper had yet to be born, so the constabulary was unaware that they were dealing with a serial murderer. Even if they had known, they would not have had a name to describe him, as the term "serial killer" would not enter common usage for several more decades.

The residents of Bucks Row later petitioned for the name of the road to be changed to erase any sign of its dark past, and it became known as Durward Street.

Durward Street (formerly Bucks Row), 1930s. The imposing building to the right is the Board School. The body was found just behind the man walking on the right-hand side

In recent years, it has been proposed that the man who found Polly Nichols' body could have been the murderer. What do we really know about the two men who were first on the scene? The first man, Charles Lechmere, told the inquest that his name was Charles Cross. His late stepfather Thomas Cross had been a police constable, so he might have felt that using his name would lend him more credence, or maybe he just preferred not to be identified, as witnesses' names were printed in the newspapers.

The second man, who arrived just moments later, and to whom Charles pointed out the body, was Robert Paul. Both Lechmere and Paul were carmen on their way to work, a profession which involved transporting goods in a horse and cart. Many jobs started well before dawn, and common occupations in Whitechapel included dock labourer, butcher, market trader, and fish porter at Billingsgate Fish Market. Others sold anything they could on the street, known as "hawking". There are many names of trades unfamiliar to us today, for example, a costermonger was someone who sold fruit and vegetables from a handcart, a chandler was a candlemaker, and a cooper was someone who made barrels.

The overcrowding in the East End meant that the number of people far outweighed the available jobs, and for many it was a hand-to-mouth existence. Polly Nichols was certainly not alone in struggling to pay for a bed for the night, and it was common for people to survive day to day, earning just enough to cover their lodgings that night, but with little left over. It is arguably unsurprising that excessive drinking was widespread, as whenever there was a little extra money to be had, it was often spent on drowning the sorrow of being trapped in a cycle of poverty, grime, and deprivation.

Lechmere and Paul neither saw nor heard anyone leaving the scene of the murder. Lechmere lived in nearby Doveton Street, just half a mile away from Bucks Row, and it would have taken less than eight minutes for him to get there after leaving his home. He worked for a company called Pickfords, which still exists today. In recent years, he has become a popular suspect, and we will explore this possibility in more detail later.

PC Neil discovering the body of Mary Ann Nichols (Famous Crimes Past and Present, 1903)

Regardless of whether Lechmere was an innocent witness or a stone-cold killer, nobody knew where Polly had been between 2:30 a.m. when she parted from Emily Holland, and 3:30 a.m. when she was killed. It would have taken less than 15 minutes to walk from the corner of

Osborn Street and Whitechapel Road to Bucks Row, so what happened in the remaining 45 minutes? The pubs were closed by 2:00 a.m. so it is assumed that she was walking around searching for customers. Whitechapel Road was busy, even in the early hours of the morning, but although she might have been seen, nobody would have had any reason to remember her at the time.

As for how the murderer struck, he could have pretended to be a client and lured her away to a quiet spot, or it could have been a sudden blitz attack with no prior communication. It was noticed that the Stable Gate to Brown's Yard was locked, so it is conceivable that the perpetrator originally planned to kill his victim in the yard, out of sight, but on finding it locked, decided with sangfroid to commit the murder in the street anyway, having gone too far to curtail his impulse for blood. Polly could have been the one to lead him there if she had previously taken clients to the Yard and knew it to be a quiet place. Either way, all the evidence pointed to her being killed on the spot, rather than dying elsewhere and then being dumped in Bucks Row, a theory which was posited at the time.

Incidentally, the reason Detective Inspector Reid, who investigated Martha Tabram's murder, has not yet appeared in this case, was that he operated in H Division, while Bucks Row fell into J Division. Unfortunately, J Division's records are not as thorough as H and no police reports survive from Polly Nichols' murder so most of the information we have is pieced together from newspaper reports of the time.

The Purkiss family, who lived just opposite the murder scene at Essex Wharf, a three-storey building used as offices, neither saw nor heard anything that night. Emma Green and her family, who resided at New Cottage right next to Brown's Stable Yard, heard nothing either. Green admitted that the street was busy but denied any knowledge of prostitution in the area. This contrasts with a report by Inspector Frederick Abberline which stated that Bucks Row was known to be frequented by prostitutes and their clients.

The grim looking Essex Wharf c. 1980s, where the Purkiss family lived

Essex Wharf in 1988 (Robin Webster, CC-BY-SA 2.0)

It was Emma Green's son, James, who helped to wash the blood stains away under the watchful eye of PC Thain. Irrespective of whether Emma was genuinely unaware of women soliciting in Bucks Row, or whether she pretended otherwise to preserve her social status, some people were of the belief that *every* part of Whitechapel was full of iniquity. Here is an extract from a lively article by writer Arthur G. Morrison, published in the Palace Journal in April 1889, in which he satirised the view that the area was wholly dreadful and reminded readers that this was a sweeping generalisation.

"A horrible black labyrinth, reeking from end to end with the vilest exhalations; its streets mere kennels of horrent putrefaction; its every wall, its every object, slimy with the indigenous ooze of the place; swarming with human vermin, whose trade is robbery, and whose recreation is murder; the catacombs of London darker, more tortuous, and more dangerous than those of Rome, and supersaturated with foul life. Others imagine Whitechapel in a pitiful aspect. Outcast London. Black and nasty still, a wilderness of crazy dens into which pallid wastrels crawl to die; where several families lie in each fetid room, and fathers, mothers, and children watch each other starve; where bony, blear-eyed wretches, with everything beautiful, brave, and worthy crushed out of them, and nothing of the glory and nobleness and jollity of this world within the range of their crippled senses, rasp away their puny lives in the sty of the sweater. Such spots as these there certainly are in Whitechapel, and in other places, but generalities are rarely true, and when applied to a district of London so large as that comprised under the name of Whitechapel, never."

But people were certainly correct to describe the area as a labyrinth. There were a dozen escape routes the killer could have taken to exit Bucks Row and melt into the darkness, some of which I will mention in the chapter on suspects later in the book. The maze-like nature of the Whitechapel streets could explain why nobody saw the murderer fleeing, including three horse slaughtermen, Tomkins, Britton, and Mumford, who were employed in nearby Winthrop Street and were questioned after they finished their shift at around 6:00 or 6:30 a.m.

At the inquest, rigorously presided over by coroner Wynne Baxter, nightwatchman Patrick Mulshaw, who was employed by the Whitechapel District Board of Works, said that on the night of the murder he was at the back of the Working Lads' Institute in Winthrop Street watching some sewage works until just before 6:00 a.m. He admitted to falling asleep a few times during the night but was adamant that he was awake between 3:00 and 4:00 a.m. and that he neither saw anyone during that time, nor heard any screams or cries for help. The first he knew of the murder was when a passerby said, *"Watchman, old man, I believe somebody is murdered down the street."* Given his proximity to the crime, it is unusual that Mulshaw did not hear anything. Either the killer had been exceptionally stealthy, or Mulshaw was dozing on duty, or he did hear something but did not realise the significance of it. On the other hand, he may have heard something but been too frightened to go and look, cognizant of the dangers the area held. The man who told the nightwatchman about the murder has never been identified.

An eleven-year-old girl named Charlotte Coldwell (incorrectly reported in the papers as Colville) who lived about halfway down Brady Street, reported hearing shouts of *"Murder! Murder! Police! Murder!"* in the early hours of the morning. She told reporters that she had also heard a scuffling and bumping against the shutters and that the shouts seemed to move in the direction of Bucks Row. Her mother confirmed the story but explained that such noises were frequent, and it would have been foolish to go outside to investigate, as on many occasions, people had been knocked down and robbed by gangs. This statement only exists in the press and is not mentioned in any surviving police files.

Another witness, Harriet Lilley, lived just two doors down from the spot where the body was found. This was her statement:

"I slept in the front of the house and could hear everything that occurred in the street. On that Thursday night I was somehow very restless. Well, I heard something I mentioned to my husband in the morning. It was a painful moan - two or three faint gasps - and then it passed away. It was dark, but a luggage train went by as I heard the sounds. There was, too, a sound as of whispers underneath the window. I distinctly heard voices but cannot say what was said - it was too faint."

It was established that a goods train did pass by at about 3:30 a.m. so Harriet was probably correct, but her statement was not printed in all the papers, and she was not called to the inquest. One could hypothesize that the sound of the passing train might have masked any screams or gasps and could also explain why nightwatchman Mulshaw did not hear anything. We don't know the exact time the train passed, as the railway company was notorious for running an inaccurate timetable, but if it really was about 3:30 a.m. then carman Charles Lechmere had missed the murderer by just a few minutes. If he had left home a little earlier, he may have chanced upon the assailant in action. The timing is confirmed by PC Neil, who passed Bucks Row on his beat at about 3:15 but saw nothing, and he had never been far away from the murder spot at any time on his route. PC Thain, who was also on duty in the area on the morning of the murder, passed the corner of Bucks Row every 30 minutes. The killer was either extremely cunning or preternaturally lucky to have committed his crime sometime after Neil passed by at 3:15, but before he returned at 3:30, a very narrow window of opportunity.

The inquest jury returned a verdict of wilful murder by person or persons unknown, and Polly was laid to rest in the City of London cemetery, witnessed by her children and her father.

New Cottage was damaged by bombing in World War II and a garage was built in its place in the 1960s, extending to where Brown's Stable Yard once stood. Essex Wharf was demolished in 1990, paving the way for redevelopment. In 2021, a new public footway was opened, linking Whitechapel Road to Durward Street via Whitechapel Station. The exit into Durward Street comes out alongside the spot where Polly Nichols was killed. Durward Street has been used as a location for scenes in a number of TV shows and films, for instance, the Board School and the junction with Brady Street can be seen in the 1981 British film Venom.

Durward Street in 2006 (photographer Matt Hucke, Licence: CC-BY-2.5). The entrance to Brown's Stable Yard was where the three cars are parked on the left.

It is repeatedly questioned why nobody else saw or heard anything of the murder, but it is clear from the statements that some witnesses did hear something. In some cases, they were doubtless scared of reprisals. Mistrust of the police may have prevented others from coming forward, or, simpler still, they may have feared losing a day's pay if they were called to the inquest. In later murders, manifold witnesses emerged, which could be due to the building hysteria as the crimes escalated in brutality, and people were more inclined to speak up when it became clear that a "homicidal maniac" was at large. The idea of The Ripper as a silent, stealthy apparition may consequently be something of a myth.

The first murder of a serial killer is a crucial one, as it defines their MO and helps him or her to identify any mistakes or weaknesses in their plan, which may evolve over time. Although the murder of Polly Nichols in Bucks Row was the first of the five canonical Ripper murders, it does not receive as much attention as the others, potentially due to the lack of surviving official reports.

At this time, the authorities still had no idea of what they were dealing with, but it would not be long before Jack the Ripper became a sinister household name. The Autumn of Terror was well and truly underway, and Whitechapel would never be the same again.

Chapter Three
Annie Chapman
Hanbury Street, 8 September 1888

On Saturday 8 September 1888, just a day after the funeral of The Ripper's first canonical victim, Polly Nichols, there was a gruesome discovery less than half a mile away from the site of Polly's murder.

John Davis lived on the top floor of 29 Hanbury Street and had woken up at about 5:45 a.m. He was sure about the time as he had just heard the Spitalfields church clock. He had a cup of tea and went downstairs to the back yard, where he discovered the body of a woman lying near the bottom step. He immediately went to fetch a policeman, and ten minutes later, Inspector Chandler arrived on the scene. News had spread fast and there were already crowds of people surrounding the house.

One of the many people thronging to hear about the latest atrocity was Mrs. Harriet Hardiman who lived on the ground floor of number 29 and ran a cats' meat shop - which sold meat for cats to eat, not meat made from cats! Some people did buy cats' meat for themselves as it was so cheap. Mrs. Hardiman had sent her son to see what the commotion was about, and according to the papers, when he returned a few minutes later he conveyed the disturbing news by telling her, *"Don't upset yourself mother, it's a woman been killed in the yard."*

Others were far from upset, and tenants of 29 Hanbury Street with windows overlooking the back yard charged curious sightseers a few pennies to gawk at the spot where the murder occurred. This sort of ghoulish tourism was common in the Victorian era, and it got worse by the time

Monday 10 September arrived. Several costermongers turned up to take advantage of the public fascination with murder, selling fruit and refreshments to the rubbernecking onlookers. Thousands of people, many of them respectably dressed, flocked to the scene until it became so crowded that the police had to move them on.

Before we look at the details of the murder and mutilation, it is worth describing the scene, as it was an unexpected place for a homicide to be committed. 29 Hanbury Street was owned by a woman named Amelia Richardson who ran a packing case business in the cellar and shared a room on the first floor with her 14-year-old son, while letting out the other rooms to several residents. There were eight rooms with a total of 17 people living in the building, but by the standards of the time, this was not considered overcrowded. It was in one of the better parts of Whitechapel and most of the residents had regular jobs, excepting an elderly widow whom Amelia allowed to stay out of charity even though she couldn't pay.

The backyard of 29 Hanbury Street

There was only one door into the building which opened into a narrow passageway, about 20 feet long but just three feet wide, leading to a staircase and continuing along to the back door.

Passageway to the back yard of 29 Hanbury Street. Photograph taken shortly after the murder (photographer unknown)

There were three stone steps down to a small, square back yard with an outside lavatory in the top right-hand corner. Both the front and back doors were kept unlocked as was the custom in the area, because there was nothing worth stealing. There were houses either side of number 29 with adjacent back yards, with no way in or out apart from through the house, as the yard was completely enclosed by thin fences around five and a half feet tall. About 18 inches from the ground, several patches of blood could be seen on the back wall of the house, between the steps and the paling. The palings were not damaged, indicating that the killer had calmly walked back through the house and exited by the front door, rather than climbing over the fence.

The wounds on the body were more severe than those seen on Polly Nichols at Bucks Row just over a week before. This is part of the report lodged by Inspector Chandler of H Division:

"I went to 29 Hanbury Street and through the passage into the yard. I saw the body of a woman lying on the ground on her back, parallel with the fencing dividing the two yards. The deceased's legs were drawn up and the clothing was above the knees. A portion of the intestines, still connected with the body, were lying above the right shoulder, with some pieces of skin. There were also some pieces of skin on the left shoulder. I sent for the divisional surgeon, Mr. Phillips, and saw that no-one touched the body until he arrived. After the doctor examined the body and it was removed, I found in the yard a piece of coarse muslin, a small tooth comb, and a pocket hair comb in a case, lying near the woman's feet. A portion of an envelope was found near her head, containing two pills."

Dr George Bagster Phillips, who attended the scene and later performed the autopsy, said that the items found in the yard had *"apparently been arranged in order."* The victim was described as five feet tall with blue eyes, dark brown wavy hair, a pallid complexion, excellent teeth with just two missing, strongly built but undernourished and suffering from a disease of the lungs and brain tissue. This might have referred to tuberculosis or syphilis, and Bagster Phillips surmised that had she not been murdered, she would have died imminently of her illnesses.

Dr George Bagster Phillips attending the crime scene
(Illustrated Police News)

She was wearing a long, black coat that came down to her knees, a black skirt, two bodices, two petticoats, lace up boots, red and white striped woollen stockings, a large pocket worn under the skirt and tied about the waist with strings, which was empty, and a white and red neckerchief. Marks on her fingers showed that she had been wearing two brass rings, but these were no longer present, having been stolen by the murderer as a grim memento.

At 11:30 a.m. a friend of the deceased woman identified her at the mortuary. The victim's name was Annie Chapman, and this is her story.

Mortuary photo of Annie Chapman

She was born Annie Eliza Smith in Paddington in September 1841, but her exact date of birth is unknown. She had four sisters and a brother, all younger than her. Her father was a soldier but later entered domestic service as a valet. Tragically, when Annie was in her early twenties and the youngest of her siblings barely more than a baby, her father committed suicide by cutting his own throat. The effect such a traumatic death would have had on the children is unimaginable. By that time, Annie had moved out of the family home and was following in her father's footsteps, working as a domestic servant.

In May 1869, aged 27, Annie married another servant at her workplace, a coachman named John Chapman, and they lived in Windsor together. They had two daughters and a son, but sadly one of the girls, Emily Ruth, suffered from seizures and died of meningitis aged just 12. Their son was disabled and was sent to live in a special home. In those days, a domestic servant would normally lose her job if she got married, so Annie must have been popular with her employers to have retained her position after her marriage. In some ways, this makes Annie Chapman's story even more poignant, as she had lived a relatively comfortable life before her sudden fall from grace.

Annie and John Chapman, 1869

She was the only victim of whom a photograph was taken when she was still alive; the only images we have of the others are mortuary photos. Annie's picture was taken in the year of her marriage and shows her sitting in a chair with her husband John at her side. At one point, John even secured a job as servant to a nobleman, a very prestigious position.

After their daughter's death in 1882, the pair began drinking heavily, and Annie spent time wandering the countryside, unaware and intoxicated. She was arrested several times and held in jail until she sobered up. Annie and John agreed to part ways two or three years later, and John retained custody of the children. The split was not on bad terms, and he continued paying her ten shillings a week until his death in 1886, from cirrhosis of the liver and dropsy, an old-fashioned term for oedema or swelling, which might have been caused by heart failure.

Many years later, Annie's sister Miriam wrote a letter to a minister in support of the temperance movement, describing how she had tried to prevent her sister's drinking:

"Just before I was six years old, my father cut his throat, leaving my mother with five children. My eldest sister took to drink when she was quite young. Twelve years ago, I heard a sermon on 'Christians and Total Abstinence.' I signed the pledge with two of my sisters and we tried to persuade the one given to drink to give it up. She was married and in a good position. Over and over again she signed the pledge and tried to keep it. Over and over again she was tempted and fell. She said it was no use, no one knew the fearful struggle, and that unless she could keep out of sight or smell, she could never be free. For years we wrestled with God in prayer for her. She could not keep sober, so she left her husband and two children. We never knew where she lived, she

used to come to us at home now and then, we gave her clothes and tried in every way to win her back, for she was a mere beggar. She said she would always keep out of our way, but she must and would have drink."

It is sad to hear how Annie struggled with alcohol addiction, and one cannot help but wonder if her life would have been different had there been access to support groups and a better understanding of mental health.

After John Chapman died, Annie moved to London's East End. She earned money by selling crochet work and flowers but eventually turned to prostitution. After her death, the Morning Post said that Annie had *"lived an immoral life for some time* [by which they were referring to her sex work], *and her habits and surroundings had become worse since her means failed".*

Although she had split from her husband, she was visibly upset when she received news of his death, and soon after this she gained the nickname Dark Annie, because she always appeared depressed or downcast. Her friend Amelia Palmer noticed she was sad whenever she spoke of her children and that since her husband's death, she seemed to have given up on life.

At this time, Annie was living with a sieve maker called John Sivvey at a common lodging house in Dorset Street, one of the worst parts of Whitechapel known for its violence and criminal element, so much so that policemen refused to go down there alone. We know it was one of the worst streets thanks to a poverty map created by social reformer Charles Booth who undertook research from 1886 to 1903, mapping out the income and working conditions of each household, colouring each dwelling according to their status, which ranged from "Upper and upper-middle classes: wealthy" to "Lowest class: vicious, semi-criminal".

Dorset Street was unmistakably one of the latter. John Sivvey left Annie soon after her husband's death.

In August 1888, just weeks before she was murdered, Annie bumped into her younger brother, Fountain Smith, on Commercial Road. She told him she was struggling financially so he gave her two shillings. That was the last time he saw her alive.

That year, Annie was in a relationship with Ted Stanley, a bricklayer's mate known locally as the Pensioner. This was not because of advanced age, as he was only 47, but because he was drawing a military pension under false pretenses, claiming he had been in the army. At the time of her death, Annie had been living at Crossingham's Lodging House at 35 Dorset Street. Crossingham was the name of the owner, who also ran several other lodging houses, and this one had room for around 300 people and was managed by a man called Timothy Donovan, who was described in the newspaper as a *"thin, pale faced, sullen looking young man, with a plentiful lack of shirt collar and a closely twisted crimson scarf around his throat"*.

Stanley the Pensioner often paid for Annie's bed there and instructed Donovan to turn her away if she ever tried to enter with another man. He spent many weekends with Annie at Crossingham's but this arrangement wasn't exclusive as he also paid for a bed for another woman, Eliza Cooper.

At the end of August 1888, Annie and Eliza got into an argument over a borrowed bar of soap. The dispute escalated in the Britannia Public House, known as Ringers, on the corner of Dorset Street and Commercial Street, culminating in Annie slapping Eliza in the face, with Eliza punching Annie in the left eye and breast in retaliation.

On Tuesday 4 September, Amelia Palmer met Annie in the street and gave her tuppence, as Annie said she wasn't feeling well and had not had anything to eat or drink that day. She said she planned to go to the casual ward, a part of the workhouse where the homeless could stay for one night in return for hard work.

On Friday 7 September, Amelia and Annie crossed paths again in Dorset Street. Amelia asked Annie if she was going to Stratford to look for clients, and Annie replied that she was feeling too ill although she reportedly said, *"I must pull myself together and go out and get some money, or I shall have no lodgings."*

She must have had no luck, because at 11:30 p.m. she returned to her lodging house and sat in the kitchen for a while. Another lodger shared a pint of beer with her, then Annie left at around 1:00 a.m. to get some food, returning half an hour later with a potato. Donovan the lodging house manager soon arrived, and their conversation went something like this:

Donovan: *"Have you got your doss money for tonight?"*
Annie: *"I haven't sufficient money for my bed. Don't let it. I shan't be long before I'm in."*
Donovan: *"You can find money for your beer, and you can't find money for your bed!"*
Annie: *"Never mind, Tim. I'll soon be back."*

Annie was still feeling ill, but she left Dorset Street at around 1:50 a.m. and walked up Little Paternoster Row in the direction of Brushfield Street.

At 4:45 a.m. at 29 Hanbury Street, John Richardson, son of the landlady Amelia Richardson, went through the passageway and sat on the steps leading into the backyard to trim some leather off his boot with a knife. He did not live there but regularly went to the house to check on the cellar which had been broken into previously. Although the sun had not fully risen, it would have been light enough for him to see a body had one been there, but he neither saw nor smelt anything out of the ordinary.

Witness John Richardson (The Penny Illustrated Paper)

At 5:15 a.m. witness Elizabeth Long, who also went by the name Mrs. Durrell, saw Annie with a man just outside 29 Hanbury Street. She heard the man say, *"will you?"* to which Annie replied *"yes"*. Long described the man as dark, about 40 years old, a little taller than Annie, and wearing a brown deerstalker hat. Some sources say Long thought the man looked like a foreigner although she only saw him from the back, while others say it was just his accent she described as foreign. This was the last time Annie Chapman was seen alive.

Sometime between 5:15 and 5:20 a.m., carpenter Albert Cadosch, who lived next door at number 27, went into his back yard to relieve himself in the lavatory. He had a urinary tract infection, so he went out twice within five minutes. On the first occasion, he heard a woman saying *"no"*, and the second time, he heard something fall against the fence. He thought little of it as the back yard of number 29 was a popular spot for prostitutes, although the owner Mrs. Richardson vehemently denied it. By now, the sun was up and had Albert looked over the fence, he would almost certainly have seen the face of Jack the Ripper.

There was some controversy over the timings as Elizabeth Long originally put her sighting of Annie and the man at 5:30 a.m. as she had just heard the church clock chime, but matching up the events and Cadosch's statement, it would make more sense if it was the quarter past chime that she heard. It is important to remember that the residents of Whitechapel would not have owned wristwatches, so they had to rely on church clocks which had a tendency to run a few minutes fast or slow, so it is difficult to be exact.

Here is an extract of proceedings from the inquest:

Police surgeon Dr George Bagster Phillips: *"The body of the deceased was lying in the yard on her back, on the left of the steps leading from the passage. The face was swollen, and the tongue protruded between the front teeth. The small intestines and other portions were lying on the right side of the body on the ground above the shoulder but attached. There was a large quantity of blood, with part of the stomach above the left shoulder. The throat was dissevered deeply, the jagged incision reaching right round the neck. On the back wall of the house were patches of blood, and on the wooden fence were smears corresponding to the deceased's head. I believe breathing was interfered with before death, and* death arose from failure of the heart's action, due to the loss of blood caused by the severance of the throat. I believe the killer took hold of her by the chin, then commenced the incision from left to right."

Coroner Wynne Baxter: *"Was the instrument used at the throat the same as that used at the abdomen?"*

Dr Bagster Phillips: *"Probably. It must have been a very sharp knife with a thin, narrow blade, at least six to eight inches in length."*

Coroner: *"Is it possible that any instrument used by a military man, such as a bayonet, would have done it?"*

Dr Bagster Phillips: *"No, not a bayonet."*

(The coroner asked this because the doctor who examined Martha Tabram's body back in early August believed that the final stab wound of the 39 on her body was consistent with a soldier's bayonet.)

Coroner Wynne Baxter: *"Would it have been such an instrument as a medical man uses for postmortems?"*

Dr Bagster Phillips: *"The ordinary postmortem case does not contain such a weapon."*

Coroner: *"Would any instrument that horse slaughterers employ have caused the injuries?"*

Dr Bagster Phillips: *"Yes, well ground down."*

Coroner: *"Would the knife of a cobbler or of any person in the leather trades have done?"*

Dr Bagster Phillips: *"I think the knife used in those trades would not be long enough in the blade."*

Coroner: *"Was there any anatomical knowledge displayed?"*

Dr Bagster Phillips: *"I think there was."*

Bagster Phillips' postmortem report provided even more appalling detail.

"The abdomen was entirely laid open; the intestines lifted out of the body and placed on the shoulder. The uterus and its appendages, the upper portion of the vagina and the posterior two thirds of the bladder, were entirely removed. No trace of these parts was found, and the incisions were cleanly cut. The work was that of an expert, who had such knowledge of anatomical or pathological examinations as to be able to secure the pelvic organs with one sweep of the knife, which must have been at least five or six inches long. I myself could not have performed all the injuries described, in under a quarter of an hour."

Coroner Wynne Baxter was thorough and incisive in his questioning and would become well known for his involvement in the inquests of the Ripper victims. Once again, the verdict was wilful murder, by person or persons unknown. Whether or not the killer really did have anatomical knowledge was, and still is, hotly debated.

Police were no closer to finding the killer of Polly Nichols, or Annie Chapman. The investigation was led by Inspectors Abberline, Helson, and Chandler, as Inspector Edmund Reid was away on holiday.

The only known illustration of Inspector Frederick Abberline who was said to look like a bank manager

The inhabitants of 29 Hanbury Street were questioned, and all the witnesses gave satisfactory accounts of their whereabouts, even Ted Stanley the bogus Pensioner, after a lengthy cross-examination by the acerbic Wynne Baxter.

The scrap of envelope with two pills inside that had been found near Annie's body seemed at first to be a tantalising clue, as it bore the seal of the Sussex Regiment and was stamped London, 28 August 1888, with a partial address visible. Any hopes that this could lead to the killer were dashed when a fellow lodger at Dorset Street, William Stevens, came forward to say that he had seen Annie pick up the discarded envelope from the floor of the lodging house, and used it to store her pills because she had accidentally broken the box that she usually kept them in.

By the end of the inquest, the Whitechapel Vigilance Committee had been formed in The Crown Public House on Mile End Road, not far from the murder sites. George Lusk, a local builder and vestryman, was elected as president. The group's mission was to help the constabulary by looking out for suspicious characters, and they asked the Home Secretary to issue a reward for information leading to the apprehension of the murderer. Their request was denied, as experience had shown that the promise of a reward routinely led to misinformation and more police time being wasted. Everyone in the area was frightened, on edge, and wound as tight as a coiled spring.

How could the killer have escaped into the light of the early morning, covered with blood? How could anyone be so bold as to commit murder in the backyard of a house inhabited by 17 people? And above all, what malevolent use did he have for the body parts he had taken from the scene?

The postmortem report may shed some light on how bloody the killer really would have been, as Dr Bagster Phillips believed that *"breathing was interfered with"* before death.

George Lusk, President of the Whitechapel Vigilance Committee (photo distributed by the late Leonard Archer, Lusk's grandson)

People tend to assume this means that Chapman was strangled, but there was no evidence of any marks on her neck, although she must have been asphyxiated in some way, as she had a swollen and protruding tongue. The clue may lie in the bruises on her jaw and the three abrasions under her left ear, which corresponded to fingers.

I submit that rather than being strangled in the traditional sense with a cord or pair of hands, the assailant held his forearm across her throat from behind to compress the windpipe, using his other hand to cover her mouth and prevent her from crying out. It would have taken less than ten seconds to render his victim unconscious in this way, even with minimal pressure against the carotid artery. The attacker then lowered her to the ground where he slit her throat prior to performing the mutilations. The low blood pressure caused by the suffocation would have resulted in minimal blood spray, which could explain why the killer did not stand out in his appearance. Whether he knew that this method would result in less blood and deliberately chose it for that reason, which would imply medical knowledge, or whether he simply thought it would be the quickest way to subdue his victim, is up for debate. It is probable that the method used for killing Polly Nichols was very similar, as her autopsy report read, *"There was a circular bruise on the left side of the face, which also might have been inflicted by the pressure of the fingers."*

Lurid articles were splashed across the newspapers, reflecting the public disbelief that a human being could murder and mutilate so heinously. This is an extract from the Daily News printed on 10 September:

"Annie Chapman's head was nearly severed from her body by one stroke of a knife, and her mangled remains disposed about her in a way that suggested delight in the slaughter. All was done in half an hour. The house teemed with life; it was near the hour of rising, yet no-one heard a cry. The swiftness, the perfect mystery of it, are heightening effects of terror.

There can no longer be any doubt that we're dealing with some form of malignant insanity. A monster is abroad. Every cut is given with the unerring precision of the slaughterhouse. The police must find for us one of the most extraordinary monsters known to the history of mental and spiritual disease.

The public are looking for a monster, and in the legend of "Leather Apron", they seem to be inventing one to look for. This should be discouraged, or there may soon be murders from panic to add to murders from lust of blood. A touch would fire the whole district, in the mood which it is now. Leather Apron walks without making a noise, with piercing eyes and a strange smile, and Leather Apron looks like a Jew. This has already had its effect in a cry against Whitechapel Jews. Already, as our columns show today, the list of savage assaults in the neighbourhood has increased alarmingly. Every man who can say a reasonable word ought to say it, or worse may follow."

The paper was wise to warn against spreading rumours. Early enquiries had turned up a suspect in the shape of a man known only as Leather Apron. Prostitutes in the area reported being harassed by him, and that he would threaten to "rip them up" with a knife unless they gave him money. This was made even more sensational by the news that a leather apron had been found in the yard at the murder scene, recently washed and left out to dry. In fact, this belonged to John Richardson, who had used it while mending the cellar door. This did not stop an angry mob nearly killing Polish Jewish boot finisher John Pizer, who was also known as Leather Apron, as were many others who worked in similar trades. He had a solid alibi and received compensation after some of the more unscrupulous newspapers cast suspicion on him.

Pizer's problems were not yet at an end, as a few weeks later he was attacked by a woman named Emily Patzwold, who insulted him and shouted, *"Leather Apron!"* at him. When he ignored her, she struck him in the face three times, knocking off his hat. As he was picking it up, she hit him again. Fortunately for Pizer, some neighbours came to help him, and the woman was fined 10s by the Thames Police Court for the attack, plus 2s costs, although Pizer would no doubt have swapped the money for a chance to walk the streets in peace.

GHASTLY MURDER IN THE EAST-END.
DREADFUL MUTILATION OF A WOMAN.
Capture : Leather Apron

Another murder of a character even more diabolical than that perpetrated in Back's Row, on Friday week, was discovered in the same neighbourhood, on Saturday morning. At about six o'clock a woman was found lying in a back yard at the foot of a passage leading to a lodging-house in a Old Brown's Lane, Spitalfields. The house is occupied by a Mrs. Richardson, who lets it out to lodgers, and the door which admits to this passage, at the foot of which lies the yard where the body was found, is always open for the convenience of lodgers. A lodger named Davis was going down to work at the time mentioned and found the woman lying on her back close to the flight of steps leading into the yard. Her throat was cut in a fearful manner. The woman's body had been completely ripped open and the heart and other organs laying about the place, and portions of the entrails round the victim's neck. An excited crowd gathered in front of Mrs. Richardson's house and also round the mortuary in old Montague Street, whither the body was quickly conveyed. As the body lies in the rough coffin in which it has been placed in the mortuary - the same coffin in which the unfortunate Mrs. Nicholls was first placed - it presents a fearful sight. The body is that of a woman about 45 years of age. The height is exactly five feet. The complexion is fair, with wavy brown hair; the eyes are blue, and two lower teeth have been knocked out. The nose is rather large and prominent.

His passive response shows that he was not violent by nature; many other men would have reacted with aggression and made Patzwold regret her boldness.

The authorities were concerned about the anti-Jewish sentiment in Whitechapel, and the Leather Apron incident had done nothing to allay their fears. There was a large Jewish community in the area, as 80,000 Jews had fled their homes in Eastern Europe after the pogroms in Russia. They had been scapegoated for the assassination of Tsar Alexander II and found their way to the East End in large numbers, thanks to its proximity to the docks. Many were successful business owners, butchers, bootmakers, and tailors, among other trades, but the influx meant worsening overcrowding in Whitechapel and Spitalfields, which increased conflict and provoked anti-Semitism. The East End was near boiling point, and senior officials feared imminent civil unrest if relations between Jews and non-Jews broke down further – and painting a shadowy, monstrous picture of the murderer as a Jew was not going to help.

It is widely believed that the press was xenophobic and anti-Semitic, but although there are undoubtedly examples of such newspapers, it was not as widespread as one imagines, and articles have been quoted out of context. For example, the Eastern Argus reported in 1887 that "*A number of men and women land on our wave-beaten shores in a destitute condition and offer to do work at any price....this drives English labour out of the labour market.*" The writer seems to have at least recognised that those arriving in England were destitute and in need of work, rather than painting them as depraved criminals. On 15 September 1888, the East London Observer reported:

"*On Saturday in several quarters of East London, the crowds who had assembled in the streets began to assume a very threatening attitude towards the Hebrew population of the district. It was repeatedly asserted that no Englishman could have perpetrated such a horrible crime as that of Hanbury Street, and that it must have been done by a Jew - and forthwith the crowds proceeded to threaten and abuse such of the unfortunate Hebrews as they found in the streets. Happily, the presence of the large number of police in the streets prevented a riot actually taking place. Since the return of the Jews to England in 1649, only two Jews have been hanged for murder, Marks and Lipski, and taking into consideration the origin of many of the poor wretches who fly to this country from foreign persecution, this is a very remarkable record. That the beast that has made East London a terror is not a Jew I feel assured. There is something too horrible, too unnatural, too un-Jewish, I would say, in the terrible series of murders for an Israelite to be the murderer. There never was a Jew yet who could have steeped himself in such loathsome horrors as those to which publicity has been given. His nature revolts at blood-guiltiness, and the whole theory and practical working of the Whitechapel butchery are opposed to Jewish character."*

This article has been taken out of context by some unscrupulous researchers who have misquoted the newspaper as having said, *"it must have been done by a Jew"*. The inclusion above of the whole paragraph contradicts this inaccuracy, as the whole point of the article was to explain and denounce the sentiment of the crowd. The idea that the Whitechapel murderer was Jewish would pervade popular thought for the next century, but this may not be the truth at all, and this will be explored in more detail later when we tackle the cast of suspects.

After Chapman's murder, police officers visited pawnbrokers in case anyone had tried to sell the stolen rings, and they visited countless lodging houses in their efforts to track down the killer, but nothing was found.

The Illustrated Police News, 22 September 1888

A curious incident took place an hour after the discovery of the body on 8 September, when Mrs. Fiddymont noticed a strange man entering the pub she ran with her husband in Brushfield Street. He was described as wearing a torn shirt, a stiff brown hat pulled down to his eyes, and he had streaks of blood on his hands, his fingers, and under his ear. He looked furtive and had a *"terrifying look in his eyes"*. This man was thought to be Jacob Isenschmid, a butcher whose whereabouts could not be accounted for at the time of the murder. He was found to be mentally unwell and was sent to a workhouse, then to an asylum. Initially, police considered him a strong suspect in Chapman's death, but he was incarcerated at the time of later killings, so he was swiftly discounted.

Jacob Isenschmid in September 1908, from the Colney Hatch Asylum records, courtesy of Lynn Cates & Chris Scott

On 10 September, a woman named Lyons, described in the newspaper as the *"class commonly known as unfortunate"*, reported that a strange man had approached her in Flower and Dean Street and asked her to accompany him to the Queen's Head Pub for a drink later that evening. She agreed and arrived at the pub for their assignation at 6:30 p.m. but was alarmed to notice that her companion was carrying a knife. He said to her, *"You are about the same style of woman as the one that's murdered,"* to which Lyons replied, *"What do you know of her?"* The man's answer was disconcerting; *"You are beginning to smell a rat. Foxes hunt geese but they don't always find them."* He then got up and left. Lyons tried to follow him, but he broke into a run and disappeared.

A sensational story appeared in the press on the same day stating that a message had been found written on a wall at 29 Hanbury Street, which read, *"I have now done three, and intend to do nine more and give myself up."* Another version written on a piece of paper which was found in the street purportedly said, *"Five – fifteen more and I give myself up."* Some papers believed these stories had been fabricated to cause undue alarm, but we cannot say for sure if this was the case.

On 27 September, a man named John Fitzgerald came forward claiming to be The Ripper but was unable to give the police any detail which would confirm it, so it became clear that it was a false confession. Around this time, the Reverend Samuel Barnett wrote a letter to the Times, calling for improved street lighting, the removal of slaughterhouses, and better policing. Indeed, the law was heavily criticized in the press, with the satirical magazine Punch publishing a cartoon of a blindfolded constable grasping helplessly at the criminals surrounding him.

Punch Magazine, 22 September 1888

The Pall Mall Budget facetiously suggested that the killer leave his business card on his victims, to give the force a fair chance of finding him. They were also vitriolic towards the Secretary of State, Henry Matthews, with the Pall Mall Gazette proposing that it was *"high time for him to go and excel somewhere else and in some other department than the Home Office".*

Annie Chapman was buried on 14 September 1888 at Manor Park Cemetery in Forest Gate, in a private ceremony attended only by her family. Today the site of her grave is completely lost, as the plot has been used to bury new bodies twice over. Her two surviving children were cared for by relatives, having lost both their parents at a young age.

According to the newspapers, another life was unexpectedly affected by The Ripper's actions. Mrs. Sodeaux, the wife of a Spitalfields weaver living in Hanbury Street, was unable to comprehend the horror of Annie Chapman's murder and hanged herself shortly afterwards. Another woman was reported to have collapsed after reading about the grotesque killing in the paper. No doubt many others were sickened and terrified in equal measure, unable to walk down a dark street without their heartbeat quickening, and a compulsion to turn and look over their shoulder in case they were to be next.

Hanbury Street has now been completely transformed into a covered car park and weekend marketplace but it can be seen as it once was in a YouTube clip, filmed in the 1960s during the making of TV programme The London Nobody Knows.

All the murder sites look vastly different now from how they did back in 1888, but if you visit in the dark and use your imagination, you can still just about envision those narrow, dimly lit passageways and the flicker of gaslights. If you listen, you might even hear the ghostly echo of the footsteps of the blood-soaked demon who still stalks the streets in our imaginations.

29 Hanbury Street in 1967 (Tower Hamlets Local History Library)

But don't forget that the killer was still being referred to at this time as the Whitechapel Murderer or the Whitechapel Fiend. He did not yet have a name...but he was just about to get one. On 27 September 1888, the London Central News Agency received a chilling letter.

25. Sept. 1888.

Dear Boss
        I keep on hearing the police have caught me. but they wont fix me just yet. I have laughed when they look so clever and talk about being on the right track. That joke about Leather apron gave me real fits. I am down on whores and I shant quit ripping them till I do get buckled. Grand work the last job was. I gave the lady no time to squeal. How can they catch me now. I love my work and want to start again. You will soon hear of me with my funny little games. I saved some of the proper red stuff in a ginger beer bottle over the last job to write with but it went thick like glue and I cant use it. Red ink is fit enough I hope <u>ha. ha</u>. The next job I do I shall clip the ladys ears off and send to the

Dear Boss Letter (National Archives)

police officers just for jolly wouldnt you. Keep this letter back till I do a bit more work, then give it out straight. My knife's so nice and sharp I want to get to work right away if I get a chance. Good luck.

        yours truly

           Jack the Ripper

Dont mind me giving the trade name

wasnt good enough to post this before I got all the red ink off my hands curse it No luck yet. They say I'm a doctor now ha ha

The reverse side of the Dear Boss letter (National Archives)

"Dear Boss,
I keep on hearing the police have caught me. but they won't fix me just yet. I have laughed when they look so clever and talk about being on the right track. That joke about Leather Apron gave me real fits. I am down on whores and I shan't quit ripping them till I do get buckled. Grand work the last job was. I gave the lady no time to squeal. How can they catch me now. I love my work and want to start again. You will soon hear of me with my funny little games. I saved some of the proper red stuff in a ginger beer bottle over the last job to write with but it went thick like glue and I can't use it. Red ink is fit enough I hope ha. ha. The next job I do I shall clip the lady's ears off and send to the police officers just for jolly wouldn't you. Keep this letter back till I do a bit more work. then give it out straight. My knife's so nice and sharp I want to get to work right away if I get a chance. Good luck.
Yours truly
Jack the Ripper
Don't mind me giving the trade name
Wasn't good enough to post this before I got all the red ink off my hands curse it No luck yet. They say I'm a doctor now- ha ha."

Chapter Four
Elizabeth "Liz" Stride
Dutfield's Yard, 30 September 1888

"A week has now passed since the last of the Whitechapel murders took place. During that period there has been something more than the customary show of police activity. The coroner has done as much as it lies in the power of a coroner to do to probe the mystery: yet not the smallest approach appears to have been made towards the apprehension of the criminal. No trustworthy clue has been obtained. We assume that the police have done their best, and we are far from charging them with incapacity because their best amounts only to failure. They have not arrested any man against whom a reasonable case could be made; but they have arrested more than one whom there never was the faintest warrant for suspecting. We express our surprise that the police have pounced on persons who were plainly innocent. That they have not succeeded in arresting the culprit is a pity; but that they have been energetic in the wrong direction is distinctly a reproach. There is a worse thing than doing nothing: that is, doing something that ought not to be done." - **Pall Mall Gazette, 15 September 1888**

Hitherto known only as The Whitechapel Murderer or the Whitechapel Fiend, the killer had now given himself an electrifying name…Jack the Ripper. Or had he? The letter was written in neat handwriting by someone with a good education, so suspicions later fell upon a journalist. After all, why would it cross the mind of a Victorian murderer to write a letter to the press? The idea is not alien to us now, with other notable examples like the Zodiac and his ciphers planted firmly in the history books and shows like CSI and Criminal Minds to tantalize the imagination. But back then, there was no concept of a serial killer, and such an egregious, bloodthirsty name sounds like it sprung from the pen of someone set to benefit from a sensational scoop. The letter was also addressed to the Central News Agency rather than the police or one specific newspaper, which would not have occurred to an average person who was unfamiliar with the inner workings of the press. It is erroneously believed that Jack the Ripper was the very first serial killer to be given a sensational moniker, but in fact, a murderer operating in Texas between 1884 and 1885 was christened the "Servant Girl Annihilator" by American author O. Henry.

Police were initially sceptical about the Dear Boss letter and thought it was a tasteless hoax. But when the monstrous events of Sunday 30 September 1888 came to light, they began to wonder if it could have been written by the killer after all. Just three weeks had passed since the brutal murder and mutilation of Annie Chapman at 29 Hanbury Street, and tensions were running higher than ever. The public felt unsafe, and 200 tradesmen from Whitechapel petitioned the Home Secretary for additional Bobbies to be deployed.

At 12:45 a.m. on Sunday 30 September, a Hungarian Jew named Israel Schwartz was walking down Berner Street on his way home, just half a mile from the scene of the last murder. Berner Street was a mostly residential road, and between number 40, which was the International Working Men's Educational Club, and number 42, was a narrow yard called Dutfield's Yard. The entrance to the yard was just nine feet wide, with access gained through a pair of wooden gates, each one just four feet six inches across. The left gate was fitted with a small door, known as a wicket, to allow people to get through when the gates were closed. The names "W. Hindley, Sack Manufacturer", and "A. Dutfield,

Van and Cart Builder" were written on the gates in white paint, although Arthur Dutfield had moved his business to Pinchin Street two years before. The cart making business and the sack manufacturer were located on the west side of the yard, next to an unused stable. On the north side of the yard was the Working Men's Educational Club, while on the south side were three artisans' dwellings converted from older buildings. On the left of the entrance were terraced cottages occupied by cigarette makers and tailors.

Nowadays, Berner Street has been renamed Henriques Street after a local benefactor, and the houses have been replaced by a school.

Berner Street and Dutfield's Yard as it was in 1909. Dutfield's Yard is directly underneath and behind the suspended cartwheel. The International Working Men's Club is immediately to the right of it.

Schwartz noticed two people standing at the entrance to Dutfield's Yard. A man was trying to pull a woman into the street, then threw her to the ground. She cried out three times, although not loudly. The assailant was around 5'5", 30 years old, broad shouldered, fair complexioned, with dark hair and a small brown moustache. He was wearing a black overcoat and a black felt hat with a wide brim, and he appeared to be slightly drunk.

Not wanting any trouble, Schwartz crossed to the opposite side of the road and heard the broad-shouldered man shout, *"Lipski!"* This was a racial slur towards Jews, following the murder the previous year of a woman called Miriam Angel, just a block away, by Jewish umbrella salesman Israel Lipski, who was hanged for the crime. As this was a derogatory term, whoever said it would not have been Jewish themselves.

On the side of the pavement that Schwartz had moved to, a man emerged from a doorway on the sidewalk near Nelson's Public House. Schwartz described him as around six feet tall, 35 years old with light brown hair, wearing a dark overcoat and a hard felt wide-brimmed hat, and holding a clay pipe.

Schwartz walked quickly away, followed by the tall man with the clay pipe, although he was not sure if he was being pursued, or if the man was just heading in the same direction. Schwartz did not know whom the shout of "Lipski" had been directed at, nor whether the two men he had seen knew each other. I propose that he could have misheard someone shouting the name "Lizzie".

Just a few minutes later, Louis Diemschutz, steward of the International Working Men's Educational Club and jewellery salesman, arrived at Dutfield's Yard in his pony and trap after a day at the market. He lived in the Club building, and he found the gates open when he arrived, which was not unusual. He would have seen a chink of light coming from the windows, and the welcoming sounds of singing and laughter from inside. There had been around a hundred people there earlier that evening attending a lecture on the reasons Jews should be socialists. It was a three-storey building which housed a stage on which amateurs performed plays by Russian revolutionaries. It was frequented by Russians, Jews, British, French, Italian, Czech and Polish radicals; anyone was welcome, provided they were socialists.

By this time, many of the club members had left, except for 28 men who were still singing and talking. Diemschutz's pony shied as if startled by something. Horses have better night vision than humans and a keener sense of smell, so the animal was the first to detect that something was wrong. It was oppressively dark, so Diemschutz used his whip handle to poke around the area, then lit a match to shed a tiny flicker of illumination over the scene.

Penny Illustrated Paper, 6 October 1888

He gasped when he saw a figure on the ground, lying on its side about six feet from the gate, just in front of the side door to the club. At first, Diemschutz thought it was his wife lying drunk on the floor. When he looked closer, he was confronted with a hair-raising shock. It wasn't a drunk woman at all. It was a dead one. He rushed into the Working Men's Club and asked for help. Two men; Morris Eagle, who had been leading that night's political debate, and Isaac Kozebrodsky, went outside and saw the woman lying in a pool of blood, a stream of it trickling down the yard.

Eagle ran down Commercial Street, while Diemschutz ran down Fairclough Street, both shouting for a policeman. Constables Lamb and Collins arrived at the scene, pushing back a rapidly gathering crowd of around 30 people, all jostling for a glimpse, including one woman who showed her child the horrific scene while reportedly remarking to her companions, *"Does it want to see the blood, bless its heart? So it shall. Take a good look at it, my pet. You may see enough of it if this sort of thing keeps up."*

Left: Louis Diemschutz, Right: Morris Eagle
(The Penny Illustrated Paper)

PC Lamb warned the onlookers against touching the body in case they got blood on their hands and incriminated themselves. PC William Smith arrived, passing through Berner Street on his beat, and immediately went to fetch an ambulance cart. PC Lamb shut the gates to Dutfield's Yard to ensure nobody escaped, then examined the rooms of the Working Men's Club, checking the hands and clothes of all the club members still inside. He then inspected the two lavatories in the yard, the cottages across the road, and the workshop of sack manufacturer Walter Hindley. Lamb's efficiency in securing the scene and his thorough police work were commendable.

A crowd gathering in Berner Street (The Pictorial News, 6 October 1888)

Dr Blackwell, who lived nearby, arrived at 1:15 a.m. and pronounced the woman dead. Her throat had been deeply slashed, cut through right down to the blood vessels, and her windpipe had been severed. This is an extract from his report:

"The deceased was lying on her left side. Her legs were drawn up, her feet three yards from the gateway. Her dress was unfastened at the neck. The neck and chest were warm, as were the legs and face. The hands were cold. The right hand was open and on the chest, and was smeared with blood. The left hand, lying on the ground, was partially closed, holding a small packet of cachous [a type of lozenge used to sweeten the breath] *wrapped in tissue paper. There were no rings, nor marks of rings, on her hands. The appearance of the face was quite placid. The mouth was slightly open. The deceased had round her neck a check silk scarf, the bow of which was turned to the left and pulled very tight. In the neck was a long incision exactly corresponding to the lower border of the scarf, commencing on the left side, nearly severing the vessels, and cutting the windpipe completely in two. The blood was running down the gutter into the drain in the opposite direction of the feet. There was about one pound of clotted blood close by the body, and a stream all the way to the back door of the club."*

Dr Blackwell surmised that Stride's attacker had seized her by the shoulders, before yanking her backwards with her scarf and cutting her throat. Dr George Bagster Phillips agreed with Dr Blackwell, and pressure marks on her shoulders combined with Schwartz's testimony confirmed this theory. Bagster Phillips later judged at the inquest that it would have taken just two seconds to cut her throat, and the killer would not have had blood on him as the injury was inflicted by someone standing behind the victim.

At around 1:45 a.m. Inspector Edmund Reid and Superintendent Arnold arrived on the scene. At 4:30 a.m. the body was removed to the mortuary. Sometime between 5:00 and 6:00 a.m., PC Lamb washed the blood away, and Inspector Abberline arrived and ordered a house-to-house search in Berner Street, which turned up nothing.

80,000 leaflets were printed and distributed by H Division asking the occupiers of each home to tell the police about any questionable lodgers, which led to over 2,000 people being investigated.

POLICE NOTICE.

TO THE OCCUPIER.

On the mornings of Friday, 31st August, Saturday 8th, and Sunday, 30th September, 1888, Women were murdered in or near Whitechapel, supposed by some one residing in the immediate neighbourhood. Should you know of any person to whom suspicion is attached, you are earnestly requested to communicate at once with the nearest Police Station.

Metropolitan Police Office,
30th September, 1888.

Printed by M'Corquodale & Co. Limited, "The Armoury," Southwark.

Meanwhile, Thames Police looked at sailors on board ships in the docks and questioned "Asiatic" men in opium dens in the area, as well as 76 butchers and horse slaughterers. Enquiries were made into an allegation of some Greek gypsies being spotted in the city, but this transpired to be false. Three cowboys from an American exhibition were also traced and their whereabouts accounted for. This implies that the police were focused on the killer being an 'outsider' or an itinerant who dwelt in lodging houses and did not have a fixed address.

The East Enders were keen to co-operate, and Robert Anderson noted in an official file that: *"The public generally, and especially the inhabitants of the East End, have shown a marked desire to assist in every way, even at some sacrifice to themselves as for example in permitting their houses to be searched."*

Inspector Reid took a description of the victim at the mortuary:

"She was 42 to 44 years old, between 5'2" to 5'5"; lean and slightly built. She had curly, dark-brown hair, attractive features, a straight nose, an oval face with light-grey or blue eyes and pale complexion. Her upper front teeth were missing. She wore a black crape bonnet and a long black jacket trimmed with black coney fur, the left side plastered with mud; a single red rose amidst maidenhair fern pinned to it. She wore an old long black skirt, a dark-brown velvet bodice, two light-serge petticoats, a white chemise, white stockings, side-spring boots, and a checked silk neckerchief. Inside a pocket in her underskirt were a padlock key, two pocket handkerchiefs, a piece of lead pencil, a comb, a broken piece of comb, a metal spoon, six large buttons and one small, a dress hook, a piece of muslin, some wool on card, one or two small pieces of paper, and a thimble."

This list evokes a certain sadness, the image of a woman with so little in life that all her worldly goods were carried in her pocket and that even a broken piece of comb and scraps of wool were kept and treasured. Israel Schwartz identified her as the woman he had witnessed being pushed to the ground by the broad-shouldered man at 12:45 a.m. Her name was Elizabeth Stride, and just like all the other victims, she was an individual with a unique story who deserves to be remembered.

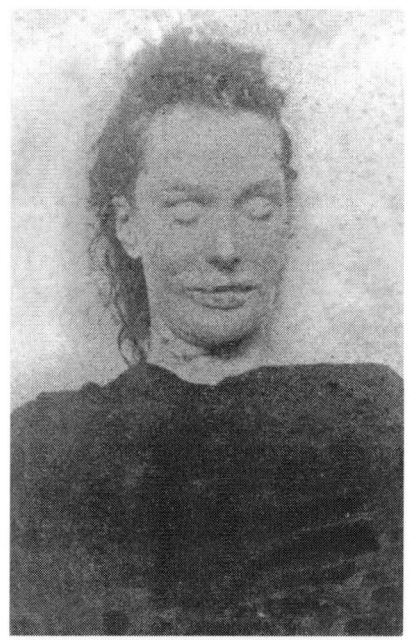

Mortuary photo of Elizabeth "Liz" Stride

She was born Elisabeth Gustafsdotter on a farm near Gothenburg, Sweden, on 27 November 1843, so she was 44 at the time of her death. She was the second of four children and at the age of 16, she moved out of the family home to work as a domestic servant. We know from Gothenburg records that she turned to prostitution a couple of years later.

In April 1865, aged 22, she gave birth to a stillborn daughter. She came to England in 1866, presumably to start a new life for herself after inheriting some money from her mother when she died. That year, she registered in London with the Swedish church at St George in the East, near the Ratcliffe Highway, which incidentally was the scene of several barbaric murders in 1811. She spoke both English and Yiddish quite well.

In 1869 she married carpenter John Stride and they ran a coffee shop together for five years until their marriage fell apart in the 1880s. Around this time, she went by the nickname Long Liz, a play on words with the phrase Long Stride, due to her surname.

In 1878, there was a horrendous accident in the Thames when two steam ships collided; the Princess Alice and the Bywell, with more than 600 lives lost. Liz later told people that her husband and two children were killed in this disaster and that she had an injury to the roof of her mouth from being kicked in the face while climbing the mast to escape. However, there is no evidence that she had any other children after her stillborn daughter, and records show that her husband died in 1884 of heart failure. After Liz was killed in 1888, the postmortem found no damage to her palate, so all or part of her story had been embroidered.

Liz drifted around Whitechapel, spending time in the workhouse, at the infirmary being treated for bronchitis, and at various lodging houses. In 1885, she began a relationship with dock labourer and army reservist Michael Kidney. They struggled financially and the clerk at the Swedish Church said he had known Liz for 17 years and that she often applied to them for help. She made money through sewing and charring (an old-fashioned word for cleaning or domestic work), as well as casual prostitution. Michael Kidney gave her money when he could afford it.

Their relationship was not a stable one, and in 1887 Liz accused Kidney of assaulting her, but she did not appear in court, so the charges were dropped. Between 1887 and 1888 they were both arrested multiple times for drunkenness. Kidney last saw Liz on Tuesday 25 September, five days before her death. He had expected her home but was not surprised when she failed to arrive, as she was in the habit of leaving and then returning. He told police, *"She always returned without me going after her. I think she liked me better than any other man."* Kidney identified Liz's body at the mortuary, but although they had been in a relationship for three years, he did not know her exact age, guessing that she was between 36 and 38.

Michael Kidney (The Penny Illustrated News)

On this occasion, Liz had taken a room in a lodging house at 32 Flower and Dean Street, one of the most crime-ridden streets in Whitechapel. She told fellow lodger Catherine Lane that she had exchanged words with the man she was living with, and that was why she had moved out, although Kidney later denied there had been an argument.

While Jack the Ripper was leaving his bloody mark on London, Dr Barnardo was visiting the city. He went to the Flower and Dean Street lodging house and met Stride, along with some of the other inhabitants. Barnardo's is now a children's charity and Thomas Barnardo was the man behind it. He was radical and ahead of his time, shocked and moved by the poverty he saw in the East End. He set up homes to care for children without families and by the time he died in 1905, the charity had 96 homes caring for more than 8,500 vulnerable children, including those with physical and learning disabilities. Implausibly, the elderly philanthropist later became a suspect himself! He noticed when he entered the kitchen at 32 Flower and Dean Street, that the women seemed frightened as they discussed the recent murders. One cried out, *"We're all up to no good, no one cares what becomes of us! Perhaps some of us will be killed next!"*

Her words were disconcertingly prescient. On Saturday 29 September, on the eve of her death, Liz Stride cleaned some of the rooms at the lodging house and was paid sixpence by the deputy, Mrs. Tanner. The two women went to the Queens Head pub together at around 6:30 p.m.

Catherine Lane, who later identified Liz's body, testified that she had last seen her alive between 7:00 and 8:00 p.m. Liz had given her a piece of velvet to look after, and when she left the lodging house, she had the sixpence on her which she had earned from cleaning rooms, which would have been enough for her doss money. Lane confirmed that Liz had recently left Michael Kidney after a disagreement, and that Liz had not been drinking that night.

At 11:00 p.m. two labourers named Gardner and Best were about to enter the Bricklayers Arms pub, not far from Berner Street, when they saw a woman with a short man who had a dark moustache and sandy coloured eyebrows, wearing a billycock hat (another name for a bowler hat). The couple were exiting the pub but seemed reluctant to leave the warmth and venture outside into the rain, and they were hugging and kissing. They then went off in the direction of Commercial Road and Berner Street. We know this from an interview Gardner and Best gave to a newspaper, but they were not interviewed by the police or called to the inquest, although they positively identified Stride in the mortuary as the woman they had seen. We don't know why they were not called, but it could have been a procedural omission or that their story was felt to be inconsequential as their sighting of Liz occurred almost two hours before she was killed.

At 11:45 p.m. William Marshall, who lived at 64 Berner Street, was standing outside his house when he noticed a man and a woman in the doorway of number 68, just a few doors down. The pair then walked down the middle of the road, talking quietly. Marshall could not see the man's face, but he noticed that he was middle-aged, had no whiskers, and wore a small dark cutaway coat and trousers. He was about 5'6" and stoutly built, and his respectable clothes made him look like a clerk. He wore a round peaked cap like a sailor, but he did not look like a sailor or a dock labourer, and his voice was that of an educated man. Marshall heard the man mutter, *"You would say anything but your prayers."* He later identified the woman as Liz Stride but mentioned that she was not wearing a flower at the time, although she was wearing one when she died. Marshall would have had a fairly good view of the couple, as there was a streetlamp outside number 70.

Matthew Packer, who sold fresh produce and sweets from the window of his home at 44 Berner Street, declared that a man and a woman bought grapes from him sometime between 11:00 p.m. and midnight, but his story changed over time, and he is now believed to have been mistaken. The postmortem report confirmed that Liz had not eaten grapes before her death, and the myth of her clutching fruit stalks when she was found has long since been refuted.

At around midnight, as Saturday 29 September gave way to Sunday 30 September, William Marshall went back into his house. Between midnight and 1:00 a.m., various people were coming and going from the Working Men's Club in Dutfield's Yard. PC William Smith, whose beat took him down Berner Street every half an hour, noticed Liz Stride and a man at around 12:35. He described him as 5'7", about 28 years old, wearing a dark coat, a deerstalker hat, and carrying a parcel wrapped in newspaper about 18 inches long and six inches wide. The pair were speaking quietly and appeared sober. Although he did not fully see the man's face, he noticed that he had no whiskers, and that he looked respectable. He spotted that the woman was wearing a flower in her jacket and when he saw the woman lying in the mortuary later that night, he recognized her immediately. He remarked that it was unusual to see couples or prostitutes in Berner Street.

Fanny Mortimer, also a resident of Berner Street, was standing outside between midnight and 1:00 a.m. She reported seeing a man walking down the road carrying a black shiny bag, which may be the first story that sowed the seed of the Gladstone Bag myth. Many films and pictures portray Jack the Ripper carrying one of these, a bit like the bags doctors typically used to transport the tools of their trade, but there was never any evidence for this, and the man Mrs. Mortimer saw turned out to be a tobacco salesman. She mentioned that the street was quiet at the time, although she could hear music and dancing from the club. She agreed that it would have been unusual to see a man and woman walking down the street together, particularly at that time of night. At around 12:35 a.m. she heard the measured, heavy stamp of a policeman passing the house on his beat, which was probably PC William Smith, whose own estimation of the timing roughly matched.

At 12:35 a.m., Morris Eagle, who had led the debate that night at the Working Men's Club, returned to Dutfield's Yard after walking his girlfriend home. He heard singing in Russian from the first floor of the Club but saw nobody. Around 12:45 a.m., dock labourer James Brown passed the junction of Berner Street and Fairclough Street on his way to get some supper from a chandler's shop, and saw a woman leaning against a wall, talking to a man who was 5'7", who wore a long black coat down to his heels. He heard the woman say, *"Not tonight, some other night."* Brown thought that neither of them were drunk and he did not notice a flower on the woman's clothes. His statement, printed in St James's Gazette on 6 October, described the man as "not stout", and the Lloyds Weekly Newspaper on 7 October reported the man as being of "average build". In a curious anomaly, Donald Swanson's report to the Home Office on 19 October described the man Brown saw as "stoutish built".

If all the witness testimonies are taken at face value, it sounds as though Liz was seen with several men that night. It was reportedly unusual to see couples walking down Berner Street, so this could be more logically explained by the theory that the witnesses were not remembering the details accurately. Memories can be affected by many factors including the power of suggestion. American cognitive psychologist Elizabeth Loftus has extensively researched human memories and proven how easy it is to make people believe they saw something that they didn't. People have a propensity to assume that our memories work like a video recorder and play scenes back to us in exactly the way they happened, but memories are reconstructed rather than replayed, so remembering something is like slotting jigsaw puzzle pieces together. The stories people recall are sometimes uncannily accurate, sometimes completely fictional, and frequently a mixture of the two. Eyewitness testimony is a useful form of evidence for convicting the accused and it was all they had to go on in 1888 before advances in forensic science were made, but even the most confident of witnesses can be subject to unconscious memory distortions and biases. There have been many instances of mistaken identity, including the famous case of Adolf Beck in the early 1900s, which is well worth reading about as it is truly stranger than fiction and led to changes to the British justice system.

I propose that William Marshall and PC William Smith both saw the same man with Liz, as their descriptions are similar and they described him as respectable, about 5'6" or 5'7", wearing dark clothes, and with no whiskers. If they did indeed see the same man, this would mean that he was with Liz for at least 45 minutes; longer if Gardner and Best's story was accurate and he was the same man she had been hugging and kissing outside the pub at 11:00 p.m. It would be absurd for a prostitute to spend so long walking up and down the road with a client, so my belief is that this was a romantic rendezvous. Stride is the only one of the canonical victims who was not described as an "unfortunate" in contemporaneous sources, so any prostitution she practiced must have been casual. She had also earned sixpence that afternoon from her cleaning work, so she would not have needed to sell herself to get a bed for the night. She had not been wearing a flower in her coat when she left her lodging house earlier that evening, but she was wearing one when she was killed, so either she bought it some time that evening, or the man she was with gave it to her. We will never know for sure, as there is no evidence that detectives spoke to flower sellers in the area. Gardner and Best had seen Liz wearing the flower at 11:00 p.m. so it may be that witnesses William Marshall and James Brown, who did not mention it in their descriptions, simply failed to notice it.

After Stride and the respectably dressed man parted ways, she could have been approached by another man wearing a long dark coat at around 12:45, as per witness James Brown's description. The conversation Brown overhead, in which Liz said, *"Not tonight, some other night,"* does not sound consistent with the friendly, softly spoken conversation she had been having with the respectable man earlier, who she clearly knew more closely than as a casual acquaintance. Shortly after the man with the long coat left, the broad-shouldered, intoxicated man seen by Israel Schwartz could have attacked her, having come out of the pub moments before, or the man James Brown saw could well have been the same man Schwartz witnessed throwing Stride to the ground.

As for why the respectable man never came forward, we could hypothesize that he was Jewish, as the area was notably a Jewish one and Liz was known to associate with Jewish people. If this was the case, he might have been too scared to admit to having been in the victim's company that evening, given what had happened to John Pizer in the Leather Apron incident. Or, he could have been a family man who did not want his indiscretion with a woman of a lower class to be uncovered. This is of course conjecture but could explain why no trace of the man was ever found.

In a quirk of chance, a woman at the inquest named Mrs. Malcolm was convinced the deceased was her sister, Elizabeth Watts. Funnily enough, she shared her first name with Stride, both were nicknamed Long Liz, had at one time kept coffee houses, were drinkers, had lived in common lodging houses in the East End, and had lost their front teeth. Uncanny similarities aside, it was proven beyond doubt that the body was Elizabeth Stride, and not Mrs. Malcolm's sister.

Liz was buried a week later, on Saturday 6 October in the East London Cemetery, and the simple funeral was paid for by the parish. So was she really killed by Jack the Ripper? There are several key differences between her murder and those of the other canonical victims:

- She was the only victim found south of Commercial Road
- She was the only victim not found on her back
- Other murders occurred in quieter locations, while this one took place in front of the bustling International Working Men's club
- Witnesses, including a police officer, confirmed that it was unusual to see couples or prostitutes walking down Berner Street. All the other canonical crime scenes were known to be frequented by streetwalkers. Berner Street was therefore a strange choice of location for The Ripper to seek a victim
- The knife that killed Stride was different and less sharp than the ones used on the other victims

- Dr George Bagster Phillips observed that the way Liz Stride's throat was cut differed from how Annie Chapman's was cut, with the latter being severed all round down to the vertebral column, with an obvious attempt to separate the bones
- Stride's body was not mutilated

Some people believe that Jack the Ripper ran out of time and had to abandon the murder after cutting her throat, not having the opportunity to slash her body like the others as he heard someone coming: Diemschutz in his pony and trap.

The Pictorial News, 6 October 1888

But The Ripper was used to working quickly and in the dark and it seems an odd place to choose to kill someone when his main goal seemed to be the mutilation of the body and removal of organs after death, for which he would need time and privacy.

Many historians now believe that Stride's death was in fact the result of a domestic dispute with partner Michael Kidney. She had not been home for five days, so we can imagine that he went out looking for her and an argument escalated into violence, particularly if he saw her walking around with another man. Perhaps he was the person whom Israel Schwartz saw in the gateway to Dutfield's Yard, throwing Liz Stride to the ground. Either way, the man Schwartz saw was almost certainly the killer, as it would have been extraordinarily unfortunate for Liz to be attacked again moments later by another man.

Modern policing wisdom teaches us that nearly half of all murdered women are killed by their partner, and in about a third of these cases, there was an argument shortly before the homicide. We know that Stride and Kidney had a difficult relationship and she had moved into a lodging house a few days before. In a shocking parallel, a woman named Sarah Brown had her throat cut by her husband in the West End of London that same night.

Kidney is also the only acquaintance of any of the canonical victims who presented himself at a police station behaving strangely. He felt he could have done a better job than the constabulary, admitting at the inquest to a run-in at the station:

"When I went to the station I was intoxicated. I told the inspector at the station that if the murder occurred on my beat, I would shoot myself. I have been in the army. I believe I could catch the man, if I had the proper force at my command. If I was to place the men myself, I could capture the murderer. He would be caught in the act."

Around 24 hours after the murder, 18-year-old Thomas Coram had been visiting a friend in nearby Bath Gardens when his eyes were drawn to something unusual as he walked past 253 Whitechapel Road, which was occupied by a laundress. A bloodied white handkerchief lay on the bottom step of the house, wrapped around the handle of a blood-stained knife, and secured with a piece of string. Coram gestured at an approaching policeman and said, *"There is a knife down here,"* and said that he had not touched it because it *"made his blood run cold"*. PC Joseph Drage of H Division escorted Coram to Leman Street Police Station along with the evidence. The blood on the handkerchief was dry and PC Drage was sure the knife had not been there when he passed the spot one hour earlier; he remembered paying particular attention as he had seen a woman coming out of the house. However, he could not say for sure whether it had been there or not on his next pass 45 minutes later. Dr George Bagster Phillips examined the nine-inch-long knife, which was presented at the inquest, and was certain that it was not the murder weapon.

The police and the press firmly believed that Liz Stride was a Ripper victim, but amid the Autumn of Terror, it would have been difficult for them to step back and think otherwise, caught up in the hysteria of the string of unsolved brutal murders. Had she been killed earlier in the year, before Martha Tabram, would investigators still have linked her murder to the others and counted her among Jack's victims? Some believe Stride really was killed by The Ripper, but others are convinced that she was not.

The reason many initially believed her murder was a hastily aborted Ripper killing became clear that very same night when another body was found at 1:45 a.m. in a corner of dark and eerie Mitre Square.

The Illustrated Police News, 6 October 1888

Chapter Five
Catherine Eddowes
Mitre Square, 30 September 1888

"Two more terrible murders are now added to the long list of East End tragedies which have filled London with horror and alarm. The audacity and cunning of the criminal is certainly unparalleled. Before the victim has time to utter a cry, one swift, deep stroke descends, and all is over except the horrible work of mutilating the lifeless body. Once round a corner into a main thoroughfare, the miscreant is safe from arrest, for he can keep a sufficient distance from the lamps to hinder any recognition of blood-marks on his clothing" – **The Echo, 1 October 1888**

Sunday 30 September 1888 marked the peak of the Autumn of Terror, when two women were killed on the same night, less than an hour apart. In the previous chapter, we learned the story of Liz Stride, whose blood ran in red rivulets into the street when her throat was cut from ear to ear at Dutfield's Yard. Less than an hour later, and under a mile from the scene of the Stride killing, Catherine Eddowes was found dead in Mitre Square, subjected to the most horrific mutilation yet.

Rather than immediately examining the details of how she met her tragic demise, let's learn a little about Eddowes and her life first. With the Jack the Ripper case, it is all too easy to become immersed in the sensational, sanguinary details, so it is incredibly important to remember that each of these women were individuals who should be remembered in their own right, not just as victims of one of the most infamous serial killers in history.

Catherine Eddowes was born on 14 April 1842 in Wolverhampton, in the Midlands of England, to mother Catherine and father George, who was a tin plate worker. She was the sixth of 12 children, but in those days such large families were not uncommon, and a high infant mortality rate, especially among the poor, meant that parents did not expect every baby to survive. In fact, three of the Eddowes children died young.

The family moved to London in 1843. Without access to any other means of transport, they walked all the way there; more than 120 miles. Catherine's mother died when she was 13 and her father followed just two years later. Orphaned and with no source of income in an unfriendly city, she made her way back to Wolverhampton to stay with her aunt. In 1862 she was caught stealing from an employer and ran away to live with an uncle in the nearby city of Birmingham, where she worked briefly as a tray polisher, before going back to Wolverhampton to live with her grandfather. Eventually she met partner Thomas Conway, a street hawker who sold cheap books and gallows ballads, and they returned to London together. Gallows ballads were exactly what they sound like: songs or poems hastily written and printed overnight about criminals who were due to hang the next day, then sold to the public literally at the foot of the gallows.

This happened elsewhere in the country too, not just London. For example, here is a verse from a ballad written about a brutal Portsmouth murder in 1829:

A barbarous foul and horrid deed,
I shortly shall recite,
Which did occur in Portsmouth town,
Upon a Sunday night,

An aged man of 80 years,
his housekeeper likewise,
Were there most basely murdered,
By a monster in disguise.
All in the night so dark and drear,
His entrance he obtained,
And with a deadly hammer he,
Beat out the old man's brains,
His throat he cut from ear to ear,
Most horrible to view,
And streams of crimson blood did flow,
The bedroom through and through.

This sort of thing would disparagingly be called doggerel these days, but back then it was considered entertainment and the public relished it. Eddowes and Conway even wrote a ballad based on the execution of Catherine's own cousin who was hanged in 1866.

The pair lived a nomadic lifestyle and Catherine sometimes claimed to be married to Conway but there is no evidence that this was true. Nonetheless, the five feet tall, hazel-eyed, and auburn-haired Kate, as she was known, had his initials tattooed in blue ink on her forearm. Conway did not earn much but drew a regular pension from his soldiering days. They had three children, Ann, Thomas, and Alfred, and they lived at 71 Lower Gower Street in Chelsea, one of the better parts of London.

The couple had split by 1881, presumptively due to Catherine's heavy drinking which was at odds with Conway's teetotalism. She took her daughter Ann, while Thomas took their sons Thomas Junior and Alfred. Catherine found her way to the East End and began living with a man named John Kelly in Spitalfields, mostly staying at Cooney's Lodging House in Flower and Dean Street; a stark contrast to Catherine's earlier life in Chelsea.

When Ann grew older and got married, she told her mother she wanted nothing to do with her and moved away to stop her heavy-drinking parent scrounging money from her. Although the deputy at Cooney's Lodging House said that Eddowes was, *"not often in drink and was a very jolly woman, often singing"*, she did appear at the Thames Police Court for being drunk and disorderly. The deputy was sure that Catherine was not in the habit of walking the streets and he had never known her to be intimate with anyone other than John Kelly. Kelly admitted that although Catherine sometimes drank to excess, he had no knowledge of her ever going on the streets to earn money.

This is interesting because popular opinion has traditionally been that all Jack the Ripper's victims were prostitutes, but there does not appear to be much evidence that this applies to Eddowes. Although many women were career prostitutes, others only practiced the "world's oldest profession" occasionally, when they fell upon hard times and had no other option. Some historians set out to distinguish whether each victim really was a streetwalker, but rather than viewing them only through that narrow lens, I believe it is more important to highlight the social and economic inequalities of the time that forced so many women into this way of life.

Every year, Kelly and Eddowes went hop picking in Kent, something many poor families from London looked forward to. Even as late as the 1950s, people would travel to hop farms in the neighbouring county for a working holiday, helping farmers to pick hops, which are flowers used for making beer. Those who could afford a train ticket could cover the 35 miles or so in style, but others had to make do with walking. Not only would they enjoy fresh, healthy air in the countryside, but on a good year they could earn enough money to keep them going over the harsh winter months.

*Sketch of Catherine "Kate" Eddowes
(Famous Crimes Past and Present, 1902)*

The year of Eddowes' death, they had not had a good hopping season and the wages were low, so they decided to leave early and walk home. They arrived in London on Thursday 27 September, just three days before Catherine would be viciously murdered. Without enough money for their Flower and Dean Street lodgings, they spent the night in the casual ward in the Shoe Lane workhouse. The next day Kelly earned sixpence, but this was not enough to pay for a double room at Cooney's, so Catherine took tuppence and said she would try the casual ward again, advising Kelly to take fourpence for a single bed at the lodging house.

The superintendent of the casual ward knew Kate well, and allegedly had a foreboding conversation with her that night:

Superintendent: *"Haven't seen you for a while Kate, where you been?"*
Catherine Eddowes: *"I've been hopping in the country, but we didn't earn very much, so we hoofed it home. Anyway, I'm going to earn the reward offered for the apprehension of the Whitechapel murderer. I think I know him."*
Superintendent: *"Well, you ought to be careful he don't murder you an' all!"*
Catherine Eddowes: *"Oh, no fear of that!"*

This makes for a striking tale, but there is no corroborating evidence for this story. At 8:00 a.m. on Saturday 29 September, Kate Eddowes and John Kelly regrouped at Cooney's Lodging House. They were still in desperate need of money, so they pawned a pair of boots they had obtained in Kent. With the two shillings and sixpence this generated, they bought breakfast, tea, and sugar, and they spent the rest of the morning together before parting in Houndsditch at around 2:00 p.m. Eddowes told Kelly she was going to look for her daughter to ask her for money. Kelly warned her to be careful, saying, *"Don't forget there's a murderer about, Kate."* She replied, *"Don't you fear for me. I shall take care of myself and I shan't fall into his hands."*

It transpired that John Kelly's fears were well-founded, and he never did get to find out whether Catherine spoke to her daughter or not. Most of the day remained unaccounted for until she was spotted at 8:30 p.m. on the Aldgate High Street, sleeping rough. She smelt of alcohol and had attracted a crowd of onlookers. PC Louis Robinson of the City Police asked if anyone knew who she was or where she lived, but nobody did. She could not stand unaided, so Robinson called for help from PC Simmons, and they took her to Bishopsgate Police Station, putting her in a cell to sleep it off. They checked on her regularly and by 9:00 p.m. she was asleep.

Even through her drunken haze, Eddowes would have noticed as she was led into the station the almost palpable smell of carbolic soap, used to clean the tiled walls and floors, designed for easy mopping if someone was brought in bleeding or vomiting. The ceilings were tall, and the building was lit with mounted gas lamps, illuminating the long wooden reception desk. In each room was a small fireplace to offer warmth to officers completing paperwork, and there would be a lamp room for keeping stock of and maintaining bullseye lanterns, a parade room where Bobbies would muster before going out on the beat, and in some of the more newly built stations, a telegraph room.

Just after midnight, Kate was heard singing softly. At 12:30 a.m. she called out to the officers:

Catherine Eddowes: *"When will I be released?"*
PC Hutt: *"When you are capable of taking care of yourself."*
Catherine Eddowes: *"I can do that now!"*
PC Hutt: *"We'll see when the Sergeant comes round."*

At 12.55 a.m. the Sergeant came by to see if any prisoners were fit to be released, and by now, Kate was found to be sober. She had refused to give her name when she was brought to the station earlier, and when asked again before her release she called herself Mary Ann Kelly. This sounds eerily like Mary Jane Kelly, who would soon become The Ripper's final canonical victim. This has given rise to some fantastic theories that the killer was targeting specific women, but it is far more logical that she gave the surname Kelly because her partner was John Kelly, and she did not want to give her real first name.

She left the station at around 1:00 a.m., speaking to PC George Hutt as she left. The conversation went something like this:

Catherine Eddowes: *"What time is it?"*
PC Hutt: *"Too late for you to get anything to drink."*
Catherine Eddowes: *"I shall get a damn fine hiding when I get home."*
PC Hutt: *"And serve you right, you had no right to get drunk. This way missus."*
Catherine Eddowes: *"All right. Goodnight, old cock."*

She did not turn right out of the station towards Cooney's Lodging House, instead turning left towards Houndsditch and Aldgate. Some have posited that she was heading to St Botolph's Church, also known as the Prostitutes Church. According to local legend, police had an arrangement with the sex workers in the area, granting them amnesty so long as they confined themselves to a limited area. Allegedly you would see a line of prostitutes walking around outside the church each night and although there is no evidence of this story's veracity, many did ply their trade in that area. Wherever she was planning to go, neither Catherine Eddowes nor the officer who released her had any idea that just 400 yards away in Mitre Square, she would become the next victim of the Whitechapel Murderer.

Mitre Square was a small, cobbled area, with a passage to its north leading into St James' Place, and to the east a passage leading to St Botolph's Church, known as Church Passage. Even now, this alleyway is only four metres wide, but back in 1888 it measured just one metre across. There were three dim gas lamps; one just off Mitre Street at the entrance to Mitre Square, one in the northwest corner of the square, and one in Church Passage, each giving off a light no stronger than a modern refrigerator. The square was surrounded by tall warehouse buildings including those belonging to Williams & Co, Horner & Son, and the famous Kearley & Tonge tea merchant. There were only a few other buildings in Mitre Square. PC Richard Pearce of the City Police lived in one of the houses with his family, another house was empty, and the third was a picture framing shop.

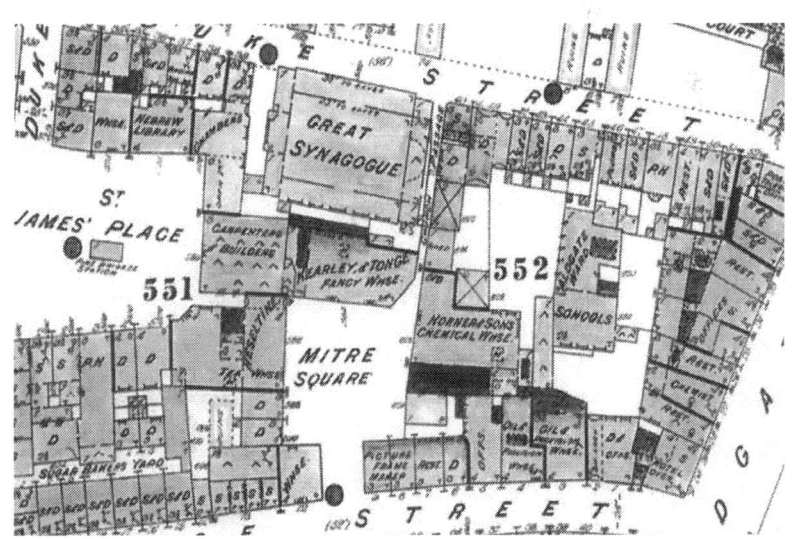

Map of Mitre Square in 1887 (Casebook.org)

It has changed significantly since 1888 and the square cobbles, known as setts, have mostly been replaced, but the approximate shape of the square remains. Even now, with better lighting, it is an unsettling place at night. In my opinion, it is the most chilling of the murder sites, which remains just similar enough to how it once looked to allow your imagination to run wild. You can visit it on one of the many Jack the Ripper walking tours on offer; I went on one of these in 2011 led by author and historian Philip Hutchinson; an extremely interesting way to spend an evening if you are within travelling distance of London.

*Seats in the corner of Mitre Square
(2010, Basher Eyre, CC BY-SA 2.0)*

At 1:40 a.m. PC James Harvey walked down Church Passage and peered into Mitre Square. As he heard and saw nothing unusual, he did not go any further in. Just four minutes later PC Edward Watkins entered the square as part of his regular beat, which involved checking that warehouses were secure, and liaising with the night watchman if necessary. Moments after Watkins entered the square, he cried out in horror and shouted for the nightwatchman.

PC Watkins: *"Oh my god! Where's the night watchman? Hey! For God's sake, mate, come to my assistance!"*
Nightwatchman George Morris: *"Stop until I get my lamp. What's the matter?"*
PC Watkins: *"Oh god, there's another woman been ripped to pieces!"*

It was 46-year-old Catherine Eddowes. George Morris, night watchman for tea merchants Kearley & Tonge, was sweeping the floor when he heard the policeman's shout. He brought his lantern and followed PC Watkins to the corner of the square, illuminating the grotesque scene with a ghostly glow. When he saw the heart-stopping spectacle in front of him, he turned and ran up Mitre Street and into Aldgate, blowing his whistle to attract attention. He bumped into PC Harvey, who had passed by just a few minutes previously but had not entered the square. Morris quickly told him of the sickening sight he had just witnessed.

PC Harvey ran to Mitre Square, enlisting another constable, Holland, on the way, telling him to fetch a doctor. Dr George Sequeira lived just two minutes away and arrived on the scene shortly before 2:00 a.m. He was sure that the victim had only been dead for a few minutes, and certainly no more than a quarter of an hour. City Police surgeon Dr Gordon Brown arrived shortly after.

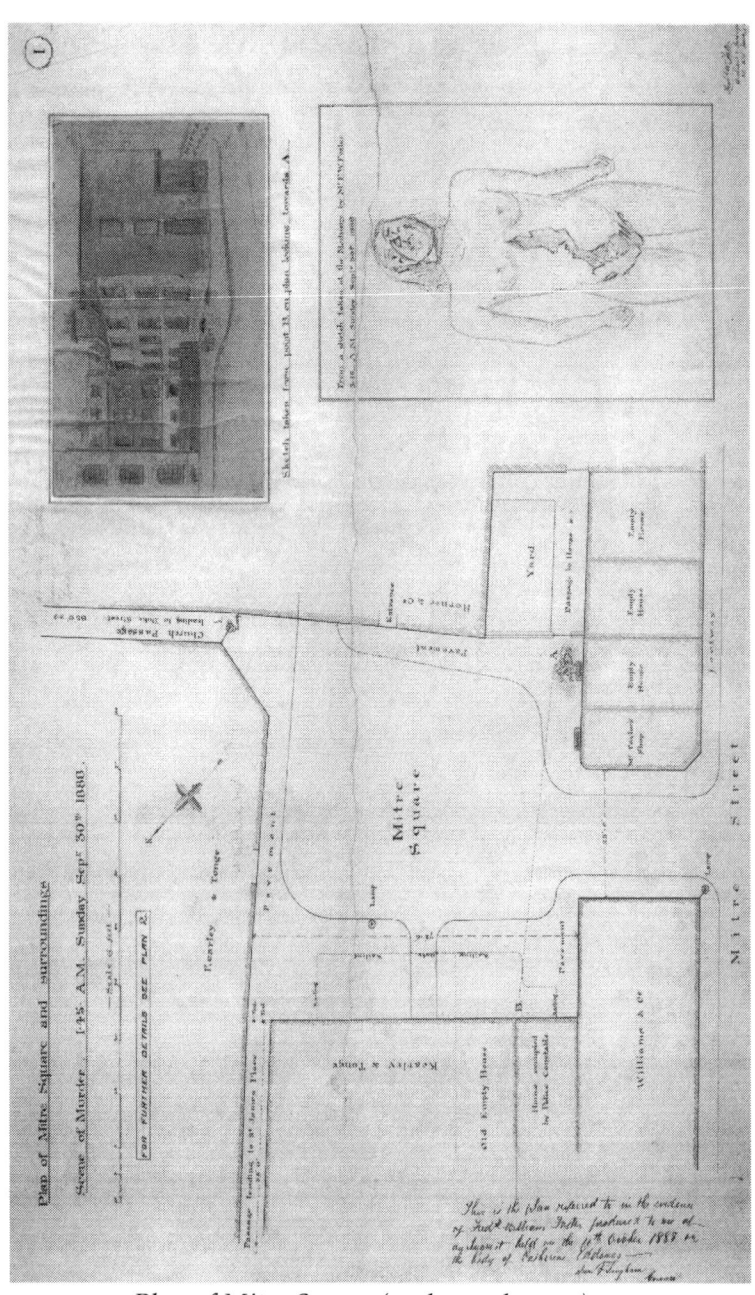

Plan of Mitre Square (author unknown)

118

FINDING THE MUTILATED BODY IN MITRE SQARE

Illustrated Police News, 6 October 1888

The wounds and mutilations inflicted on Eddowes' body were the worst anyone had yet seen. This is an extract from Dr Brown's postmortem report:

"The throat was cut across. The intestines were drawn out and placed over the right shoulder. A piece of about two feet was detached from the body and placed between the body and the left arm. The right ear was cut obliquely through. When we removed the body to the mortuary, a piece of the deceased's ear dropped from the clothing. The face was very much mutilated. There were cuts to both eyelids. There was a deep cut over the bridge of the nose, extending from the left border of the nasal bone down near the angle of the jaw on the right side of the cheek, going into the bone. The tip of the nose was detached. Another cut divided the upper lip and extended through the gum. There was on each side of the cheeks a cut which peeled up the skin, forming a triangular flap about an inch and a half. The throat was cut across to the extent of *six or seven inches. The big muscle across the throat was divided through on the left side. The large vessels on the left side of the neck were severed. The larynx was severed below the vocal cords. The carotid artery had a fine hole opening, the internal jugular vein was opened. All these injuries were performed by a sharp, pointed knife of at least six inches long. The cause of death was haemorrhage from the left carotid artery. The death was immediate, and the mutilations were inflicted after death. The front walls of the abdomen were laid open. The liver was stabbed by a sharp instrument. There was a stab of about an inch on the left groin. The left kidney and the uterus were carefully taken out and removed."*

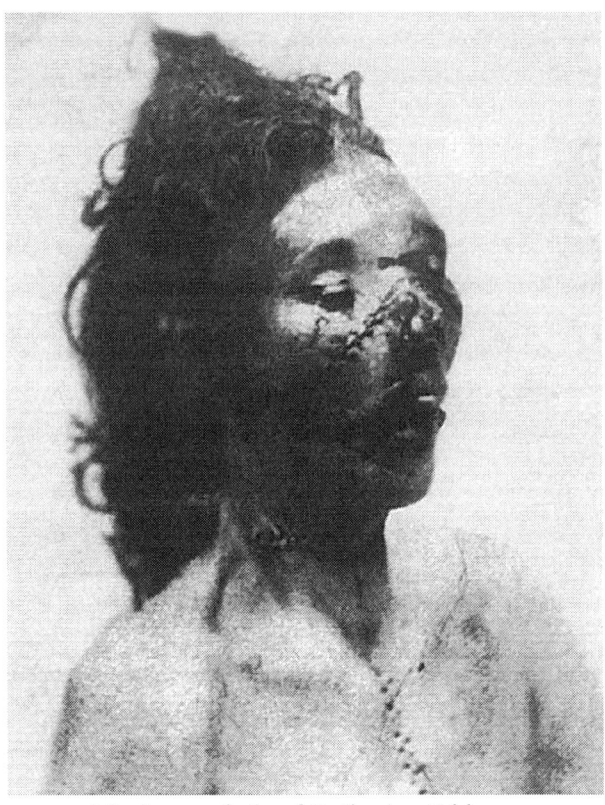

Mortuary photo of Catherine Eddowes

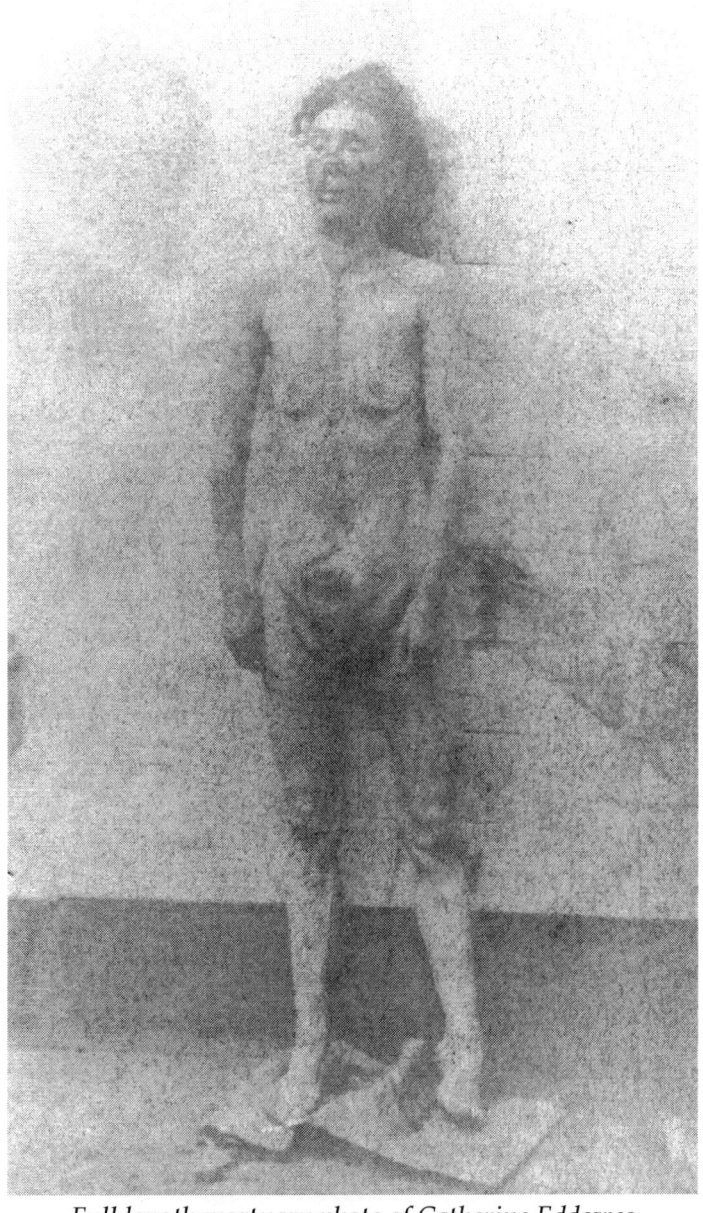

*Full length mortuary photo of Catherine Eddowes
(Original photograph in collection of Royal London Hospital
Archives and Museum, catalog number MC/PM/5/2/5)*

Dr Brown felt that the perpetrator must have had expert anatomical knowledge, although Dr Sequeira and medical officer William Saunders disagreed. At the inquest, Dr Brown was forced to admit that somebody used to cutting up animals could have done it, although he pointed out that the kidney was not easy to stumble upon unless you knew where it was. Brown thought that making all the mutilations must have taken at least five minutes, although Dr Bagster Phillips believed it would have taken at least 15 minutes to inflict Annie Chapman's injuries, and she was not mutilated as severely as Eddowes. However, Bagster Phillips was judging this based on his experience as a surgeon, and he was used to taking care over his job to ensure no permanent damage was caused to his patient, while the killer had no need for caution and would have been filled with the frenzy of bloodlust and the need to escape.

As Eddowes died instantly when her throat was cut, she would have been unable to make a sound, and as the mutilations were inflicted after death, there may not have been much blood on the killer. One of the most puzzling aspects of this crime was that nobody had heard anything, and Constables Watkins and Harvey had not seen anyone when they passed by. Watkins, who had 17 years' experience as an officer, walked through Mitre Square every 15 minutes on his beat, so the killer had somehow committed his atrocities in a very narrow window and escaped detection by moments. This has added to the mystique of Jack the Ripper as a spectre who was swallowed up by the night, leaving no trace behind.

Nightwatchman George Morris was certain he would have heard a cry or shout if there had been one. Unbelievably, he had been smoking his pipe just outside the door of the warehouse at the time of the murder. This is part of his statement:

"Before being called, I had no occasion to go into the square. I did not go there between one and two o'clock; of that I'm certain. There was nothing unusual in my door being open and my being at work at so late an hour. I had not seen PC Watkins before during the night. I do not think my door had been ajar more than two or three minutes when he knocked. It was awful. It looked as though she'd been cut up like a pig or any other animal you see in the market."

George Clapp, a caretaker at 5 Mitre Street, did not hear anything all night, even though the back of his house looked directly into Mitre Square. The first he heard of the murder was at around 5:00 or 6:00 in the morning.

The southwest corner of Mitre Square where Catherine Eddowes' body was found

Constable Richard Pearce of the City Police lived in one of the two private houses in the square. He went to bed at 12:20 a.m. on the night of the murder and was not disturbed by anything until he was called at 2:20 a.m. after Eddowes' body had been found. From his window, he could even see the spot where she was killed. How had so many people been in or around the square and yet heard nothing? It is reminiscent of the frustrating situation at Hanbury Street when Albert Cadosch heard a thump against the fence. If he had looked over, he might have seen the face of Jack the Ripper. Yet again at Mitre Square, the killer had been supernaturally fortunate, as PC Pearce, caretaker Clapp or nightwatchman Morris could have looked outside at any moment and seen the slaughter in progress.

The Pictorial News, 6 October 1888

Just before 3:00 a.m. PC Alfred Long made a disturbing discovery in Goulston Street, five minutes from the murder scene on foot. As he walked past a doorway leading to a staircase up to room numbers 108-119 of the recently built Wentworth Model Dwellings, he noticed a piece of apron lying on the floor, just inside the doorway. It was smeared with blood and faecal matter and looked like it had been used to wipe the blade of a knife. He was sure it had not been there when he passed by 40 minutes before. Had the killer dropped it while fleeing the scene, on his way back to wherever he lived, the headquarters of hell? This was the only physical clue he ever left behind.

The plot was about to thicken even more. As PC Long picked up the abandoned piece of bloody apron, he spotted something even more baffling. A message was scrawled in white chalk on the door jamb at shoulder height, which read, *"The Juwes are the men that will not be blamed for nothing."* The letters measured just under an inch in height, and had been written in a "rounded, schoolboy hand" according to the police files. It appeared to be fresh and would have been rubbed out over time by people brushing past it had it been there for very long.

This has become known amongst Ripper researchers as the Goulston Street Graffito; it is only called graffiti if it is plural, while just one piece is graffito. There has been much debate about this over the years and nobody is entirely sure whether this is exactly what the message said or not, as it does not make sense. Metropolitan Police Constable Alfred Long, who had been seconded from Westminster's A division to supplement H division, wrote down the message as, *"The **Juews** are the men that will not be blamed for nothing"* – note the different spelling of the word 'Jews'.

The entrance to the Wentworth Model Dwellings (photographer unknown). The white marks on the right-hand side have been added to the photo to illustrate where the graffito would have been.

Wentworth Model Dwellings as they looked in 1980 (From the documentary "The Final Solution")

In Chief Inspector Donald Swanson's letter to the Home Office on 6 November, he wrote it as "Juwes" and this has become the most quoted version of the spelling. Detective Constable Halse of the City Police, in whose territory of just one square mile Catherine Eddowes was killed, wrote it down as *"The Juwes are **not** [my emphasis] the men that will be blamed for nothing."* The curious spelling of the word Jews has given rise to outlandish conspiracy theories about freemasonry over the years and historians argue over the baffling double negatives to this day.

We will never know what the original version said, thanks to a clash of jurisdictions. DC Halse wanted the writing to be photographed and for Acting City Police Commissioner Major Henry Smith to see it before it was erased. The Metropolitan Police, in whose territory Goulston Street fell, were concerned that this would mean waiting until it was light to obtain a reasonable picture, and by then, people would be awake, and the message would be seen; something they wished to avoid. Tension between Jews and non-Jews was already simmering, so leaving a piece of anti-Semitic graffito on the wall was out of the question, particularly as Goulston Street was inhabited predominantly by Jews.

While the debate continued, PC Alfred Long hastily searched the stairs for clues but found no traces of blood. While he went to deliver the bloody piece of apron to Leman Street Police Station for examination by Dr Bagster Phillips, a brother officer was stationed in front of the Wentworth Dwellings to ensure nobody entered or left. DC Halse later made enquiries of all the tenants in the Wentworth Building, but no witnesses or persons of interest were found.

Metropolitan Police Commissioner Sir Charles Warren arrived on the scene, and as the doorway was officially on

Met Police territory, his orders stood. The graffito was to be washed away immediately, in the face of a sensible compromise proposed by DC Halse that they remove the first part of the graffito only, which referred to Jews. It is bizarre that Warren was so intent on removing the graffito, when the details were discussed publicly at the inquest and printed in the newspapers soon after. The Pall Mall Gazette printed a description of the whole affair on 12 October and were very critical of Warren's decision.

The Illustrated Police News, 20 October 1888

Meanwhile, Major Henry Smith had been summoned and went to view the scene at Mitre Square. He never did get to see the graffito. Smith was a flamboyant character and something of a raconteur, who later wrote about the case in his memoirs, From Constable to Commissioner, published in 1910. As this was some 22 years after the Ripper murders, we must question the validity of his account, but his style of writing makes for an entertaining read. Here are some of his memories from the night of the "Double Event".

"The night of Saturday, September 29, found me tossing about in my bed at Cloak Lane Station, close to the river and adjoining Southwark Bridge. Suddenly the bell at my head rang violently. "What is it?" I asked, putting my ear to the tube. "Another murder, sir, this time in the City." Jumping up, I was dressed and in the street in a couple of minutes. A hansom- to me a detestable vehicle- was at the door, and into it I jumped, as time was of the utmost consequence. This invention of the devil claims to be safe. It is neither safe nor pleasant. In winter you are frozen; in summer you are broiled. When the glass is let down your hat is generally smashed, your fingers caught between the doors, or half your front teeth loosened. Licensed to carry two, it did not take me long to discover that a 15 stone Superintendent inside with me, and three detectives hanging on behind, added neither to its comfort nor to its safety."

Having survived his uncomfortable journey in the hansom cab and arrived at Mitre Square, Smith noted that not a single drop of blood was found at the scene. Smith and DC Halse later met at the mortuary and noticed that part of the murdered woman's apron was missing. Around the same time, the portion of apron found at Goulston Street was being examined by Dr Bagster Phillips, and he confirmed that it belonged to Catherine Eddowes.

After finding nothing at Mitre Square, Major Smith explored the local area and made an interesting discovery in Dorset Street:

"In Dorset Street, with extraordinary audacity, the killer washed his hands at a sink up a close [referring to Miller's Court] *not more than six yards from the street. I arrived there in time to see the blood-stained water. I wandered round my stationhouses, hoping I might find someone brought in, and finally got to bed at 6 a.m., after a very harassing night, completely defeated. The revolting details of this murder would shock my readers; but there are certain facts-gruesome enough in all conscience-which have never appeared in print, and which, from a medical and scientific point of view, should certainly be put on record."*

Given that Miller's Court became the next murder scene a little over a month later, this recollection could be extremely important, indicating that the killer already knew that area very well, or lived close by. No Metropolitan Police records corroborate this story, but this could be because Smith worked for the City of London Police and information was not shared between the two jurisdictions, which is one of the reasons experts cite for the failure of either to catch The Ripper.

Major Smith was disappointed by the Met Police's decision and felt that the erasure of the graffito was unjustifiable. It could have yielded a clue, no matter how small, and he had even been prepared to send one of his officers to stand over the writing and shield it from view until it could be photographed. As for which version of the message is accurate, I believe that DC Halse's version, *"The Juwes are not the men that will be blamed for nothing"* is probably more accurate than PC Long's rendition. As a plainclothes detective, Halse would have been more experienced, and we know from his statement at the inquest that he spent time door-knocking to make enquiries of the Wentworth tenants, even though Goulston Street did not fall into his jurisdiction. In contrast, PC Long only gave a cursory search of the stairs. Halse had also advocated for the graffito to remain and is accordingly more likely to have grasped the significance of it and taken care to copy it accurately.

Many people, including Major Henry Smith, believed that Jack the Ripper had purposefully written the cryptic statement as a mocking red herring, to turn attention away from himself and towards the Jewish community. Others class the dropping of the apron under the graffito as a coincidence. The writing on the brickwork was much smaller than is usually portrayed in documentaries and films, so if it was deliberate, it was lucky that anyone spotted it. It would have been a Machiavellian move for a killer of the time to dream up the idea of writing a piece of graffito as a diversionary tactic, and some historians have pointed out that graffiti was surprisingly common, proponing that a disgruntled customer of a Jewish shop in nearby Middlesex Street had written it in anger after a bad experience. After all, the previous day (Saturday) had been market day.

At the time of writing, the graffito site is now a fish and chip restaurant called Happy Days, occupying 44 – 46 Goulston Street. Inside is a collection of Jack the Ripper memorabilia including a replica of the writing, which stands just inside and to the right of the front customers' entrance.

Whether or not the message was really written by Jack remains a polemic issue. The Whitechapel Murderer had already proven his boldness, so it is not unreasonable to think that he spared a few moments to divert attention from himself as he ran from Mitre Square.

Petticoat Lane Market c.1890
(Tower Hamlets Local History Department)
"Petticoat Lane" does not actually exist, but referred to the area covered by both Middlesex Street and Wentworth Street

Writing messages at crime scenes is not unusual. For example, the Zodiac Killer wrote a message in a black marker pen on the door of his victims' VW Karmann Ghia at Lake Berryessa, claiming responsibility for the previous killing and the method. In 1913, Jim Conley, supposedly in collusion with his manager Leo Frank, penned a note pointing the finger of guilt at a black man in the murder of little Mary Phagan, one of the most famous cases in the state of Georgia. This ruse was a deliberate attempt to cast suspicion on someone they thought would be readily accepted as the killer due to the colour of his skin. Australian serial killer Paul Denyer also left a threatening message on a mirror belonging to Donna Vanes, whose home he ransacked prior to his escalation to murder. Keith Jesperson killed eight women in the 1990s, many of them sex workers, and left graffiti in the form of smiley faces at the crime scenes.

I mention these modern examples to illustrate that killers can and do use tactics like this to taunt the police or sidetrack an investigation. The average person might consider it illogical for a murderer to delay his escape by stopping to write a message, but modern precedent proves there is no shortage of criminals willing to take this risk. Some people argue for the unlikelihood of Jack the Ripper just happening to have a piece of chalk in his pocket, but one could say the same about the Zodiac, who had clearly planned ahead and carried a black marker pen.

As for why the killer took a piece of Eddowes' apron, it could have been to wipe the blood off his hands and knife, and he could not do this at the scene because he heard someone approaching, so he cut the apron to clean himself up as he ran, before disposing of it in a quiet place. Alternatively, he could have used it to carry the kidney and uterus he removed from the body. This begs the question of what he did with the organs after he discarded the apron. Did he carry them in his bare hands or put them in his pocket, and if so, why take the scrap of material in the first place? This remains unanswered over a century later, as nobody has been able to present a well-accepted explanation.

As for what happened to the kidney afterwards, George Lusk, chairman of the Whitechapel Vigilance Committee found out a couple of weeks later when he received a nauseating package in the mail, along with the now-famous From Hell letter. Inside a stained, grubby looking cardboard box measuring three inches square, was half a human kidney preserved in wine. The accompanying letter read:

From hell
Mr Lusk
Sor
I send you half the Kidne I took from one women prasarved it for you tother piece I fried and ate it was very nise I may send you the bloody knif that took it out if you only wate a whil longer
signed, Catch me when you Can
Mishter Lusk

Dr Openshaw of the London Hospital confirmed that it was a left human kidney belonging to a heavy-drinking woman of about 45, and that it had been removed from the body within the last three weeks. The victim had also suffered from Bright's Disease, just like Catherine Eddowes. This was a kidney inflammation known as nephritis today, which affected many people in the 19th century, including engineer Isambard Kingdom Brunel, the first wife of Theodore Roosevelt, the Birdman of Alcatraz, and Booker T. Washington.

The handwriting and phrasing of the letter were vastly different from the Dear Boss missive, with the words barely legible and poorly spelled. This is one reason why the From Hell letter is considered more likely to have come from the real killer than any of the others, although many believe none of the letters were genuine, and most researchers now agree that Dear Boss came from a journalist seeking a scoop.

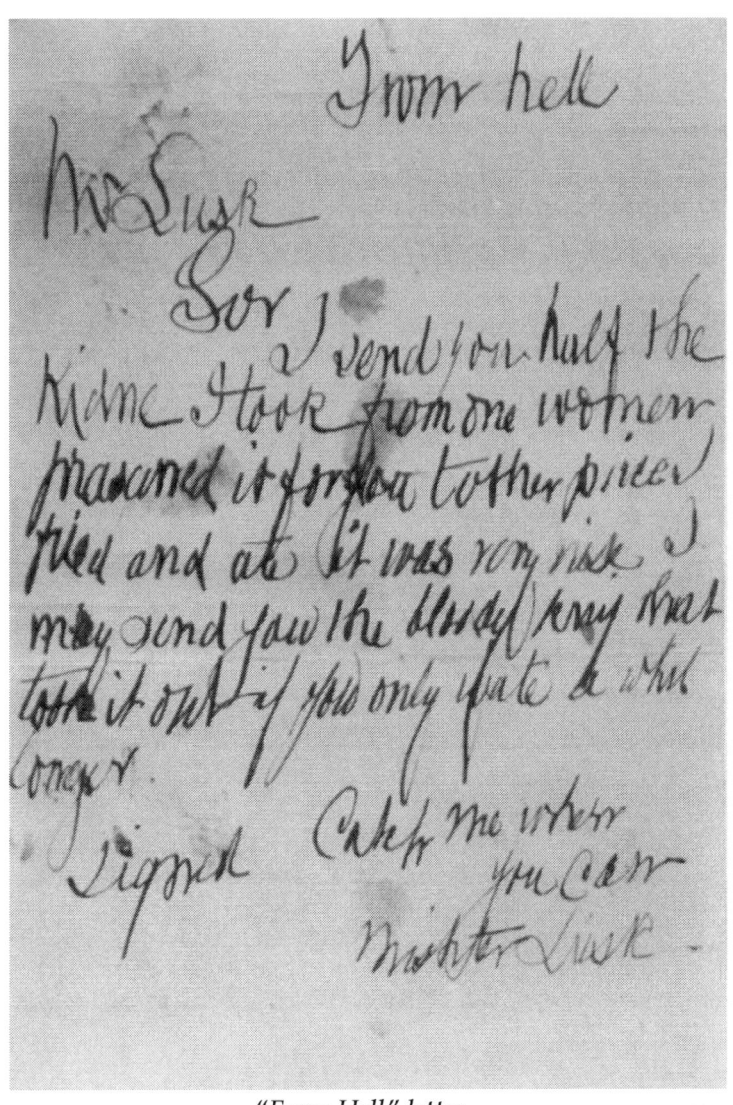

"From Hell" letter
(Records of Metropolitan Police Service, National Archives)

This was not the first time George Lusk had received a hoax letter, although we can assume it was the first occasion he had been mailed a body part, but by the end of October, the incident was widely viewed as a tasteless practical joke by a medical student.

Penny Illustrated Paper, October 13 1888

The Lusk letter was not the only one received after the night of Stride and Eddowes' deaths. This one became known as the Saucy Jacky postcard:

I was not codding dear old Boss when I gave you the tip, you'll hear about Saucy Jacky's work tomorrow, double event this time number one squealed a bit couldn't finish straight off had not the time to get ears for police. thanks for keeping last letter back till I got to work again.
Jack the Ripper

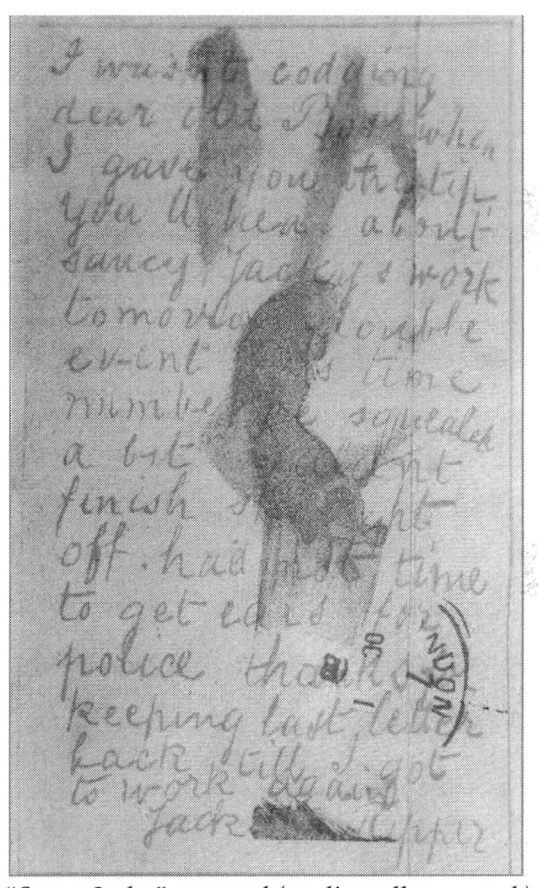

"Saucy Jacky" postcard (mediencolleg-rostock)

The writing was similar to the Dear Boss letter so it is commonly believed that this also came from a journalist, especially in light of the more modern theory that Liz Stride was not a Ripper victim, and therefore it may not have been a "Double Event" at all. In 1931, journalist Fred Best of The Star claimed that he and a colleague had written all the letters signed Jack the Ripper to *"keep the business alive."* At some point after the murders, the Saucy Jacky postcard and the Dear Boss letter went missing from the files. Dear Boss was recovered in 1987 but Saucy Jacky has never been located.

No clues were found at the crime scene and detectives were still dumbfounded. The whole neighbourhood was searched, including lodging houses, men were stopped in the streets, and there was a house-to-house enquiry in and around Mitre Square. The investigation turned up very little, although they did find some witnesses with interesting stories to tell.

James Blenkinsop, a nightwatchman overlooking the roadworks in St James' Place behind Mitre Square, said a respectably dressed man had approached him on the night of the murder, and asked him if he had seen a man and woman pass through, to which he answered he had seen people but had not paid any attention to them.

At 1:35 a.m. three men left the Imperial Club in Duke Street and were walking towards Aldgate High Street in the rain. They were commercial cigarette trader Joseph Lawende, butcher Joseph Hyam Levy, and furniture dealer Harry Harris. They saw Catherine Eddowes talking to a man near Church Passage, one of the narrow alleyways leading into Mitre Square. Lawende described the man as of rough and shabby appearance, about 30 years old, 5'7" in height, of medium build, with a fair complexion and a moustache. He was wearing a *"salt and pepper coloured loose-fitting jacket, a grey peaked cloth cap, and a reddish handkerchief knotted around his neck"*. He had the appearance of a sailor, but Lawende told police he would be unable to identify him if he saw him again.

The Illustrated Police News, 20 October 1888

Joseph Levy obviously thought the person he saw was less than respectable, as he commented to his friend Harris as they walked past, *"Look here, I don't like going home by myself when I see those characters about."*

Lawende said the woman they saw had her hand on the man's chest, but not as if to push him away, and they noticed that he was taller than her. They were talking quietly and did not seem to be arguing, but Lawende could not hear what they said. After he and his friends passed, he did not look back to see where they went.

The murder was mystifying. PC Watkins, who first discovered the body, entered Mitre Square on his beat at 1:30 a.m. and saw nothing unusual. He had gone to the southwest corner to check that nobody had removed the covers of the coal holes belonging to the buildings in the square, and then shone his bullseye lantern around to the other corners before continuing on his way. Somehow, between 1:30 a.m. and 1:44 a.m. when Watkins returned and found the desecrated figure of Catherine Eddowes, the killer had appeared, lured his victim into the square, slit her throat then carried out his obscene outrages on her corpse including the removal of her uterus and left kidney, before disappearing into the night, all in under 15 minutes.

Considering the doubt over whether Kate was a prostitute, the killer could have been someone she knew who had approached her for some reason, or maybe she really was looking for a client on this occasion as she and John Kelly were so short of money. Following the bloodcurdling events in Whitechapel over the last few months, women were far more cautious about who they stopped to converse with so late at night, especially in secluded areas, and police had advised them to travel in pairs, so would Eddowes really have taken the risk of encountering The Ripper by speaking to a total stranger in the early hours of the morning? The answer might have been yes, if the anti-Semitic word on the street was enough to convince most people that the killer was a Jew, which might have made her feel safe had she been approached by a non-Jew, even in a dark, quiet spot. The constabulary had been focusing their efforts on searching Jewish homes in the East End, peering into cupboards and underneath beds, and demanding to inspect any knives kept in the house. Sometimes they stayed outside, but asked householders whether they had any lodgers, how long they had been living there, and whether they were respectable.

Fear and tension were at an all-time high and almost 1,000 people descended on Victoria Park to join a demonstration calling for the resignation of Sir Charles Warren. The public had lost faith in his ability to find the murderer who was spreading terror unchecked through the East End. Police received letters from across the country from keen but misguided citizens compelled to share their certainty that the killer was, to name just a few, a Jewish minister, a Frenchman, or an Indian tribe! Someone suggested photographing the victims' eyes in case the image of the killer had been preserved there, while another more sensible character proposed fitting policemen's boots with Indian rubber soles, as *"his tramp can be heard a quarter of a mile away. He might just as well ring a bell all the time!"*

There followed a series of intriguing and sometimes comical recommendations of how the killer could be caught, including pugilists walking the streets dressed in women's clothes to tempt the killer into an attack. Failing this, it was recommended that the police themselves dress up as ladies, but as most officers had facial hair and many were over 5'9" in height, this might have been a bit of a giveaway. The Lloyds Weekly on 14 September reported that Detective Sergeant Robinson disguised himself in women's clothes to watch a suspect in Clerkenwell whom he thought was Jack the Ripper. A man called William Jarvis saw through his ruse and asked him, *"What are you messing about here for?"* Robinson took off his lady's hat and answered, *"I am a police officer."* Clearly unsatisfied with this explanation, Jarvis punched the detective, then stabbed him in the left eye before being taken into custody thanks to the timely arrival of several constables. He was indicted for maliciously wounding an officer of the law, notwithstanding his claim that it was all a misunderstanding. Thanks to Jarvis spoiling the stakeout, we shall sadly never know whether Detective Sergeant Robinson was onto something with the man he was watching.

Sir Charles Warren decided that instead of dressing up, it would be easier to enlist the help of animals. He organized a trial of two bloodhounds named Barnaby and Burgho and put them through their paces in rigorous tests, even giving them his own scent and allowing them to chase him through a public park, which afforded the press and public much amusement. Sadly, Barnaby and Burgho never did get the chance to prove their mettle.

The idea of using bloodhounds was not a new one. The first recorded case of tracker dogs being used in a homicide investigation was in 1876, when two canines successfully found the missing body parts of dismembered seven-year-old Emily Holland in Blackburn, stuffed up the chimney of a barbershop owned by the killer. Ironically, this murderer became the subject of a gallows ballad when he was hung for the crime.

Shortly after Catherine Eddowes' murder, her ex-partner Thomas Conway learned that City of London Detectives were looking for him, so he went to the police station and explained who he was. He was taken to see their daughter, Annie, who identified him as her father.

The trial of the bloodhounds
(The Penny Illustrated Paper, 20 October 1888)

He stated that he had left Catherine eight years before due to her heavy drinking, and although he had seen her a couple of times since, he had kept away from her. He does not appear to have ever been considered as a suspect.

Kate was buried in the City of London Cemetery in a funeral paid for by Mr. Hawkes, a vestryman of St Luke's Church. Her interment was witnessed by a vast crowd which included several of Kate's friends and relatives, including John Kelly. Her grave was officially commemorated with a plaque in 1996, 108 years after her death, but like Annie Chapman, her grave site has long since been reused.

Less than a month later, The Ripper would steal the life of final canonical victim Mary Jane Kelly, in a slaying yet more bloody and more inconceivably brutal than any murder that had been seen so far. In the next chapter we will uncover the heinous, abhorrent details of the climax of the Whitechapel Fiend's trail of terror, the coup de grace of the months of hell on earth he had unleashed on the East End.

Chapter Six
Mary Jane Kelly
Miller's Court, 9 November 1888

In the lead up to the horrendous climax of the Whitechapel Murderer's rampage, we have explored the deaths of Emma Smith and Martha Tabram, who were almost certainly not victims of The Ripper, before examining the stories of each of the Canonical victims: Polly Nichols, Annie Chapman, Elizabeth Stride and Catherine Eddowes, although I have put forward the argument that Stride was not killed by the same man.

The fifth canonical murder was the most abhorrent, frenzied attack of the series, marking the height of Whitechapel Jack's bloodlust and the end of the string of murders, although some later killings have been put forward as a possible continuation of his sinister work. The death of Mary Jane Kelly is perhaps the most memorable, not because any victim is more important than the others, but because her death was different in two ways, firstly because it took place indoors, and secondly because it was the most grotesque and inhuman act of mutilation in the sequence.

At this time, the police were no closer to finding the killer, but myriad peculiar characters seemed to be looking for trouble. A man was arrested on 21 October after entering a shop in Charing Cross and placing a black bag on the table before announcing, *"You must not be surprised to hear I'm Jack the Ripper. I'm a most mysterious man. I'm used to cutting people up and can put them back together again."* He left the bag in the shop, which was found to contain a dagger and a razor blade. Another man was remanded in custody for confessing to the murders while drunk. Others managed to find themselves under suspicion for the thinnest of justifications. The Morning Post reported that an American man was arrested in Ireland on 15 October, for nothing more than carrying a black leather bag. For reasons best known to himself, the man refused to offer any information, which did not help matters, and it took 48 hours for him to be discharged, along with the woman and child who were with him, once police had accounted for his movements.

Meanwhile, the landlady of a house at 22 Batty Street reported on 17 October that she had been disturbed by the early morning movements of her lodger, who was *"a foreign man"*, and that he had changed his clothes and gone away, claiming he would return later. He left her with a bloody shirt to be washed, tied up in a bundle with several other garments. The house was put under surveillance to await the man's return, then he was taken into custody and questioned for an hour before being released.

After the "Double Event" of 30 September, it was more than a month before The Ripper struck again, this time in Miller's Court. The court was entered through a narrow brick archway, no more than three feet wide, off the north side of Dorset Street. This path extended about 20 feet into a courtyard, which housed a poky, closed-in collection of poorly maintained cottages on both the left and right sides, with a wall and toilets at the end. This was a place where some of London's poorest lived and it was plagued by poverty and crime; even the police avoided going down there unless they were in pairs. Around 1,500 men slept in lodging houses in Dorset Street each night, and a city missionary, distressed by the deprivation he saw, was astounded on one occasion to find 11 women sheltering overnight in the staircase of one house. Just a couple of years earlier, Dr Loane, the Medical Officer of Health, had been asked by the council to inspect the homes in Miller's Court, as they were *"in a condition dangerous to human health, so as to be unfit for human habitation, and request that you will forthwith inspect the said premises and report thereon as required by section 12 of the Artisans' and Labourers' Dwellings Act 1868"*. Dr Loane agreed, reporting that the houses in the Court were *"most dilapidated, and the furniture of the most worthless description, but very large rents are paid by tenants. The structural condition of the houses, as far as could be judged, does not afford the opportunity to condemn them"*.

Dorset Street, entrance to Miller's Court c. 1928
(The Mystery of Jack the Ripper by Leonard Matters)

There were several pubs nearby including the Horn of Plenty, the Blue Coat Boy, and the Britannia, known as Ringers. Across the road on Commercial Street was Christ Church, Spitalfields, and its graveyard, christened Itchy Park by the locals. Homeless people slept there on the grass or against the gravestones during the day when the gates were open if they hadn't found a bed overnight. Huddling in doorways was not an option, as the police would move them on. The word "itchy" referred to the lice that many of these people carried, as if their grinding poverty, and life without a roof over their heads was not enough to contend with.

A homeless woman
(The Illustrated London News, October 1888)

Number 13 Miller's Court was a 10' x 12' room containing nothing more than a bed, two small tables, a fireplace, and a washstand. The bed was behind the door, running the length of the partition wall where it joined onto the back of 26 Dorset Street, which was used by the landlord to store goods. Upstairs were more tenants. The fireplace was on the opposite wall to the door, and there were two mismatched windows, one higher than the other, both set into the wall that looked out onto the court. One of these had two broken panes of glass which had been stuffed with newspaper and rags to keep out the wind and rain. Just past number 13 was a small area with a water pump and refuse facilities.

13 Miller's Court (unknown photographer). This photo was first discovered c. 1966 by Donald Rumbelow in the City of London photographic archive

John McCarthy, landlord of number 13 and several other properties, ran a chandler's shop in Dorset Street, just to the left of the Miller's Court archway, selling candles, oils, and groceries.

At 10:45 a.m. on 9 November 1888, McCarthy sent his employee Thomas Bowyer to collect the six weeks' worth of rent money owed to him by Mary Kelly at number 13 Miller's Court, totalling 29 shillings. Bowyer did as he was asked, but nobody answered when he knocked.

Left: John McCarthy, Right: Thomas Bowyer (The Penny Illustrated News)

He knew the windowpane was broken so he pulled out the paper and rags covering the hole, drew aside the sheet that was draped across the window, and peered into the room. It took a moment for his eyes to adjust to the darkness. What he saw would stay with him for the rest of his life. The first thing he spotted was a mound of flesh on the small table near the bed. The next thing he noticed was the blood streaked all over the walls. Then he saw a body lying on the bed. He ran back up to Dorset Street trembling with horror and told McCarthy what he had seen. Both men returned to the window, and McCarthy looked in and saw for himself what had shaken Bowyer so badly.

Famous Crimes Past and Present, Volume 2, No. 18

The body on the bed was a mass of blood and flesh, chopped and slashed beyond recognition. They ran to the Commercial Street Police Station, and Inspector Beck and

Detective Constable Dew immediately went to Miller's Court. Inspector Beck squinted through the window into the dimly lit room and said to DC Dew, *"For God's sake, don't look!"* Dew needed no further warning. Later, landlord John McCarthy described what he had seen:

"It looked more like the work of the devil than of a man. I'd heard a great deal about the Whitechapel murders, but I declare to God I had never expected to see such a sight as this. The whole scene is more than I can describe. I hope I may never see such a sight as this again."

The Illustrated Police News, 17 November 1888

Police closed off the court to everyone including the journalists hovering like a plague of locusts and waited for instructions from their seniors. There was a rumour that bloodhounds Barnaby and Burgho, who Met Police

Commissioner Sir Charles Warren had recently trialled, were on their way, so the crime scene remained untouched. What they had not realised was that Sir Charles Warren had resigned his post the previous day, so the bloodhounds were not coming. The man who looked after the dogs, Mr. Taunton, later admitted that they would have been of no use anyway in Miller's Court, because the streets were too crowded, and to have any chance of success they needed to be put on the trail before too many people were about.

A crowd flocking to Miller's Court
(The Pictorial News, 17 November 1888)

At around 1:30 p.m., almost three hours after the discovery of the body, it was agreed that they could wait no longer. On the orders of Superintendent Arnold, McCarthy prised open the door with a pickaxe.

In pitiful contrast with the blood-soaked tableau before them, Mary Jane Kelly's clothes lay folded neatly on a chair, her boots arranged in front of the fireplace as if she would be coming back to put them on at any moment. A roaring fire had been burning in the grate, so hot that it had melted the spout of the kettle. Several items of clothing had been burnt, later found to belong to one of Mary Kelly's friends, Maria Harvey, who sometimes stayed with her. Harvey had left behind a curious array of garments; an overcoat, two dirty cotton shirts, a boy's shirt, a girl's white petticoat and a black crape bonnet, which was not so curious after all given that she was a laundress. Police deduced that the killer had burned some of these items to keep the fire going to light up the room while he carried out his depraved defilement.

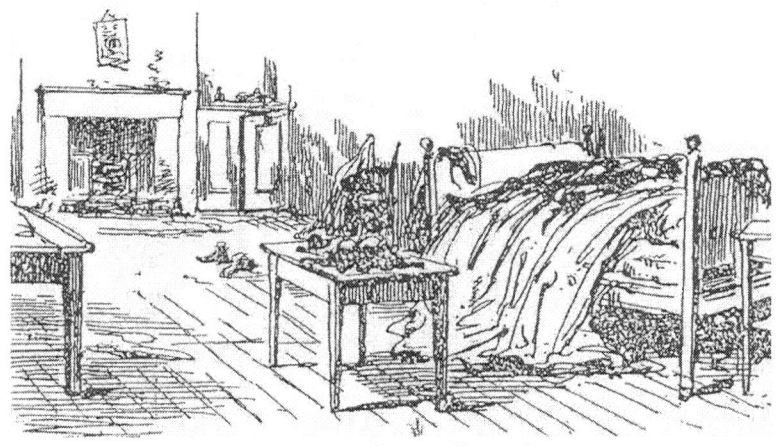

Interior of 13 Miller's Court
(Reynolds News, November 1888)

Once the body arrived at the Shoreditch Mortuary, it took six hours to piece the remains together and inspect the injuries in detail. Mary's boyfriend, Joseph Barnett, identified her from her ears and her eyes, as all other facial features had been destroyed. Police surgeon Dr Thomas Bond's report was a lengthy one. Here is an extract:

"The body was lying in the middle of the bed. The legs were wide apart. The whole of the surface of the abdomen and thighs was removed, and the abdominal cavity emptied of its viscera. The breasts were cut off, the arms mutilated by several jagged wounds and the face hacked beyond recognition. The tissues of the neck were severed all round down to the bone. The viscera were found in various parts; the uterus, kidneys and one breast under the head, the other breast by the right foot, the liver between the feet, the intestines by the right side and the spleen by the left side. The flaps removed from the abdomen and thighs were on a table. The bed clothing was saturated with blood, and on the floor beneath was a pool of blood covering about two feet square. The wall by the right side of the bed and in a line with the neck was marked by blood which had struck it in a number of separate splashes. The face was gashed in all directions, the nose, cheeks, eyebrows and ears partly removed. The lips were cut by several incisions running obliquely down to the chin. There were numerous cuts extending irregularly across all the features. The neck was cut through the skin and other tissues right down to the vertebrae. Both breasts were removed by circular incisions. The intercostals between the fourth, fifth and sixth ribs were cut through and the contents of the thorax visible through the openings. The skin and tissues of the abdomen were removed in three large flaps. The left calf showed a long gash through skin and tissues to the deep muscles, reaching from the knee to five inches above the ankle. Both arms had extensive, jagged wounds. On opening the thorax, it was found that the lower part of the right lung was broken and torn away. The heart was absent."

It was clear they were dealing with a killer the like of which they had never encountered before. The mutilations to the first victims had been harrowing enough, but now, in the shelter of a private room with no need to rush or the fear of being stumbled upon in the street by a passer-by, The Ripper had fulfilled his urge to butcher a body completely and utterly.

Some people argue that this shows a clear escalation from the murder of Polly Nichols onwards, as the disfigurement of each corpse worsened each time, except for Liz Stride, who, as discussed in Chapter Four, may not have been a Ripper victim.

The body of Mary Jane Kelly at the crime scene (City of London Police Archives)

Others believe this was what he had craved all along and that he would have done so had the opportunity arisen; this was just the first time he had been able to attack his victim indoors with less chance of being caught.

There is a myth that the victim's entrails were hung from picture hooks in the room, but there is no evidence of this, although it is easy to see why some people think it, as they misinterpret the shadows and marks in the poor-quality photos.

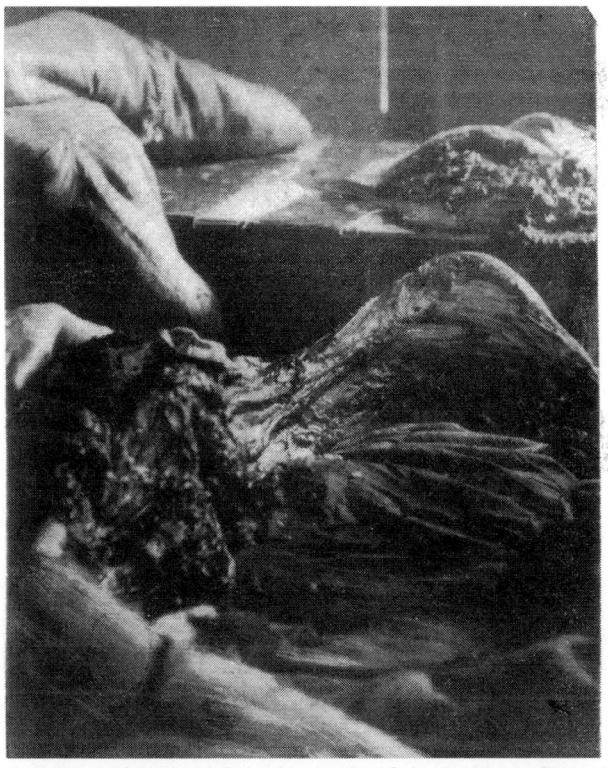

Original photograph in Records of the Metropolitan Police Office, National Archives. It was in a private collection for a time, before being returned to Scotland Yard in 1988 by the heirs of Ernest Millen, Deputy Assistant Commissioner of Police

What was Mary Kelly's story and what happened in the days leading up to her death? Although they may not have realised it, this was the final chance for detectives to find any clues and catch the faceless killer who had been stalking the East End for months. Was there anything that could have shed light on the hideous riddle?

Mary Jane Kelly, although we do not know for sure if that was her real name, was born around 1863, so she was 25 at the time of her death. We know little about her life except for what she told her friends, and sadly, we don't even know exactly what she looked like due to the extent of the mutilations.

She said she was born in Limerick, Southern Ireland, with six or seven brothers and one sister. One brother, Johnto, was serving in the Second Battalion Scots Guard. The family moved to Wales when she was a young child and her father, John Kelly, worked as a foreman at the iron works. Nobody knows whether she would have had an Irish accent or a Welsh one, or even a hybrid of both. She married a collier, another name for a miner, when she was just 16, but he tragically died in a pit explosion two or three years later. She then moved to Cardiff and stayed in an infirmary for nine months, although it is unclear what illness she was suffering from.

In 1884 she arrived in London and began working as a prostitute in a West End brothel. She said she visited France at least once with a wealthy gentleman, but that she did not enjoy it, so she returned to London, at which point she found herself in the East End. The stories of the various places she lived have not all been verified, but it is generally accepted that she lived with plasterer Joseph Fleming for a time, near Bethnal Green Road around 1886.

After breaking up with Fleming, she stayed in Cooney's Lodging House (not the one in Flower and Dean Street where Catherine Eddowes lodged, but the one in Thrawl Street). While lodging there in April 1887 she met Joseph Barnett, a porter at Billingsgate Fish Market, and they began a relationship. They had a painfully low income and were regularly behind on their rent, moving from place to place when they were unable to pay their bills. In spring of 1888, they moved to 13 Miller's Court.

Lloyds Weekly Newspaper, 11 November 1888

Mary Kelly was 5'7", taller than many women of the time. She had blonde hair, blue eyes, and pale skin, and although she was known for her stormy temper when drunk, she was quiet and friendly when sober. She is said to have spoken fluent Welsh and a friend described her as *"much superior to that of most persons in her position in life"*. Another acquaintance said she was *"not a notorious character"* and was well-liked by everyone she met.

Drawing of Mary Jane Kelly
(The Penny Illustrated Paper, November 1888)

One of Mary's previous landladies described her as coming from a well-to-do family, and said she was an excellent scholar and an artist. She once told someone she had a relative who acted on the stage. When she first arrived in London, it is thought that she had stayed with nuns at a refuge on Crispin Street, scrubbing floors and cleaning for them, before going into domestic service in a shop. It is unknown how she ended up turning to prostitution on the Whitechapel streets, when she had previously had a more comfortable place at a high-end brothel, but without any family or a support network in the area, she must have found herself in a difficult situation.

Joe Barnett would later state that her brother had visited once and her father had tried to find her, but Mary hid from him. A city missionary said she had shown him letters from her mother in Limerick so she may have been on good terms with her, but as far as anyone knows, she had little contact with the rest of her family. Friend Lizzie Albrook told the inquest about the last conversation she had with Kelly:

"About the last thing she said to me was, 'Whatever you do, don't you do wrong and turn out as I did.' She had often spoken to me in this way and warned me against going on the street as she had done. She told me, too, that she was heartily sick of the life she was leading and wished she had money enough to go back to Ireland where her people lived. I do not believe she would have gone out as she did if she had not been obliged to do so to keep herself from starvation."

Giving advice to Lizzie was not the only occasion on which Mary Kelly showed her kindness. Joseph Barnett stated that he had left her on 30 October 1888, less than two weeks before she was killed, because he was unhappy about her habit of allowing prostitutes to stay in their room. He told the inquest:

"*She would never have gone wrong again, and I shouldn't have left her if it hadn't been for the prostitutes stopping at the house. She only let them stay because she was good hearted and did not like to refuse them shelter on cold bitter nights. We lived comfortably until Mary allowed a prostitute named Julia to sleep in the same room, then another named Maria Harvey. I objected and took lodgings elsewhere.*"

It was during an alcohol-fuelled argument about this that either Mary or Joe had thrown something and broken the window of 13 Miller's Court. Barnett and Kelly were remembered as a friendly and pleasant couple who did not cause any trouble unless they were inebriated, but this was one of the occasions when their tempers got the better of them. The broken window came in useful when the key to the room was lost, and Kelly and Barnett developed a system of reaching through the hole from the outside to access the door handle. This raises some questions if this were true, such as why did McCarthy need to use a pickaxe to prise the door open, rather than just reaching through the window himself?

Even though he had moved out, Joe Barnett continued to visit Mary on an almost daily basis, giving her money when he could afford to, although he had lost his fish porters license a few months before, so he no longer had a regular job at the market. Fish porters needed a license to work, and they were the only ones allowed to transport fish in the city. They wore numbered badges on their aprons to identify them and spent their days carrying around heavy boxes of fresh fish, a physically demanding and smelly job. There were fish porters at Billingsgate right up until 2012 and those who worked there were proud of their camaraderie and the shared heritage of their profession, up until the City Corporation of London stripped away their licenses to hire a cheaper workforce.

When Mary Kelly was last seen, she was wearing a dress made of a plain, cheap fabric called linsey, with a red shawl pulled around her shoulders and no hat. She was known to always wear a spotlessly clean white apron and generally went around with two or three friends.

On Thursday 8 November, Joe Barnett visited Mary at Miller's Court at around 7:00 p.m. When he arrived, her friend Lizzie Albrook was present, and Maria Harvey had been there earlier but had left shortly before Joe's arrival. Lizzie left at around 8:00 p.m. and Joe went back to his lodging house. He apparently told Mary he was sorry, but he had no money to give her that day, and they parted on good terms. Julia Venturney, who lived at 1 Miller's Court, gave evidence that Barnett was very kind to Mary, in contrast with her ex-partner Joseph Fleming. Mary had told Julia she was very fond of Fleming but that he *"often ill-used her because she cohabited with Joe Barnett"*.

At 11:45 p.m. Mary Ann Cox, a widow living in Miller's Court, had been out looking for clients but decided to go home to warm up for a while as it was cold and wet. She noticed Mary Kelly and a man of large build walking ahead of her. She described the man as in his mid-thirties, 5'5", shabbily dressed in dark clothes and a long, dark overcoat with a billycock hat (another name for a bowler hat), a blotchy face, small side whiskers and a carroty moustache. He was carrying a pot of beer and both he and Mary appeared to be drunk.

Cox followed them down the passage into the court and passed Kelly as she was about to go inside number 13, although intriguingly, she made no mention of seeing her putting her hand into the window to reach the handle and open the door. Either she didn't notice or didn't think it worth mentioning, or Kelly had left it unlocked or on the latch, having nothing of value to steal. Mary Kelly told her she was going to sing for the man she had brought home, and a few minutes later, Cox heard her singing "Only A Violet I Plucked From Mother's Grave."

Cox went out again around midnight and heard Mary still singing the same song. Around this time, she must have had a meal of fish and potatoes, which the coroner found partially digested in her stomach during the postmortem. This could have been bought at McCarthy's store round the corner, as chandlers' shops also sold takeaway food like fish and chips. Although if she owed him 29 shillings, she might have been reluctant to show her face in there, unless someone went in and bought it for her. It is also worth noting that lack of sleep can slow down the digestive process, which could confuse the calculation for time of death.

It was not long before her singing began to irritate the neighbours. Everything in the court was crammed in so closely that everyone would have been able to hear what was going on in their neighbours' rooms, which makes what happened later, with reputedly no noise whatsoever, all the more unsettling. Flower seller Catherine Pickett was about to knock on Kelly's door to complain, but her husband told her not to, telling her to *"leave the poor woman alone."* Pickett later told the inquest that Mary was a *"good, quiet pleasant girl, and well-liked by all of us"*.

At 1:00 a.m. Mary Ann Cox returned once again to Miller's Court to warm up for a while. Mary Kelly was still singing, and a light was coming from behind her window.

After a few minutes in her room, Cox left again, still in search of a client so she could earn some money.

Elizabeth Prater lived directly above Mary Kelly's room, and she too supported herself through sex work after her husband left her five years previously. There were only floorboards keeping her room and Mary's apart so every sound from downstairs could be heard by Elizabeth. Between 1:00 and 1:30 a.m. Prater was standing at the entrance to Miller's Court waiting for a client, before returning to her room. She heard nothing from Mary's room below. At 1:30 a.m. Prater placed two chairs against her door to keep out intruders and went to bed.

This is where the story becomes rather colourful, in an intriguing turn of events which has led to much debate over the years. At 2:00 a.m., out-of-work groom George Hutchinson was making his way down Commercial Street after walking back from Romford, about 11 miles east of Whitechapel. He reportedly lodged at the Victoria Working Men's Home, but its doors were already closed for the night. They sold nightly tickets for beds between 5:00 p.m. to 12:30 a.m. but to gain admittance after that time, you would need to possess a weekly pass, which not everyone could afford. Author Jack London is said to have lodged at the Victoria Home in 1902.

It charged 4d for a single bed or 2s a week, but if you wanted extra comfort and privacy, you could pay 6d a night or 3s a week for a "cabin", which was little more than a cubicle but at least had some form of thin wall separating your bed from the others. Common Lodging Houses, which operated under certain regulations, closed for cleaning each day, usually sometime between 2:00 and 5:00 a.m. The Victoria Home was privately run so it did not have to follow those rules and seemed to be a better class of lodging house than some. It did not permit women, provided warm baths, and threatened to eject any lodgers who *"interfered with the comfort of others"*. It was completely destroyed during an air raid in World War II.

The Victoria Home for Working Men c1900

Hutchinson said that as he passed Flower and Dean Street, he saw Mary Jane Kelly, whom he knew. The conversation supposedly went like this:

Mary Jane Kelly: *George, will you lend me sixpence?*

George Hutchinson: *Sorry Mary, I spent all my money down Romford today.*
Mary Jane Kelly: *Good morning then, I must go and find some money.*

She continued walking in the direction from which Hutchinson had just come, and a man appeared and approached her. He put his hand on her shoulder and she laughed, and Hutchinson heard parts of a muttered conversation, including Mary Jane Kelly saying *"alright"* and laughing, and the man saying rather cryptically, *"You will be alright for what I have told you."*

Hutchinson then watched as the pair walked back towards Dorset Street. By this time, Hutchinson was standing under a lamp post near the Queen's Head Pub, and he watched the man intently; rather more intently than would have been normal, if his vividly detailed description was anything to go by:

"He was aged about 34 or 35 and was 5'6" tall. His complexion was pale, with dark eyes and eyelashes, a slight moustache curled up at each end, and dark hair. He was very surly looking and returned my gaze with a stern glare. He was wearing a long, dark coat, and the collar and cuffs were trimmed with astrakhan, with a dark jacket underneath. A light waistcoat, dark trousers, a dark felt hat turned down in the middle, button boots, and gaiters with white buttons. He wore a very thick gold chain. He had a white linen collar and a black tie with a horse-shoe pin. He was of respectable appearance, but shabby genteel I should say. He walked very sharp and was of Jewish appearance. I could identify him again if I saw him."

The Daily News, Evening News, East London Advertiser and The Star did not directly quote Hutchinson's description of the man as "Jewish", instead printing the phrase "foreign looking", possibly in a bid to prevent further anti-Semitic feeling.

Hutchinson only came forward with this description after the inquest was over, and his story was subsequently embellished with extra details including bushy eyebrows, a large seal on the gold chain with a red stone hanging from it, a pair of kid gloves carried in the right hand, and a small package in his left. His assertion that he could identify the man if he saw him again turned out to be a little too hopeful, as detectives escorted him around the area for two days in the hope that he could point him out, and paid him handsomely for his time, but the shabby genteel man had vanished into thin air.

Hutchinson alleged that he saw Mary Kelly and this character, who is referred to in the Ripper community as "astrakhan man", turning towards Miller's Court. At the entrance to the court, Kelly said, *"Alright my dear, come along. You will be comfortable."*

She then kissed him, before remarking that she had lost her handkerchief. The man gave her a red one and they made their way towards her room at number 13. Hutchinson, according to the story he told police, remained under the lamp post opposite the archway, near Crossingham's Lodging House, for about an hour.

When the bells of Christ Church marked 3:00 a.m., he decided to leave and find somewhere to sleep. What he was doing there is the subject of much contention, but many believe that as he'd claimed to know Mary, he was hoping she would let him stay for the night once her client had left, but eventually got bored waiting.

Hutchinson's story about astrakhan man is implausible for a few reasons. Firstly, the lighting in the area was poor and even though he was standing under a streetlamp, it

Illustrated Police News, 24 November 1888

would have been difficult for him to pick out so many details of the man's clothing, especially when he did not see him for very long. Why would he have even troubled to remember the man's appearance? At the time, he had no idea he could have been looking at Jack the Ripper and would have seen him as just another of Kelly's clients. Even if he had an excellent memory and powers of observation, a man of such distinctive appearance would have been noticed by others. Someone dressed so well with gaiters, kid gloves, a gold chain and astrakhan trimmings would have been very distinctive in this part of the East End, at the very least finding himself the object of unwanted attention and having his pockets emptied by thieves, or worse.

There was a witness named Sarah Lewis who saw a man standing where Hutchinson had been.

Photo of a woman who is thought to be witness Sarah Lewis (Casebook.org)

She said at the inquest, *"Between 2 and 3 o'clock this morning I came to stop with the Keylers at number 2 Miller's Court as I'd had a few words with my husband. When I came up the Court there was a man standing over against the lodging house on the opposite side in Dorset Street. He was not tall, but stout, and was wearing a black wideawake hat* [a broad-brimmed, Quaker style hat]. *Shortly before 4 o'clock I heard a scream like that of a young woman, and seemed to be not far away, she screamed out 'murder!' I only heard it once. I did not look out at the window. I did not know the deceased."*

The man she saw was probably Hutchinson and some have theorized that Hutchinson himself could have been The Ripper, and that he only came forward after the inquest because he read about it in the paper and realised he had been seen. It was not unheard of for a detail or two to be strategically held back by the police, so he could have been worried that someone had seen him closely or even recognised him, and thus decided to come forward with his tale about the astrakhan man to turn attention away from himself. As an alternate explanation, he could have been partially telling the truth and was waiting to see if Kelly would give him shelter for the night but did not want to admit to this, for fear that it would make him sound even more shady. He maintained he had known her for three years and that he had given her a few shillings whenever he could, which seems a lot of money to give a casual acquaintance, when he was apparently out of work himself. His biography is patchier than Mary Kelly's and nobody knows what became of him later. We will return to Hutchinson as a suspect in more detail in the next chapter.

The description of astrakhan man lacks plausibility and conveniently echoed the word on the street and public belief that the killer was a foreigner. Neither the blotchy faced man with the carroty moustache, nor astrakhan man, matched any of the other descriptions of men seen with the victims just prior to the murders. Hutchinson conceivably created this description by combining bits from previous witness reports, for example the red handkerchief he mentioned sounds like the red neckerchief seen by Joseph Lawende in the Eddowes murder, the parcel he said astrakhan man was carrying is reminiscent of the policeman who saw someone carrying a package near the scene of the Stride murder, and the phrase "shabby genteel" emulated Elizabeth Long's description of the man with Annie Chapman outside Hanbury Street.

Not long after Hutchinson departed, Mary Ann Cox returned to her room and remained there for the rest of the night. By now, there was no sound or light coming from number 13. Cox could not sleep and heard men going in and out of the court several times and someone leaving one of the rooms at 5:45 a.m. but she did not hear a door close afterwards and was unsure exactly where the sound came from.

At 4:00 a.m., Elizabeth Prater, asleep in the room above Mary Kelly's, was startled awake by her kitten Diddles and shortly afterwards heard a faint cry of *"Oh, murder!"* which could have been the same cry that Sarah Lewis heard, helping to narrow down the time of Kelly's death, but this kind of shout was a common occurrence in the area, so it is not necessarily connected. Considering how thin the partitions were between the walls, one would have thought Elizabeth would have been able to tell if it came from directly below.

At 7:30 a.m., flower seller Catherine Pickett, who had been kept awake late by the singing, wanted to borrow a shawl from Kelly. She knocked on her door several times but got no answer. More confusion has been added to an already muddy set of circumstances, by two people who thought they saw Mary alive later that morning. Caroline Maxwell, wife of a lodging house keeper, believed she had seen her at 8:30 a.m. on 9 November and then again at 9:00 a.m. outside the Britannia, and that Mary was suffering the effects of too much alcohol and vomited. Caroline did not know the victim that well and her testimony was not taken seriously. Maurice Lewis, a tailor by profession, was playing Pitch and Toss with friends in Miller's Court at around 10:00 a.m.; a game which involved throwing coins at a certain mark. The person whose coin landed nearest the mark won all the money that had been tossed. A boy called out, *"Copper!"* so Lewis and his companions scarpered and went into the Britannia pub. He thought he saw Mary inside, but about 30 minutes later, he heard that she had been found dead.

It would not have made sense for her to be out at 9:30 in the morning, then to have gone home, undressed, and folded up her clothes neatly as if to go to sleep. Nobody else from the pub came forward to say that Mary had been there that morning, and if the murder had been committed after 10:00 a.m. rather than under cover of darkness, somebody would surely have seen the killer leaving her room. As for Maxwell's story about her vomiting, this is inconsistent with the fish and potatoes found in her stomach, unless she ate them afterwards, but that would not have allowed much time for the killer to do his work and escape before Thomas Bowyer arrived to collect the rent.

These inexplicable sightings and the fact that the body was so badly desecrated that the face was unrecognisable, have led to conspiracy theories that the victim was not Mary Kelly after all. It is more likely that Maxwell and Lewis just got their timings muddled up and had really seen Kelly the day before. Her remains were identified not only by Joe Barnett, but also by George Hutchinson and landlord John McCarthy. Mrs. Paumier, who sold roasted chestnuts nearby, also had a curious set of events to relate:

"I was approached at about midday on 9 November by a well-dressed man. He said, 'I suppose you have heard about the murder

in Dorset Street?' I said that no, I hadn't. He grinned at me and said, 'I know more about it than you.' He stared me in the face then walked down Sandy's Row, looking back over his shoulder at me as he went. He was about 5'6" with a black moustache, wearing a black silk hat, a black coat and speckled trousers. He also carried a black, shiny bag, about a foot in depth and a foot and a half in length. He's been going around accosting young women these last few nights, and when they asked him what he had in the bag, he replied, 'something the ladies don't like!'"

This was corroborated by Sarah Lewis, the witness who had seen George Hutchinson opposite Miller's Court on the night of the murder. She said that a week before in Bethnal Green, she and a female friend had been approached by a strange man carrying a black bag.

Joe Barnett was questioned but had an alibi. He was at his lodging house, Buller's, in New Street, playing whist until 12:30 a.m. and then went to bed. When he heard about the murder, he voluntarily went to the police, who were satisfied with his statement. He became unwelcome at Buller's when the attention from journalists grew overwhelming, so they asked him to leave, and he went to stay with his sister.

In the days following the murder, Dorset Street and Miller's Court were packed with people trying to get a glimpse of the murder scene, but they were denied entry by two constables guarding the entrance to the court. There was even a story that landlord John McCarthy had been offered £25 by a showman akin to P.T. Barnum who wanted to use the room for a month. Apparently, McCarthy rejected the offer.

Since Catherine Eddowes' murder, the constabulary had received around 1,500 letters pertaining to the case, many of which were hoaxes, while others appeared to be genuine tips. The Penny Illustrated Paper printed a proclamation from Scotland Yard offering a pardon to any accomplice who gave evidence leading to the conviction of the murderer. Meanwhile, a so-called medical man painted his face black in a misguided attempt to become an amateur undercover sleuth. A mob got hold of him, but the police intervened and took him to the station to check his identity.

Another mob, although for all we know it was the same one, chased a German immigrant who had recently arrived in the country, after a woman took a dislike to his appearance and shouted that he was Jack the Ripper. Thankfully no blood was spilt, as the police came to the rescue, questioned him with the help of an interpreter, and let him go.

A macabre mania seems to have beset Whitechapel at this time, as several men were arrested for shouting, *"I'm Jack the Ripper!"* Another man was caught by a policeman in the middle of breaking into a house. Unperturbed by the prospect of arrest, he calmly assured the officer that he was looking for The Ripper. Elsewhere, George Bartlett was charged with unlawful possession of a silver sceptre which he had stolen from a church and hidden in a shiny black bag with a padlock on it. Saving the best for last, John Brinckley was charged for being drunk and disorderly when a constable found him wearing a woman's skirt over his clothes. He shouted, *"I'm Jack the Ripper and I'm going down City Road tonight and I'll do another there!"*

More graffito was discovered in the form of some chalk writing on the Wren's buildings in Thomas Street, which read, *"Dear Boss – I am going to do three more murders. Yours Jack the Ripper."*

Later, another man was arrested for dressing up as a woman, claiming he *"did it for a lark"*, and although there was no mention of The Ripper in this particular incident, the force was by now heartily sick of timewasters, so they charged him with an unlawful act anyway – presumably not for wearing a dress, but for obstructing the police.

The letters and witness testimonies led only to an impasse. They knew no more about the killer with any more certainty than they had when the first canonical killing took place at the end of August in Bucks Row. The one thing they did know was that they were dealing with a dangerous, vicious ghoul who appeared seemingly from nowhere, to commit his barbarous acts, before disappearing once again into the shadows. He had breath-taking audacity and an astonishing streak of luck. How had he slaughtered Mary Jane Kelly in her room, with nothing but paper-thin walls between him and her nearest neighbours, yet nobody heard a thing? There was only one way in and out of the court so he must have had nerves of steel as he walked away after the bloodbath, knowing he risked passing other residents as he left. As he did so, he might even have been clutching his victim's still-warm heart, as this was missing from the scene, unless he had cooked and eaten it in the room.

Coroner McDonald pronounced a verdict of *"wilful murder against some person or persons unknown"*. The inquest was concluded more rapidly than those which had been presided over by Coronor Wynne Baxter, who was known to ask lots of questions and scrutinize statements carefully.

News of the murder even reached the other side of the Atlantic. This is an extract from an article printed in the New York Herald on 11 November:

"Thirty-six hours have passed since the ghastly discovery in Miller's Court, Dorset Street, and nothing more has become known about the murder or murderer than what was sent to the Herald last night. Neighbors have been fancifully garrulous,

absurdly ineffectual arrests have been made and sensational journals have printed a number of absurd, groundless rumors. It is still said "the police are reticent." Quite so, and for the best of all reasons - they know nothing. Sir Charles Warren has issued a proclamation offering a pardon to any accomplice, as if so secretive a murderer possessed accomplices. A story is afloat that the victim was seen outside in the morning shortly before the shocking discovery, but medical evidence shows that this was impossible, as from postmortem signs, she had been dead some hours."

Mary Jane Kelly was laid to rest at St Patrick's Roman Catholic Cemetery in Leytonstone on 19 November. Henry Wilton, sexton of a local church, paid for the funeral himself and set up a fund for people to contribute, but in such an impoverished district, he never received enough to reimburse him for the costs. News of the murder was published internationally so her family may have learned of her tragic death, but they did not attend the funeral. It is possible that Mary Jane Kelly was a pseudonym, so they may not have realised it was her. Mary was a common name at the time, as was Kelly, as an Irish surname.

Crowds of people lined the streets to watch Mary Jane take her final journey in the hearse. For many years, nobody was sure where her grave was, and someone even erected a memorial at the wrong plot in 1986. A few years later, a new one was put up at the correct spot.

Dorset Street later became the site of more murders. In 1901, Mary Ann Austin was stabbed to death at number 35, where Annie Chapman had once lodged, and five years later, Katie Roman had her throat cut at 12 Miller's Court. Dorset Street was renamed Duval Street in 1904, and in the 1960s, a man was shot in the building opposite, almost exactly where George Hutchinson had stood.

John McCarthy, the Miller's Court slumlord, attended Detective Abberline's retirement dinner in 1892, and in 1901 he delivered a rousing speech at a public meeting at the Duke of Wellington pub, refuting the Daily Mail's allegations that Dorset Street was the worst street in London and the centre of crime. A fascinating piece of trivia is that John's granddaughter was the actress Kay Kendall, who married actor Rex Harrison, and played the role of Rosalind in the film Genevieve. The Kay Kendall Leukaemia Fund was established after her death in 1959 at the age of just 32. Somehow, knowing that a famous figure of a modern time was related to a man involved in the story of Jack the Ripper, brings McCarthy and his contemporaries to life in our minds even more, transforming them into three-dimensional grandmothers and grandfathers; real, full-colour people who leap off the page far more than their black and white sketches portray.

Today, people still leave plastic flowers, rosaries, ornaments and even bottles of gin at Mary Kelly's grave, a symbol of the lasting effect that the brutal manner of her death has on anyone who learns her story. Will we ever know the truth and be able to bring justice to the victims of the ruthless string of inhuman murders in the East End? Let's look at the aftermath before we finally tackle the major suspects, debunk some myths, and talk about incarnations of Jack the Ripper in film throughout the decades.

Chapter Seven
Aftermath

Following the murder of Mary Jane Kelly, police continued unsuccessfully to seek a viable suspect, while interest in the case grew both at home and internationally.

A tip was received from an American German named Julius Lowenheim, who claimed to have spoken to a Polish Jew called Wirtkofsky, who told him that he had an urge to kill prostitutes. Meanwhile, a Swedish man named Nikaner Benelius was charged with entering a private house in Mile End for an unlawful purpose. He refused to account for his actions, but Detective Inspector Reid was certain he had nothing to do with the Whitechapel murders.

On 19 November, a man purporting to be a doctor was arrested at Euston Station having arrived from Birmingham. It is not known whether he was proven to be a medical man or not, nor why he was thought to be a person of interest, but he had alibis for the times of the murders and was released.

Joseph Isaacs, a Polish Jew, was apprehended in December for stealing a watch, but the Northern Daily Telegraph libelously wrote that his arrest was in connection with the murders. Apparently, an Inspector was heard to say, *"Keep this quiet, we have got the right man at last. This is a big thing."* They must have been disappointed when it transpired that the sole reason for the misgivings about Isaacs was that his lodging house deputy had reported that he *"had a violin and four or five other musical instruments but was never known to play any of them"*.

On 23 December 1888, The Sunday Times zealously printed the news that Theo Hanhart, a German school master near Bath in southwest England, had confessed to being Jack the Ripper. He was examined by a doctor and certified insane. The false confessions did not end there. In March 1889, John Fitzmaurice told police he was the guilty man, then in July, William Wallace Brodie said the same thing, despite not having been in England at all during the ten weeks of hell in Whitechapel. He was later re-arrested for fraud.

In October 1890, a woman told the Whitechapel Vigilance Committee that a man who had lodged with her in 1888 must have been Jack, as she had seen him wrapping up pieces of liver with the intent to post them to the newspapers. He also had multiple items of clothing, a collection of guns, stayed out late at night and did not have a job. In fear of her life, she did not report him at the time, but was convinced of his guilt.

Newspapers received tips that Jack the Ripper had fled to Algeria, Spain, and Paris, while the Lloyds Weekly Newspaper wrote of the Ripperesque mutilation of a woman in Berlin. Edward Larkins, who worked as a clerk for HM Customs Statistical Department, repeatedly wrote to the police to outline his opinions on the case. He had an unorthodox idea that The Ripper was not one man, but a group of Portuguese cattlemen who came to London by boat; a theory which proved to be foundationless.

Whilst none of this helped to clear up the case, leaving it as muddy and polluted as the River Thames, what it does illustrate is that many of the people being pursued and deemed worthy of investigation were "foreigners" or outsiders. Authorities, for the most part, were apparently unwilling to believe that an Englishman could have committed such atrocities, but this blinkered perspective did not help them arrive at a solution, and we are none the wiser today.

In the 1950s, the Metropolitan Police and Home Office files were transferred to the Public Records Office at Kew, now called the National Archives. These have been available to researchers since 1976 but lamentably, many of the files have since disappeared. Paul Bonner, who worked for the BBC and was involved in the creation of a Jack the Ripper documentary in the early 70s, made notes on some suspect files, reference MEPO 3/141 32-135, which vanished before anyone had a chance to copy them. Bonner, who had the benefit of reading them before they were either lost or purloined, observed that *"Many men, at least a hundred in the file, were taken to police stations just for carrying black bags, having foreign accents, accosting women, or talking about the Ripper in pubs, but were then released on being able to prove their identity. There was no mention, in this file or anywhere else, to Macnaghten's candidates: Druitt, Kosminski, or Ostrog."*

Had there been fewer confounding false confessions and vindictive lodging house keepers, and law enforcement less intent on pursuing men with black bags and foreign accents, could the Whitechapel Fiend have been caught? We will never know.

Some researchers believe that the killer did not stop after the slaughter of Mary Jane Kelly, but continued to operate with a modified MO. For the sake of completeness, I will include here a brief description of some of the later murders which have been pinned on The Ripper at one time or another, although many theorists do not believe these are attributable to Whitechapel Jack. If you wish to read in more detail about the homicides mentioned below, I recommend the Casebook website, which offers a wealth of information and discussion. I have deliberately excluded The Whitehall

Mystery, Elizabeth Jackson, Carrie Brown, Ada Wilson, and Annie Farmer, due to significant differences in method and location, as well as a consensus among the Ripper community that these were unrelated.

Catherine Mylett a.k.a Rose Mylett, Catherine/Rose Millett, Lizzie Davis

Catherine Mylett was born on 8 December 1859. She married a man called Davis and they had one daughter, but she split from her husband and went by several different aliases. Catherine spent time at various lodging houses around the Poplar and Spitalfields areas and spent six weeks at the Bromley Sick Asylum. She was known to practice prostitution.

She was last seen alive, visibly drunk, on 20 December 1888 at around 2:30 a.m. outside the George Tavern in Commercial Road, with two men who looked like sailors. Her body was discovered by two policemen just a couple of hours later, in Clark's Yard in Poplar High Street. There were ligature marks around her neck and the cause of death was strangulation with a cord. There was no sexual assault, nor mutilation.

Dr Thomas Bond and Assistant Commissioner Robert Anderson put forward a peculiar theory that Mylett had fallen while drunk and was choked to death by her stiff velvet collar. Coroner Wynne Baxter was perturbed that several doctors had gone to view the body without his knowledge or sanction. Of the five doctors who saw the body, Dr Bond was the only one who believed it was an accident, and Wynne Baxter diplomatically pointed out that Bond did not see the body until five days after Mylett's death, which put him at a disadvantage. Dr George Bagster Phillips, who completed the postmortems in several of the Ripper murders, firmly believed they were dealing with a homicide and that *"the murderer had studied the theory of strangulation, for he evidently knew where to place the cord so as to immediately bring his victim under control."* The verdict was recorded in the way so many others recently were, as 'wilful murder by person or persons unknown.'

Alice McKenzie a.k.a. "clay pipe Alice"

Like Mary Jane Kelly, Alice McKenzie's background is hazy, but she was born around 1849 and spent her early life in Peterborough, before moving to the East End in the 1870s. She was 5'4", had a fair complexion with brown eyes and brown hair, and a propensity for drinking and smoking a pipe. The top of her left thumb had been cut off in an industrial accident.

By 1888, Alice was working as a charwoman and prostitute, and lived with a man called John McCormack at a lodging house in Gun Street. On 16 July 1889, McCormack returned home at around 4:00 p.m. and gave Alice money to pay the landlady Mrs. Ryder. Alice left the room but did not pay the rent, instead visiting the pub accompanied by a blind boy called George Dixon. While there, Dixon heard Alice speaking to a strange man who wanted to buy her a drink.

At 8:30 p.m. Mrs. Ryder saw Alice back at the lodging house and noticed she was drunk. She observed that Alice and McCormack had an argument (which we might reasonably assume was about her having spent the rent money at the pub), but McCormack claimed the last time he saw Alice alive was 4:00 p.m. At 11:00 p.m., McCormack left the lodging house.

At around 1:00 a.m. the following morning, Alice's body was found in Castle Alley off Whitechapel High Street, by PC Walter Andrews of H Division. It was a well-lit area and Alice was lying just under a streetlamp. Just 45 minutes before, Andrews and another PC, Joseph Allen, had passed by and had not noticed anything out of the ordinary. The pavement beneath her body was still dry, which helped narrow down the time of death, as it had started to rain at 12:45 a.m. Dr George Bagster Phillips estimated the time of death at 12:25 a.m. to 12:45 a.m., and the cause of death was severance of the left carotid artery. There were some superficial cuts to her abdomen, but Phillips believed she had not fallen foul of The Ripper, as the knife used in this case was smaller and not as sharp as the one used in the canonical killings. Once again, the verdict was "wilful murder by person or persons unknown."

The Pinchin Street Torso

On Tuesday 10 September 1889 at 5:15 a.m., a policeman made a gut-wrenching discovery in Pinchin Street, which runs parallel to Commercial Road. The torso of a woman, with head and lower limbs removed, had been dumped underneath a railway arch. The officer had passed the spot about half an hour before but had seen nothing. The organs appeared to be intact. Even at that time, people felt that the case was too dissimilar to the canonical murders to be blamed on Jack. Tragically, the woman was never identified, and she was buried in an unmarked grave in the

East London Cemetery, very close to Liz Stride's final resting place.

Similar examples of dismembered bodies were found in Rainham and Whitehall in 1887 and 1888 respectively, and along with Pinchin Street, this trio of unsolved cases is collectively known as the Thames Torso Murders, which were almost certainly committed by someone other than The Ripper. It is not unusual for more than one serial killer to be operating in an area. For example, the FBI estimates that there are around 50 active serial killers in the United States at any given time; a chilling statistic that does little to put one at ease. In light of this, it does not stretch credulity that both Jack the Ripper and the Thames Torso Killer were operating at the same time.

Frances Coles a.k.a. Frances Coleman

Frances Coles was born in 1865 to a Somerset boot maker. She earned a few shillings a week putting stoppers on medicine bottles for chemists in Whitechapel, but she left her job and turned to prostitution, and began drinking heavily.

On 11 February 1891, Coles met client James Sadler, a 53-year-old merchant seaman and fireman on the SS Fez. Sadler had just been discharged from duty and had found his way to the Princess Alice pub. They spent the following day together, visiting one pub after another. On 13 February at 1:45 a.m., Coles met a client who also looked like a sailor, and wore a "cheese cutter hat," which was a sort of flat cap. Another prostitute named Ellen warned Coles away from the man, but they walked off together in the direction of the Minories.

Between 1:00 and 2:00 a.m., James Sadler got into a fight with some dockworkers who tried to rob him. Later, he attempted to board his ship and was observed to have blood running down his forehead. He was also seen by a policeman who confirmed that he was bleeding, intoxicated, and unable to walk straight.

At 2:15 a.m., PC Ernest Thompson of H Division spotted a shape in the darkest corner of Swallow Gardens, a thoroughfare connecting Chamber Street to Royal Mint Street. It no longer contained anything resembling greenery, although it had once housed trees and gardens before the railway line was built. With the light from his lamp, Thompson saw a body lying on the ground, blood flowing from the neck. It was Frances Coles. He thought he could hear footsteps in the distance, moving away from the scene. At 3:00 a.m., Sadler returned to his lodging house in White's Row, heavily blood stained, but was refused entry.

The postmortem revealed that Coles had been thrown to the ground before her throat was cut in a sawing motion. There were no abdominal wounds. A folded piece of paper containing two shillings was found near the body. Dr George Bagster Phillips, who had been kept very busy indeed over the last couple of years, was certain that the killer had no anatomical skill.

James Sadler was charged with murder but was later acquitted, as he would not have been capable of killing Coles in such an inebriated condition. PC Ernest Thompson did not have such a happy ending. The following year, he was stabbed to death by a man named Abrahams while trying to prevent a crime. He had been with the force for a decade and left behind a wife and four children.

What became of some of the key characters?

Detective Inspector Edmund Reid retired from the force in 1896 due to ill health. He and his wife moved back to Kent, where he was born, but his wife's mental health deteriorated and she was admitted to an asylum, dying in 1900 of chronic organic brain disease, which would be called dementia today. Reid continued working as a private eye and in 1903, moved to a small Kentish village called Hampton-on-Sea. He set up a wooden kiosk in his garden and jovially called it the Hampton-on-Sea Hotel, selling drinks and postcards to locals and tourists. He campaigned to save the village, which was being threatened by coastal erosion, but it was eventually swallowed up by the sea in 1916. He was one of the few investigators who did not believe the killer was a Jew, and criticized his peers for their theories, stating firmly that none of the speculation was true and the identity of the murderer remained unknown.

"I was on the scene and ought to know. One thing is to my mind quite certain, and that is that he lived in the district. The police, of course, did everything possible with a view to the arrest of the man. A set of rules was laid down as to the sending for assistance immediately upon any discovery, not only to Scotland Yard, but to everyone who was likely to be of assistance. And there was always a sort of interesting speculation as to who would reach the scene of a new crime first. There were vigilance societies formed, the members of which used to black their faces, and turn their coats inside out, and adopt all sorts of fantastic disguises. To one of the officers of this organisation the late Queen Victoria sent a letter of commendation, and the public subscribed very liberally. Officially and otherwise, many thousands of pounds were spent in the effort to catch 'Jack', but he eluded us all."

Edmund Reid died in 1917 at the age of 71. The character of Detective Dier, created by writer Charles Gibbon, was based on Reid.

Postcard showing Edmund Reid at Hampton-on-Sea in 1912 (Fred C. Palmer, Herne Bay Records Society)

This is me visiting Hampton-on-Sea, looking towards the area where Reid once stood. The white building in the background on the right is the Hampton Inn, which can also be seen in the Reid postcard, and where I enjoyed a hearty plate of scampi and chips which sustained me through an afternoon of writing!

Surgeon Thomas Bond committed suicide in 1901 at the age of 60. He threw himself from the bedroom window of his home and was buried in a churchyard in Somerset. He is known for creating a profile of the killer based upon reports compiled by his predecessors and the knowledge he obtained during the postmortem.

Frederick Abberline was promoted to Chief Inspector in 1890 but resigned from the Metropolitan Police in 1892 after having served for nearly 30 years. Not content to let go of law enforcement for good, he relocated to Bournemouth and became a Pinkerton Detective. He died in 1929, but his character lives on, having been portrayed many times in film and television.

Sir Robert Anderson was appointed Assistant Chief Commissioner of the Metropolitan Police Criminal Investigations Department on 1 September 1888, the day after the murder of Polly Nichols, succeeding James Monro who had recently resigned. Anderson retired in 1901 and later received a knighthood. He died from Spanish Flu in 1918 aged 77.

Sir Robert Anderson

Sir Charles Warren had come under fire many times for his handling of the Whitechapel murders and was ridiculed in the press, with many believing that the bloodhounds Barnaby and Burgho, who he had so enthusiastically hired, would have done a better job than him as Police Commissioners. Warren resigned on the day of Mary Jane Kelly's murder on 9 November 1888 and returned to the army, fighting in the Second Boer War in 1899 where he commanded the fifth division of the South African Field Force.

Sir Charles Warren

It turned out that being put in charge of things he was not capable of managing was a common occurrence, as he had limited experience of leading troops into battle. He botched the attempted relief of Ladysmith in January 1900 and made further errors of judgement at the Battle of Spion Kop, resulting in disaster for the British forces. He even slowed down the march by bringing a cast iron bathroom and a well-equipped kitchen. In 1908, Warren became involved in the beginnings of the Boy Scouts alongside Robert Baden-Powell. As an interesting aside, Robert Baden-Powell's great-grandson Gerard Baden-Clay was charged with murder in 2012 of his wife Allison, one of the most infamous recent cases in Australia. Sir Charles Warren died of pneumonia at his home in Weston-super-Mare in 1927 aged 86.

Donald Swanson was promoted to Superintendent in 1896 and retired from the force in 1903. He died in 1924.

Sir Charles Melville Macnaghten was appointed Assistant Chief Constable of the Metropolitan Police in 1889 and wrote his famous memorandum in 1894 naming his three favoured suspects: Druitt, Kosminski, and Ostrog. He served as Assistant Commissioner of the Met Police from 1903 to 1913 and played a role in the exoneration of a wrongly convicted man, Adolf Beck, and the capture of murderer Harvey Crippen. Macnaghten published his memoirs in 1914 after retiring due to ill health, and he died in 1921 aged 67.

Dr George Bagster Phillips, who was described as a leading police surgeon in London by the Lancet, conducted postmortems on some of the later murders in Whitechapel which were not ascribed to Jack the Ripper, including Frances Coles, Alice McKenzie, and the Pinchin Street Torso. He died in 1897 of apoplexy, which would be called a stroke today.

Coroner Wynne Edwin Baxter presided over the inquest into the death of "Elephant Man" John Merrick in April 1890, as well as the deaths of 11 German spies captured in Britain during the First World War. He was an enthusiastic plant collector, a Fellow of the Geological Society of London, and a Fellow and Treasurer of the Royal Microscopical Society. In the 1890s he translated several scientific books from French to English, and he was an avid antiquarian, amassing a library of 3,000 books about author John Milton, about whom he wrote academic papers. He was a member of the archaeological societies of Middlesex, Surrey, Kent, Sussex, and Gloucestershire, and as if this was not enough to fill his time, he was Clerk to two City Guilds: The Worshipful Company of Shipwrights and The Worshipful Company of Farriers. He continued to serve on myriad committees and held various public offices, and he was also a prominent Freemason. In 1907, he was quoted as saying, *"I have held over 30,000 inquests, and have not had one body exhumed yet."* Baxter died in 1920 aged 76. His legal practice in Lewes, East Sussex, still exists today as Mayo Wynne Baxter LLP. The Brighton and Hove Bus Company named their number 657 bus after him, which was unveiled during a Jack the Ripper conference held in the city in 2005.

Chapter Eight
The Suspects

I have listed below a short summary of each of the five canonical murders, to serve as a reminder before we embark on examining the suspects.

Mary Ann Nichols (née Walker) a.k.a. Polly Nichols
26 August 1845 – 31 August 1888
Estimated time of death: 3:40 a.m.
Place of Death: Bucks Row, in front of Brown's Stable Yard
Details of death: Asphyxiated before throat was cut, severing the jugular vein and carotid artery. Multiple incisions to the abdomen, with intestines later discovered to be erupting from the abdominal wound. Two small stabs to the private parts. High risk crime due to regular police beats, and a nightwatchman was on duty in nearby Winthrop Street.

Annie Chapman (née Smith) a.k.a. Dark Annie
25 September 1840 (or 1841 according to some sources) – 8 September 1888
Estimated time of death: 5:15 a.m. to 5:30 a.m.
Place of Death: Back yard of 29 Hanbury Street which housed 17 people.
Details of death: Asphyxiated before throat was cut. Intestines lying above right shoulder. Uterus, vagina and two thirds of the bladder were removed by the killer. Two brass rings were presumably stolen by the killer. High risk crime as escape would have been difficult as there was only one way in or out of the backyard, which was through the

house. People were getting up for work at this time and tenants' windows overlooked the yard.

Elizabeth Stride (née Gustafsdotter) a.k.a Long Liz

27 November 1843 – 30 September 1888
Estimated time of death: 12:45 a.m. to 1:00 a.m.
Place of death: Dutfield's Yard, off Berner Street.
Details of death: No evidence of suffocation. Victim's scarf was used to pull her backwards before her throat was cut. Unlike previous murders there were no bruises about the face. High risk crime as 28 people were at the International Working Men's Club and there were regular police beats in the area. Dr George Bagster Phillips confirmed that the weapon and method were different from the other victims.

Catherine Eddowes a.k.a. Kate Kelly

14 April 1842 – 30 September 1888
Estimated time of death: 1:35 a.m. to 1:45 a.m.
Place of death: Dark corner of Mitre Square
Details of death: No evidence of suffocation. Cause of death was severance of the left carotid common artery, with the jugular vein opened by about an inch and a half. The intestines were removed and placed over the right shoulder. The left kidney and uterus were removed from the body. Facial mutilations were carried out. High risk crime due to frequent police beats, nightwatchman working at Kearley & Tonge, and houses overlooking the square.

Mary Jane Kelly a.k.a. Marie Jeanette Kelly

C. 1863 – 9 November 1888
Estimated time of death: 3:30 a.m. to 4:00 a.m.

Place of death: 13 Millers Court; a single room in a quiet court off Dorset Street, one of the most dangerous roads in Whitechapel.

Details of death: No evidence of suffocation. Cause of death was severance of the carotid artery. Facial mutilations were carried out. The heart was removed from body and never found. Intestines were placed on the right side of the body, and various other parts such as breasts and liver were positioned around her. Medium risk crime as police did not customarily walk down this road and the killer had more time and privacy to carry out his debauchery.

One of the few things that is apparent from studying this sequence of horrific killings, from the initial Whitechapel Murders through to the canonical five, and those who came after, is that The Ripper seemed to be protected by almost preternatural forces. Despite the increased police presence on the streets and the vigilance of ordinary citizens, he came and went without detection, committing his heinous outbursts of violence under cover of shadow before disappearing, all against a backdrop of rising tension between Jews and Gentiles, and the bubbling, fomenting anger and unease that authorities feared would spill into civil unrest at any moment.

The Puck Magazine of September 1889 printed an illustration of the killer looking into a mirror, with a selection of possibilities staring back at him in caricature, including a doctor, a woman, a clergyman, and a couple of unspecified rogues, not to mention a stereotypical Jewish man. You can also see a policeman's helmet just above the killer's right arm, suggesting that the idea of "Jack the Peeler" had also been contemplated.

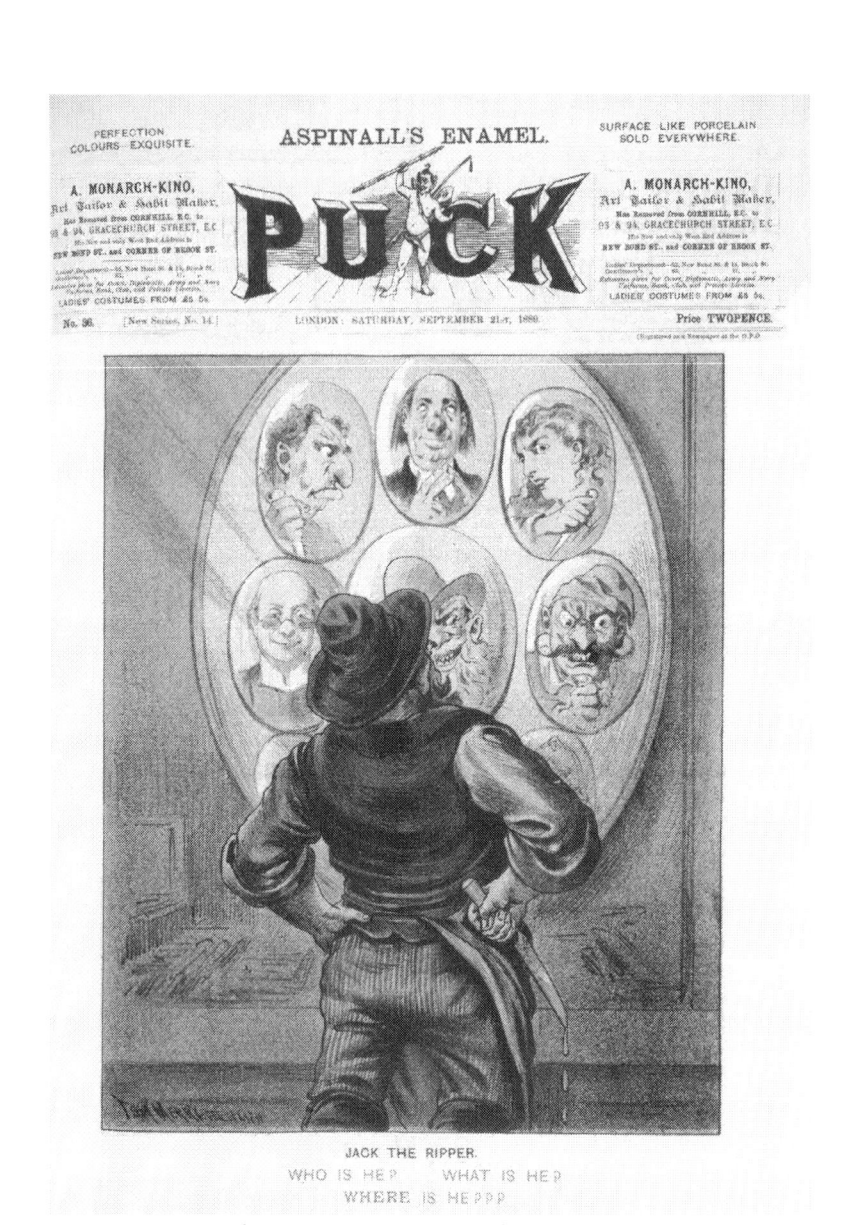

Puck magazine, 21 September 1889

The idea of a policeman as the Whitechapel Murderer is sometimes floated by those who are new to the case and looking at it with fresh eyes, unfettered by bias or their own favourite suspect. It is easy to see why this is an attractive theory. In all the canonical murders, except for that of Mary Jane Kelly, a policeman had either discovered the body or had been patrolling in the vicinity, yet none of them saw anyone fleeing the scene. If the killer was a police officer, he would have been able to walk around freely, concealed by his uniform and comfortably above suspicion whilst his colleagues desperately hunted for him. When you add to this the fact that the official files were quietly closed in 1891, it almost looks as though the police knew who Jack was and that he was no longer a threat.

However, their routes were set in stone, and they had to meet their colleagues on regular joining beats. They also had to keep their uniforms clean or risk the wrath of a punctilious superior. In the example of PCs Mizen, Neil and Thain, who patrolled in and around Bucks Row, their beats came within yards of each other, which would have made subterfuge very difficult. There were also no eyewitnesses who reported seeing a policeman speaking to any of the victims.

When we consider who The Ripper might have been, we need to ask ourselves why he stopped. We know that in most cases, serial murderers only cease their activities if they are incarcerated, die, or find a healthier outlet for their aberrant desires. Some people believe that the Whitechapel Fiend continued to practice his evildoings, citing examples like those we saw in the Aftermath chapter, such as Frances Coles, and the Pinchin Street Torso. Some guess that Jack the Ripper ended his days in an asylum, others believe he travelled overseas and continued to kill in other countries, while another conclusion is that the debauched slaughter at Miller's Court allowed him to reach the climax of his crazed thirst for blood and there was nothing left that he desired to achieve.

Over the last century, the pile of suspects put forward has grown into a mountain and includes by some counts as many as 500 individuals. The majority of these were based on minimal evidence and have been discounted for the most part, with some weird and wonderful proposals ranging from Alice in Wonderland author Lewis Carroll to the Royal Family, to the "Jill the Ripper" theory of a female killer - a mad midwife or abortionist. It would be a Herculean task to review them all in one book, so we will examine those more generally considered to be serious possibilities.

When I first discovered this case some 25 years ago, I'm sure I was not alone in finding the most exciting aspect to be the thrill of trying to pick out the killer from the lineup of eccentric suspects. I leaped from one character to the next, each time convinced I was correct, before moving on to favour a different person the next year. I now appreciate that cracking the enigma is a virtual impossibility because the evidence is too disparate, circumstantial, and frequently spurious. Countless theories have been put forward and more emerge all the time, usually leaving more questions than answers in their wake.

I aim to focus on what we know to be true from the records of the time. I will make it clear when an argument or opinion is based on speculation, rather than trying to sell fiction as fact, because although conjecture can be fascinating, it only serves to perpetuate the aura of mystery around Jack. We will rip our way through the facts and try to apply modern insight to establish if any of the most well-known suspects are more credible than others. Hardly a week goes by when a new publication does not emerge with a fresh theory or a novel explanation. Can we ever answer the 130-year-old question that still plays on the minds of true crime enthusiasts all over the world: who **was** the elusive phantom who stalked the streets of Whitechapel?

Before we investigate the key suspects and their merits, it is important to look through the lens of the 21st century knowledge of which we now have the benefit, to assess what kind of killer we are dealing with. Firstly, I believe it is vital to understand whether The Ripper was an organized or disorganized killer. Much of the knowledge base that criminal profilers rely on was developed by the FBI's John Douglas and Robert Ressler, who conducted around 30 unstructured interviews with California serial killers in the 1970s to get a feel for their character traits and whether they were organized or disorganized. Although the credibility of this study has been questioned due to the small sample size and the fact that it yielded qualitative, rather than empirical data, the concept of organized versus disorganized has proven to be broadly useful in categorizing killers.

To identify a killer as organized, criminal profilers look for evidence of methodical thinking, planning the crime in advance, and the ability to employ a ruse to gain the trust of their victim. Organized killers are generally intelligent, have a job, and are likely to be in a relationship, whereas disorganized killers may be unemployed, live alone or with parents, and attacks may be random and unplanned. Disorganized criminals may suffer from a mental illness or from drug or alcohol misuse. They tend to have less well-developed social skills and often come from dysfunctional families where abuse and a lack of stability are factors, although this can be the case with organized killers too. In the real world, people display a combination of these traits.

It is my opinion that Jack the Ripper was predominantly an organized killer for the following reasons:

- He always brought a murder weapon with him, showing premeditation
- He must have had the social skills to approach the victims and convince them that he wanted to pay for their services, without appearing to be a threat. This was particularly important as time went on, as women alone at night would have been increasingly wary
- He must have ensured he had sufficient privacy so that any blood or odd behaviour would go unnoticed, and he may have had more than one set of clothes and the facility to wash them. He would have needed money to approach prostitutes, or at least have the appearance of someone who would be able to pay. All of this indicates someone who had a job and lived independently, practicably not in a workhouse or as a lodger in someone else's home
- The crime scenes were in quiet, dimly lit locations, excepting Dutfield's Yard, which may not even be a Ripper murder site
- Irrespective of the increased police presence, he always found an escape route which suggests strong knowledge of the local area, police beats, and careful planning (or extraordinary luck)
- In Miller's Court, evidence points to him lighting a fire using Mary Jane Kelly's clothing so that he could see better in the dark as he mutilated her body. He then closed the door as he left, indicating that he knew delaying the body's discovery was important.

Although most of the murders were high risk crimes in that there were police nearby and the killer could have been caught at any moment, we must remember that in the context of the time, The Ripper would have had limited options. Today, killers are more likely to have their own home, offering them privacy, and a car or other method of transport to dispose of the cadaver. In the East End in 1888, people lived cheek-by-jowl and would not have had a private vehicle, so there would have been no question of taking the body elsewhere to conceal it. Had the canonical murders taken place in the 21st century, we might well consider the killer to be disorganized, but in the Victorian era, this was simply the best he could manage.

Let's look briefly at some other killers to assess whether their behaviour was organized or disorganized. I have selected some of the most grotesque cases I could find, as a point of comparison with the brutal violence seen in the Whitechapel murders.

The Greyhound Bus Murder

In 2008, 22-year-old carnival worker Tim Mclean was returning home to Winnipeg on a Greyhound bus after working at a fair in Edmonton, Canada, when 40 year old Vince Li launched a sudden, vicious attack on him with a knife. As the other passengers looked on in horror, Li held up Mclean's severed head before eating his heart and eyes, and placing the victim's ear, nose, and tongue in his pocket. The RCMP heard him say, *"I have to stay on the bus forever."* Li's demeanour before the attack was described as calm and robotic, and he had been seen sitting bolt upright at the bus station with his eyes wide open. Li had moved to Canada from China seven years prior to the attack. English was not his first language and he sometimes struggled with communication, working various jobs which did not make the best use of his skillset, as he had been a software engineer in his home country. While one manager described Li as hardworking and reliable with no signs of anger, he had been fired from another job at Walmart following a disagreement with colleagues. The defense team argued that Li had been hearing voices since 2004 and that God had instructed him to kill Tim McClean, who he believed to be a demon. He was judged not to be criminally responsible for the killing. Tim brought joy to all who knew him with his sunny disposition, and he is greatly missed by family and friends.

Due to the suddenness of the attack, the mental illness, and the fact that it occurred in a very public place with no attempt to hide his crime, we can establish that Vince Li was a disorganized killer.

Richard Chase a.k.a. The Vampire Of Sacramento

Richard Chase was an American serial killer who murdered six people, both men and women, in the late 1970s. He was known to be a hypochondriac and believed that he could absorb Vitamin C by holding oranges to his head. He suspected his cranial bones had been somehow separated without his knowledge, so he shaved his head to monitor the situation. As a teenager, he displayed all three elements of the MacDonald Triad; fire starting, bedwetting and animal cruelty, which were proposed by psychiatrist J.M. Macdonald in 1963 as early predictors of future sociopathy. Chase was also a heavy drug user. A psychiatrist he saw in his early life believed that he suffered from repressed rages.

As his mental health deteriorated, his personal hygiene suffered, and he lost weight. He ultimately began killing and his preferred method was to shoot his victims before using a knife to carve them up and cannibalize them. When the police eventually arrested him, they found the walls, ceiling, refrigerator, and cutlery in his apartment caked in blood and rotting flesh.

In jail, other prisoners were scared to go near Chase, and he eventually received a formal diagnosis of paranoid schizophrenia. In December 1980, aged just 30, he was found dead in his cell, having taken an overdose of antidepressants prescribed by the prison doctor that he had been saving up for weeks.

Richard Chase's character profile is often used as the archetype for a disorganized killer because he had a serious mental illness, there was little cooling off period between the murders, and he left a mountain of evidence in his home, making no attempts to hide or deny his crimes.

Jeffrey Dahmer a.k.a. Milwaukee Monster

Dahmer murdered 17 men, mostly African American, between 1978 and 1991. He lured them into his home with the promise of money or sex and gave them alcohol laced with drugs before strangling them. He then dismembered their bodies, keeping parts as souvenirs. Signs of his sociopathy had appeared in childhood when he began collecting dead animals, and he was described as detached and vacant. He began struggling with alcoholism in his teenage years and became intoxicated prior to each murder.

He stalked his victims, assessing their suitability by engaging them in conversation at local bars, choosing those on the lowest rungs of society who were less likely to be missed. He also posed the corpses after death.

When the police searched his home, they discovered body parts in his refrigerator and photographs of his victims. Dahmer resisted arrest and was quoted as saying, *"for what I did I should be dead."* Others evidently thought so too, as he was killed in prison in 1994. A forensic psychiatrist testified during his trial that Dahmer knew right from wrong but suffered from paraphilia, while another expert portrayed him as amiable and courteous. It is generally understood that Dahmer killed homosexual men because he was trying to destroy a part of himself that he did not understand or accept. Alcohol would have served to lower his inhibitions as it affects the limbic system, the part of the brain which regulates emotions and behaviour.

Although Dahmer was a college dropout and left significant evidence in his home, he was an organized killer as his victims were carefully chosen and he was able to appear as an ordinary, friendly person, allowing him to lure his victims without arousing suspicion.

Albert Fish a.k.a. The Werewolf of Wysteria

Albert Fish was an American serial killer and cannibal who was born in 1870 into a family which had a history of mental illness. His uncle suffered from "mania", his mother experienced hallucinations, and three other relatives had mental illnesses. When his father died, Fish was sent to an orphanage where he was abused and witnessed sadistic treatment of other children. As an adult, he began kidnapping young boys, but sometimes girls too, mostly African American or those with learning disabilities.

Although he knew by this time that he was gay, his mother arranged for him to be married to a woman named Anna Hoffman and they had six children, so Fish's life appeared normal on the surface, and he worked as a painter and decorator. What was not apparent to the outside world was his fascination with mutilation and torture, which he practiced on his victims with a butcher's knife and hacksaw. He was able to befriend people and inspire their trust, in one notable case convincing the parents of 10-year-old Grace Budd that he was going to take her to his niece's party, which was of course a lie. After Fish killed Grace, he sent an anonymous letter to her mother detailing how he had killed and eaten her daughter.

Fish was found to be sane and was executed in 1936. He had a sadistic personality disorder and derived sexual gratification from his acts of mutilation. Although Fish may have had a diagnosable mental illness, he closely matches the characteristics of an organized killer as he was able to get away with his crimes for a long time and planned the murders carefully, coming across as a trustworthy, normal citizen.

I hope these examples have been helpful to explain that although killers may exhibit a combination of traits, they can usually be described as mostly organized or disorganized. Had Jack the Ripper suffered from a serious mental illness or delusions like Richard Chase or Vince Li, he would have run a far greater risk of being noticed and commented on, the murders would have been more spontaneous and committed at random times rather than consistently in the early hours of the morning, and he would have been more easily caught due to leaving evidence behind and an inability to cover his tracks or make his escape.

For these reasons, I contend that it is improbable, but of course not impossible, that The Ripper suffered from an overt mental illness like paranoid schizophrenia, whose symptoms can include perceiving sights and sounds which others do not, having a persistent and unusual belief system, decline in hygiene, lack of motivation, poor speech patterns, and being highly distrustful of other people.

It is important to point out that people with paranoid schizophrenia are not usually violent unless the influence of hallucinations and delusions becomes acute, which may happen in cycles alternating with periods of few or no symptoms. As Jack the Ripper usually killed on or close to the weekend in the early hours of the morning and selected dark, quiet places to do so, it is unlikely that he could have had an illness like this, as his symptoms would have been unpredictable, rather than only becoming apparent on specific days and times. We should keep this in mind as we look at each of the main suspects.

The Profile

Police surgeon Dr Thomas Bond created a profile of the killer, one of the earliest of its kind. He believed the mutilations were carried out by someone with no scientific or anatomical knowledge, and he thought they did not even have any experience of cutting up animals. He hypothesized that the perpetrator was physically strong, with a calm, cool demeanour, but subject to attacks of homicidal mania or unstoppable sexual desire.

Dr Thomas Bond

According to Bond, his appearance would have been inoffensive, he would have been neatly and respectably dressed, and he was likely middle-aged. He wore an overcoat or cloak, which would have covered the worst of the blood marks as he fled the crime scenes. He would have been solitary and eccentric and may not have had a regular job. Sadly, Dr Bond took his own life in 1901, thirteen years after completing Mary Jane Kelly's postmortem.

While many believe that profiling is a pseudoscience and is not a useful tool for solving crimes, it is important to remember that Criminal Minds and CSI do not represent real life. Human beings are innately programmed to profile people, and this is evident in all kinds of social situations. For example, when a new intake of children starts school for the first time, they will subconsciously identify which of their classmates they are most likely to resonate with, and they very quickly fracture off into separate friendship groups. The same pattern can be seen in adults, and everybody has experienced the sensation of taking an instant dislike to someone without an obvious reason for it, or in contrast, feeling immediately at home in someone's company, as though you've known them for years. It is not magic, but a combination of psychology, intuition, and statistics. Although it should only ever be used alongside other evidence, profiling can be a valuable way of painting a picture of a suspect's likely characteristics.

As for Bond's belief that Jack the Ripper was unemployed, I am not convinced by this. If Detective Inspector Reid's views are to be believed and the killer found his victims in one of the many pubs in the area and followed them out at closing time, then he must have had money. All the canonical murders took place towards the end of the week or at the weekend, so we could submit that he had a job which paid weekly, and that on receipt of his wages, he went to the pub for a drink and to search for his victims. Witness Joseph Lawende thought the man he saw with Catherine Eddowes resembled a sailor. Could he have been a dock worker, a strong manual labourer who knew the area well? Whatever his occupation, he would have fitted in; someone to whom his victims would talk freely, and considered one of their own.

A Whitechapel citizen named Toby, who had apparently known Liz Stride, gave an extraordinarily insightful interview in the Star newspaper on 1 October

1888. When asked what type of man he thought had committed the murders, he replied:

"It weren't none of the kind that puts up at a six-penny doss. That chap's got a room to wash himself in. He don't live far off neither. I shouldn't be surprised if he was walking up and down in the crowd out there now. He's a cool one he is, and it would be just like him to call and see if he could identify the bodies."

Toby would no doubt have been surprised to be told by a criminal profiler of the future that he had hit upon a very accurate definition of an organized serial killer! If only he had worked for the police, Jack the Ripper might have been named and we would have no need to write books about him in the 21st century. This is my attempt at a profile, based on all the evidence we have discussed so far:

- Organized rather than disorganized
- Socially adept at convincing his victims he was not a threat, and therefore could not have had an overt mental illness
- Had a regular job and enough money to spend at the pub
- Had lodgings which offered at least some privacy, allowing him to come and go without attracting attention
- Working class or lower-middle class
- Above average intelligence
- Heterosexual, but possibly with an issue of some kind around gender. The primary focus seemed to be on the removal or destruction of female organs such as the vagina and uterus. In the patriarchal Victorian era, anyone with gender dysphoria or who simply did not fit the stereotypes of masculinity would have been unable to express their feelings. The desire to

destroy that which you hate in yourself is not uncommon, for example in the case of Paul Denyer's 1993 killings which we will return to briefly later in the chapter.

The first time any suspects were officially named was in the Macnaghten Memorandum, written in 1894 by Assistant Commissioner of the Metropolitan Police, Sir Melville Macnaghten. He was not involved with the investigations at the time, having only joined the police force in June 1889. He had no prior experience in law enforcement but had spent time in India managing his father's tea plantation.

Sir Melville Macnaghten

His Memorandum was created in response to a sensational article in the Sun newspaper about a suspect called Thomas Cutbush. Macnaghten wanted to set the record straight, although his Memorandum was not made public at the time, only emerging several decades later.

"No one ever saw the Whitechapel murderer; many homicidal maniacs were suspected, but no shadow of proof could be thrown on anyone. I may mention the cases of three men, any one of whom would have been more likely than Cutbush to have committed this series of murders:

(1) A Mr M. J. Druitt, said to be a doctor and of good family -- who disappeared at the time of the Miller's Court murder, and whose body (which was said to have been upwards of a month in the water) was found in the Thames on 31st December -- about seven weeks after that murder. He was sexually insane and from private information I have little doubt that his own family believed him to have been the murderer.

(2) Kosminski -- a Polish Jew – and resident in Whitechapel. This man became insane owing to many years' indulgence in solitary vices. He had a great hatred of women, especially of the prostitute class, and had strong homicidal tendencies: he was removed to a lunatic asylum about March 1889. There were many circumstances connected with this man which made him a strong suspect.

(3) Michael Ostrog, a Russian doctor and a convict, who was subsequently detained in a lunatic asylum as a homicidal maniac. This man's antecedents were of the worst possible type, and his whereabouts at the time of the murders could never be ascertained."

Montague Druitt

Montague John Druitt, known as Monty, was not actually a doctor as Macnaghten alleged, but the son of a surgeon. He was born on 15 August 1857, the third child of seven, to a wealthy family who lived at Westfield House, a Victorian manor on a six-acre estate in Dorset, southwest England. Monty's father and grandfather were both surgeons, while his older brother and uncle were solicitors. His mother, Ann, suffered from mental illness and moved from asylum to asylum in the last few years of her life, before dying in December 1890 of "melancholia" and "brain disease."

Montague Druitt, courtesy of Suzanne Foster at the Winchester Archives

Monty received a scholarship to Winchester College at the age of 12. He was an avid sportsman, taking part in track and field, rugby, cricket, and handball. Cricket was his favourite and he was a medium-paced bowler, although not always accurate, with a tendency to bowl a number of wides. When he wasn't playing sports, he found time to serve as treasurer and secretary of the debating society. Winchester College boasts several notable alumni, including Douglas Jardine, the cricket captain who led England to the

Ashes, and notoriety, in 1933 with his questionable Bodyline tactics.

In July 1876, Montague Druitt secured a place at New College, Oxford, where he graduated four years later with a third-class Honours degree in Classics. We can speculate that his family were less than impressed with these results, comparing him to the successful surgeons and barristers among the Druitts. Monty decided that he would like to study for a law degree, perhaps having realised that he would struggle to make a lucrative career out of Classics. There was an agreement that Monty could have the £500 needed to pay for his legal studies, but his father insisted that it would be deducted from his future inheritance. It must have left a bitter taste in Monty's mouth that the money for his studies was given so reluctantly, leaving him nothing on his father's death in 1885 except for pictures, clocks, jewellery, ornaments, and books, while his eldest brother received a farm, and his three sisters each received £6,000 (around £788,000 in modern money).

Druitt passed his law exams and was called to the Bar in April 1885, just a few months before his father's death. In the 1887 Law List he was described as a Special Pleader, a title which no longer exists. This involved working on behalf of a plaintiff to demonstrate how he or she had suffered due to a defendant's actions. Some people say he was a failed barrister, but this is untrue; his practice was successful enough that he could afford to pay for chambers at 9 King's Bench Walk, which cost £60 a year (£7,000 today) and he continued his work as a Special Pleader until his death.

He supplemented his income by taking up an additional job as an assistant schoolmaster at a boarding school at 9 Eliot Place, Blackheath, in southeast London. This is popularly referred to as Valentine's School, as it was run by a Mr. George Valentine. It catered for just 30 to 40 pupils between the ages of 9 and 17, with no more than 10 supporting staff and two or three other schoolmasters. Monty covered nighttime duties, for which he was paid £200 a year less board and lodging, which was an above average wage for a schoolmaster at the time, but we do not know what his duties entailed. He lived at Eliot Place but spent his days at his King's Bench Walk chambers, returning to the school each evening.

On Friday 30 November 1888, Druitt was dismissed from the school. His brother William said that it was for a "serious offence", but nobody knows any further details. Some have advanced the notion that as there was no record of his having any relationships with women, that he was gay or had been caught molesting pupils. There is no evidence for this at all, but it must have been something that concerned Valentine sufficiently to remove Druitt from his job after eight years of service.

If there *had* been any suggestion of Druitt being gay, this alone would have been enough to warrant his dismissal in an era of intolerance and prejudice. He would have been ostracized from society and if the news got out, he would have risked losing his chambers, his clients, and his cricketing connections.

Nobody knows what Druitt's movements were after his dismissal, until his body was found floating in the Thames near the Thornycrofts shipyard on 31 December 1888, having been in the river for three or four weeks. He left a very brief suicide note in his room at Eliot Place, which read, *"Since Friday I felt I was going to be like mother, and the best thing for me was to die."* This reference to Friday almost certainly refers to the day he lost his job at the school, and alluded to his mother's mental illness, which had begun just a few months earlier. The following items were found on Monty's body:

- Four large stones in each pocket
- £2 17s 2d cash
- A cheque for £50 and another for £16 (probably for any due wages and/or a severance payment from the school)
- Silver watch on a gold chain
- Pair of kid gloves
- White handkerchief
- First-class half-season rail ticket from Blackheath to London
- A second-half return ticket from Hammersmith to Charing Cross dated 1 December 1888

We do not know what Monty did in Hammersmith, nor what he had intended to do in Charing Cross, but we do know that he did not use the Hammersmith to Charing Cross part of his ticket. Some question why he bought a return ticket if he was planning to end his life, but he could have been operating on autopilot, mindlessly going through the motions as he made his final journey.

His mother's mental breakdown shortly before the first of the Jack the Ripper murders is cited as a potential trigger for Druitt to commence a string of murders, and that his deteriorating mental state and strange behaviour led to the loss of his job and his subsequent demise, very shortly after the murder of Mary Jane Kelly.

Melville Macnaghten apparently suspected him for these reasons, but also claimed that Druitt's own family believed him to be guilty. This may have stemmed from a newspaper article printed in February 1891, which is the earliest known documentation to mention Druitt as a suspect. The Bristol Times and Mirror published a story from West Dorset MP (Member of Parliament) Henry Farquharson. Farquharson was the same age as Monty and lived just a few miles from the Druitt family home, so it is not farfetched to think they had known each other. The article read:

"I give a curious story for what it is worth. There is a West of England member who in private declares that he has solved the mystery of 'Jack the Ripper.' His theory - and he repeats it with so much emphasis that it might almost be called his doctrine - is that 'Jack the Ripper' committed suicide on the night of his last murder. I can't give details, for fear of a libel action; but the story is so circumstantial that a good many people believe it. He states that a man with blood-stained clothes committed suicide on the night of the last murder, and he asserts that the man was the son of a surgeon, who suffered from homicidal mania."

Although the suspect is not named, it is believed that this article referred to Monty due to the mention of suicide and his being the son of a surgeon. The timing of his death is incorrect though, as Mary Jane Kelly was killed on 9 November, and Druitt did not die until the beginning of December. It has been attested by some sources that there exists a more detailed account of Druitt as a suspect, held by Macnaghten's daughter Christabel, the Dowager Lady Aberconway. This version is reportedly a draft of the 1894 memo which listed Macnaghten's three favoured suspects, Druitt, Kosminski, and Ostrog. The story goes that Lady Aberconway showed this draft to author and broadcaster Dan Farson in 1959, who was making a Ripper documentary. In the official police memo, Macnaghten expressed no opinion on which of the three suspects was more likely than the others, but in the Aberconway version, he allegedly wrote:

"I enumerate the cases of three men against whom police held very reasonable suspicion (Druitt, Kosminski and Ostrog). Personally, after much careful and deliberate consideration, I am inclined to exonerate the last two, but I have always held strong opinions regarding the number one, and the more I think the matter over, the stronger do those opinions become. The truth, however, will never be known, and did indeed, at one time lie at the bottom of the Thames, if my conjections [sic] be correct."

This matches a statement from Macnaghten's 1914 memoirs Days of My Years, declaring that Jack the Ripper had died on or about 10 November 1888 after *"his brain gave way altogether and he committed suicide; otherwise the murders would not have ceased"*.

We cannot track down and confirm Macnaghten's sources, as he reported in a Daily Mail interview in 1913 that he had destroyed all his documents and there was no longer any record of the information that had come into his possession.

Others deem Druitt a good candidate for the Whitechapel Fiend because he was well-educated and able to speak articulately, so he conformed to the picture of an organized killer. Although not a doctor himself, the presence of surgeons in the family may have allowed him access to knives or anatomical knowledge gleaned from medical books. Is it possible that he was exposed to age-inappropriate experiences, hearing his father and uncle share gruesome surgical anecdotes around the dinner table as a young boy? Did he stumble across images in books that distressed and disturbed him? Either of these things, combined with a genetic predisposition to mental illness, could have set the stage for a descent into violence and could explain the killer's fixation with removing organs and disembowelling his victims.

Although the circumstances of Monty's death appear damning on the surface and there are good reasons to investigate him, there is little evidence for his involvement. Macnaghten made several errors in his report, such as stating Druitt's age as 41, when he was 31, and claiming he was a doctor, when he was a teacher and a barrister. The allegation that Druitt's own family suspected him is based on hearsay and has never been backed up by anything solid.

Monty did not fit the witness descriptions and had a busy timetable holding down his teaching role and law career, not to mention his hobby of playing cricket, so he would have struggled to find time for late night trips to the East End. Nevertheless, this does not rule him out completely and the match records do not offer him watertight alibis. For instance, he was playing cricket in Bournemouth on 1 September 1888, but Polly Nichols was killed at around 3:40 a.m. in the early hours of 31 August. Annie Chapman died at around 5:30 a.m. on 8 September, and although Monty was playing cricket the same day, he only had to travel to Blackheath for the match, so he would have had time to get there before play commenced. However, according to Ripper historian Philip Sugden, there was no night train service between Blackheath and London, so Druitt would have had to lurk around the area before the trains started again in the morning, which would have been risky and increased his chances of being seen. I suspect the only victims Monty took on 8 September were the 3 for 38 runs! He did have his King's Bench Walk chambers, which were only a 15-minute walk from the canonical crime scenes, so he could have used this building as a base, but the problem is that it is a mile west of Mitre Square, while the murderer travelled east towards Goulston Street after the Eddowes murder.

Detective Inspector Abberline did not think Monty was Jack the Ripper. He said, *"It is simple nonsense to talk of the police having proof that the man is dead . . . I know all about that story. But what does it amount to? Simply this. Soon after the last murder in Whitechapel the body of a young doctor was found in the Thames, but there is absolutely nothing beyond the fact he was found at that time to incriminate him."*

We can see from this statement that Abberline made the same error as Macnaghten, describing Druitt as a doctor. This indicates that he was only ever a minor character of interest, and nobody investigated him closely enough to correctly establish his profession.

Macnaghten had written that Druitt was "sexually insane" which is a point worth exploring. In the Victorian era, being gay was considered ample justification for describing someone in this way. If he was indeed homosexual, this would almost completely exonerate him, as it would be extremely unusual for a gay man to kill women. Heterosexual male serial killers target women, virtually without exception, while homosexual killers like Jeffrey Dahmer prey on men. Or, and this is purely conjecture on my part, is it conceivable that Druitt suffered from gender dysphoria, like Australian serial killer Paul Denyer? It transpired that Denyer, who was born male, had never felt at ease with his biological sex, and he admitted that he killed women because he wanted to destroy the part of himself that he did not understand or accept. He transitioned while in prison and now lives as a woman. Could this be what was meant by Druitt being "sexually insane?" Is this why the mutilations of the Ripper victims focused on removing female organs?

According to a 2012 Forensic Science International study of 483 serial killers, 6% were documented to have committed suicide, while other data sets quote lower numbers. When killers do take their own lives, statistics show that they generally do so in prison, and are more likely to be mass murderers and to have grown up in dysfunctional homes. Being found to be gay, or to simply not fit into the Victorian stereotype of masculinity, could have been enough to drive Monty to suicide, as attitudes to both at the time would have made his personal and professional life unbearable. It is more likely that this, along with his mother's recent incarceration in an asylum and then his dismissal from the school, whether it was due to his sexual orientation or not, were what pushed him into taking his own life. Monty's aunt had also attempted suicide and one of his sisters had jumped to her death from an attic window, so we know that the Druitt family suffered from mental health issues. At the inquest, the jury returned a verdict of "drowning whilst of unsound mind".

Monty was buried at Wimborne cemetery in a very private ceremony, with only his immediate family and two close family friends in attendance. He left a considerable estate valued at £2,600 (around £345,000 today). Some have propounded that he did not kill himself and was murdered by his family, either to gain wealth by making their mother's inheritance go further when she died, or because they genuinely believed he was the Ripper and did not want shame to be brought on the family. Proponents of this theory mention the cliché of stones in Monty's pockets as one of the reasons for believing his death to be dubious. Small stones would not have done much to weigh him down and it sounds like an ill-thought-out measure to make people think he had drowned himself. The note Monty left in his room at Eliot Place was extremely brief and was found by his brother, prompting theories that his brother wrote it and planted it there himself.

Sadly, we will never know the truth. Whilst Montague John Druitt is a good suspect in many ways, it seems that he was just a tortured soul who was plagued with sadness and fear after his mother's mental breakdown, which ultimately led to his own.

Michael Ostrog

Michael Ostrog was born in 1833, making him 55 at the time of the murders; older than any of the witness descriptions suggested, as well as much taller, at around six feet. He was imprisoned for theft more than once, on one occasion pulling out a gun and threatening to shoot the police officers who were arresting him. He served his longest stretch between 1874 and 1883, but a few years later he was sentenced to six months' hard labour for stealing again. At this time, he was described as suffering from "mania".

He was released in March 1888 and declared to be cured, although he was described by the constabulary as a dangerous man. He was committed to the Surrey County Lunatic Asylum in 1891 but once released, continued to pilfer various small items including books and a microscope from the London Hospital.

This does not correlate with MacNaghten's account of him, which said, *"Michael Ostrog, a mad Russian doctor and a convict, and unquestionably, a homicidal maniac. This man was said to have been habitually cruel to women and was known to have carried about with him surgical knives and other instruments. His whereabouts at the time of the Whitechapel murders could never be satisfactorily accounted for."*

Nobody was sure exactly where he came from as he was described severally as Russian, a Russian Pole, and a Polish Jew. There does not seem to be any evidence that he was a doctor at all, and little else is known about him.

Michael Ostrog in the 1870s

Aaron Kosminski

Aaron Mordke Kosminski was born on 11 September 1865 and was 23 at the time of the killings. He was a Polish-born immigrant who arrived in London around 1880 or 1881. As an interesting aside, although the area in the Western part of Russia near the German border where he was born would become known as Poland after the First

World War, it did not yet exist as a country. His father, Abram Josef Kosminski, was a tailor but we know very little about Aaron's early life. He had two older brothers, Isaac and Wolf, and four sisters. It is believed that the family came to England to escape the pogroms in Russia; the vilification and scapegoating of Jews. We do not know for sure which year Aaron arrived in London, but the evidence points to him being a teenager when he came, by which point his father had died. His brothers had come to London a few years earlier. Isaac became a tailor like his father and is believed to have gone by the more anglicized surname Abrahams. The family moved around the East End frequently and had numerous addresses over the years. At the time of the murders, Aaron lived with his brother Isaac. His medical records noted that he was a hairdresser by occupation but had not worked for many years.

In 1889 he was summoned to court and fined for having an unmuzzled dog on a public thoroughfare. He denied ownership of the dog and refused to pay the fine on the Sabbath, but subsequently paid on the following Monday. By mid-1890 he was showing signs of mental illness and was admitted to Mile End Old Town Workhouse on 12 July 1890, for which the reason given was "two years insane". He only stayed there for three days and was discharged to his brother's care but was readmitted on 4 February 1891. Shortly afterwards he was sent to the Middlesex County Lunatic Asylum at Colney Hatch.

Understanding of mental health in those days was extremely limited. Asylums were primitive versions of modern psychiatric hospitals, and before they were established, people suffering from mental illnesses were forced to rely on family to care for them. Many ended up begging for food and shelter or relied on local parishes who sometimes offered places at charity-funded asylums. Others who were not so fortunate ended up in workhouses or even prisons. In the late 1700s and early 1800s, conditions in asylums were punitive, unsanitary, and inhumane, with patients spending much of their time in uncomfortable restraints and being subjected to attempts to "cure" them. Thanks to campaigners and reformers like Harriet Martineau and Samuel Tuke, attitudes were slowly changing. Although asylums still left a lot to be desired and would horrify us today, they were better than they once had been, and patients could expect a little more freedom, in some cases being given therapeutic jobs like helping with garden work or cooking.

The Colney Hatch admission book made it clear that Aaron Kosminski was not a danger to others. This is how they described him:

"He declares that he is guided and his movements altogether controlled by an instinct that informs his mind. He says he knows the movements of all mankind, he refuses food from others because he is told to do so, and he eats out of the gutter for the same reason."

Jacob Cohen, a business partner of Aaron's brother, Wolf Kosminski, reported that:

"He goes about the streets and picks up bits of bread out of the gutter and eats them, he drinks water from the tap and he refuses food at the hands of others. He took up a knife and threatened the life of his sister. He is very dirty and will not be washed. He has not attempted any kind of work for years."

While at Colney Hatch, Aaron was described as *"deluded, apathetic, and morose"*, and was transferred to another asylum three years later, where he stayed until his death on 24 March 1919. Modern experts have deduced that Kosminski suffered from a combination of schizophrenia, delusions, and paranoia. He was sometimes described as excitable, but never violent. He was the only person in the asylum records with the surname Kosminski. Much of this information is known due to the thorough research of Martin Fido, a well-known Ripperologist who is sadly no longer with us.

It seems implausible that someone with such serious mental illness could have planned and executed five murders without being caught, particularly if we propose that The Ripper was an organized killer. If Kosminski's illness was so overt and he looked as though he would not have had any money, sex workers would have been reluctant to accompany him to a dark corner, especially after the news of the first murders hit. He would have been considered even more of a threat in view of the general consensus among Whitechapel's inhabitants that a Jew was responsible.

Although many students of the case no longer feel Kosminski is a viable suspect, he remains near the top of the list for others, partly due to some writing in the margins of Assistant Commissioner Dr Robert Anderson's book, The Lighter Side of My Official Life, published in 1910. This writing, added by Chief Inspector Donald Swanson, was discovered by Swanson's grandson in 1981 and has become known as the "marginalia". Swanson had been given overall responsibility for the Whitechapel murders investigation in September 1888, covering for Anderson who was on sick leave.

Anderson did not name his favoured suspect in the book, but mentioned that this suspect was a Polish Jew, and the only witness to have had a good look at him had positively identified him at a police convalescent home known as the "seaside home", but this witness had refused to testify. Swanson scribbled in the margins of his old colleague's book:

"*As to why the witness wouldn't give evidence... because the suspect was also a Jew, and witness would be the means of murderer being hanged, which he did not wish to be left on his mind. The suspect, with his hands tied behind his back, was sent to Stepney Workhouse and then to Colney Hatch. Kosminski was the suspect.*"

Chief Inspector Donald Swanson

The Swanson marginalia may not be reliable, as the phrase *"Kosminski was the suspect"* was written in a different pencil and may have been added to the annotation at a later date, by which point, his memory may or may not have been accurate. The reason for his having written this note has been deliberated by historians, without resolution. Furthermore, the marginalia stated that the suspect died shortly after being admitted to Colney Hatch. Aaron Kosminski, however, was eventually transferred to

Leavesden Asylum and did not die until 1919. We cannot excuse this as faulty memory, because Swanson had said The Ripper was dead in a Pall Mall Gazette article in May 1895, so he was convinced of it even then. Macnaghten also made an error in his memorandum, as he wrote that Kosminski was transferred to a lunatic asylum in March 1889, although he went to Colney Hatch in February 1891.

Dates and inaccuracies aside, Swanson may have believed Kosminski was the suspect due to a lack of understanding around mental health. His Jewishness, his delusions, his habit of eating food out of the gutter, and the threat he made upon his sister with a knife, were presumably enough to convince Swanson of his guilt.

In September 1946, the Reynolds News published an extract from City of London Detective Robert Sagar's memoirs. Sagar wrote:

"We had good reason to suspect a man who worked in Butcher's Row, Aldgate. We watched him carefully. There was no doubt that this man was insane, and after a time his friends thought it advisable to have him removed to a private asylum. After he was removed, there were no more Ripper atrocities."

Kosminski was a hairdresser, not a butcher, and Colney Hatch was not a private asylum. Sagar's account does correspond with documentation from City of London Detective Inspector Harry Cox, who wrote in 1906 that he had been involved in the surveillance of a Jewish suspect for three months after the Mary Jane Kelly murder, and that this suspect owned a business in the East End. Cox alleged that this suspect's motive was revenge, as he had been *"wronged by a woman of the lower classes"*. He also stated that this suspect had spent time in a Surrey asylum and was known to take walks at night, and there were no further murders because he knew he was being watched. The accounts of

Sagar and Cox agree on some points, so we can be satisfied that a suspect in Aldgate was under surveillance, but the description of the man they were pursuing does not match Kosminski. The Jewish residents of the area became aware of the police presence and challenged the detectives, who responded by pretending to be factory inspectors checking for illegal child labour.

The discrepancies in the Swanson marginalia led Martin Fido to put forward a compelling idea that Swanson was mistaken when he wrote the name Kosminski, and that he was referring to another Polish Jew called Nathan Kaminski, also known as David Cohen. Kaminski was at Colney Hatch asylum and the dates of his incarceration matched MacNaghten's report much more closely than Kosminski's, and he died in 1889. Macnaghten erroneously said that Kosminski died shortly after going to Colney Hatch which was certainly true of Nathan Kaminski.

We know very little about Kaminski, apart from his year of birth, which was 1865, like Aaron Kosminski, and he lived at 15 Black Lion Yard. He was admitted to the Whitechapel Workhouse Infirmary on 24 March 1888 suffering from syphilis and was discharged as cured six weeks later.

The Seaside Home Witness and the Jewish debate

The discussion about a Jewish man being identified by a witness at the seaside home who then refused to testify, as expressed in the marginalia, goes round in circles. If Swanson believed the witness refused to appear in court because he did not wish to be the cause of a fellow Jew being hanged, this must mean the witness was a Jew himself.

There are a limited number of possibilities that we are aware of.

Israel Schwartz saw a man throwing Liz Stride to the ground in Berner Street, and three people saw Catherine Eddowes with a man outside Mitre Square. One of the three, Harry Harris, saw so little that he was not even called to the inquest. Joseph Hyam Levy only saw enough to state that the man was three inches taller than the woman. Joseph Lawende provided a little more detail but was adamant that he would not recognise the man again, so it would not make sense for any of the three to be the witness. This leaves Schwartz as the most likely "seaside home" witness. Incidentally, it is unclear why the witness was taken to a police convalescent home to make the identification, and to date, nobody has been able to track down this home or even confirm its existence.

The problem with Schwartz as the witness is that there is a weight of evidence that Liz Stride was not killed by The Ripper. Her murderer could well have been a Jew; after all, she was killed just outside the Working Men's club which was frequented predominantly by Jews, but although it is equally important to name her killer and mourn the tragic loss of life as it is with any other victims, the information from Schwartz may be immaterial in the hunt for Jack. The puzzle that remains is why the man who murdered her would shout the racial slur "Lipski" in Schwartz's direction, if he were a Jew himself. As mentioned earlier, this could be explained by the proposition that he did not shout "Lipski" at all, but was calling out the name "Lizzie", which Schwartz misheard. If the killer knew Liz's name, it would add credence to the theory that she was killed by Michael Kidney in a domestic incident.

In his marginalia, Chief Inspector Swanson names Kosminski as the suspect who had been identified at the seaside home, but we know that after this, Kosminski was discharged from the Mile End Old Town Workhouse to the home of his brother Isaac. If he was genuinely believed to be guilty, it seems nonsensical that he would be released. In those days, rules about holding suspects were far less strict than they are now, and it seems unlikely that the police would give up and let the killer go so easily, simply because the witness refused to testify; and they would not have been averse to heavy-handed tactics to "encourage" the witness to do so. Another point of interest is that if the identification at the seaside home took place as Swanson claims, apparently in July 1890, this was more than 18 months since the last of the canonical murders. After so much time had passed, how reliable would the witness identification have been?

Although the concept of Whitechapel Jack as a Jew refuses to die, I am very sceptical. Anti-Jewish sentiment at the time was high and although the "Fourth Estate" was not unanimously guilty of stirring up hatred in the press, there were certainly newspapers which did. The East Enders found it too hard to swallow that one of their own could have perpetrated such outrages, so they needed an outsider as a scapegoat. The only evidence for the killer being a Jew was tenuous at best. Witness Elizabeth Long described the man she saw with Annie Chapman outside 29 Hanbury Street as "foreign looking" but she only saw him from the back, while George Hutchinson's description of astrakhan man bordered on being a caricature of a Jew, and as we discussed earlier, many people are mistrustful of his tall tale.

Due to the racial tension throughout London, prostitutes would surely have been reluctant to accept Jews as clients and go with them to dark, secluded places, more so than ever after the newspaper coverage of the first murders. The rumours on the street combined with the hysteria sweeping the Whitechapel community would have made women more wary of being approached by someone of Jewish appearance, no matter how desperate they were to earn their doss money.

Detective Inspector Edmund Reid was also unconvinced. He spoke to the Lloyd's Weekly News in 1912 about his theory:

"The murders were done after the public-houses were closed, the victims were all of the same class and living within a quarter of a mile of each other, all were murdered within half a mile area, all were killed in the same manner. That is all we know for certain. My opinion is that the perpetrator was a man in the habit of using a certain public house and remaining there until closing time. Leaving with the rest of the customers, he would leave with one of the women, attacking her with a knife in some dark corner and cutting her up. Having satisfied his maniacal bloodlust, he would go home and the next day know nothing about it. During the whole time I had charge in Whitechapel, I never saw a drunken Jew. I always found them industrious, and good fellows to live among."

His theory holds water, as Jews would not have socialised and drunk in the same venues as non-Jews, if they drank at all, and the killer must have been able to gain his victims' trust; possibly someone they regularly met in the pub. Reid went on to say that Anderson's ideas about Kosminski were wrong:

"I challenge anyone to produce a tittle of evidence of any kind against anyone. The earth has been raked over and the sea has been swept, to find this criminal 'Jack the Ripper', always without success. It still amuses me to read the writings of such men as Dr Anderson and many others, all holding different theories, but all of

them wrong. I have answered many of them in print and would only add here that I was on the scene and ought to know."

So Edmund Reid, one of the lead detectives working the crime scenes at the time, believes that not only was The Ripper not a Jew, but that nobody could know who he was with any certainty. So why did Anderson and Swanson seem so sure about Kosminski? This is a question that remains unanswered.

Jewish or not, if none of the suspects mentioned in the Macnaghten Memorandum are viable, then who were the other suspects who might fit the bill?

George Chapman

George Chapman was born Seweryn Klosowski in Poland on 14 December 1865. After he left school, he spent five years working as a surgeon's assistant. We don't know what his duties entailed, but some sources report that he was involved with bloodletting using leeches. He spent a few months studying surgery at Warsaw Praga Hospital but decided to become a hairdresser instead.

He arrived in London around 1887 or 1888 and worked for barber Abraham Radin at 70 West India Dock Road. After Radin moved to Aldgate, Klosowski took over the running of the shop for a while, before opening his own establishment at 126 Cable Street, about a mile from the murder sites.

He married fellow countrywoman Lusie Baderski on 29 October 1889 and they lived at 20 Scarborough Street in Whitechapel. Their first child died in March 1891 and sometime after this, the couple moved to New Jersey in the US, where Klosowski found work in a barber's shop.

Lusie fell pregnant again and in February 1892, Klosowski attacked her with a knife, threatening to kill her and cover up the murder. She returned to London and moved in with her sister, giving birth to her daughter Celia in May 1892. Klosowski followed her back to London, but by 1893 he was living with a woman named Annie Chapman (not the Annie Chapman who fell prey to The Ripper).

It was at this time that Seweryn Klosowski became known as George Chapman. After living with Annie for a year, George brought another woman to stay with them in a bizarre ménage à trois. Annie, who was pregnant, decided to leave the house a few weeks later and George offered no support for her or the baby. Remorselessly continuing his philandering, George took Mary Spink as his mistress and moved to Hastings, where he opened another barber shop. Mary died on Christmas Day of 1897 after suffering from weight loss, vomiting, and diarrhoea. After her death, George inherited £500, the equivalent of £65,000 today.

Chapman moved to Bishop's Stortford in Hertfordshire where he ran a pub called The Grapes with barmaid Bessie Taylor, who called herself his wife. After they relocated to Southwark to run the Monument Tavern, Bessie began to complain of stomach pains and vomiting. When her friend Mrs. Painter paid her a visit, she was mockingly told by Chapman that Bessie was dead, a tasteless joke which came true on 14 February 1901. On Mrs. Painter's next visit, Chapman advised her that her friend was *"much about the same"*, even though she had already passed away.

Wasting no time, Chapman employed Maud Marsh to help him at the Monument, and before long, the old pattern emerged once more when romance flourished, and he began referring to Maud as his wife. She confided in her sister that Chapman was violent towards her, and he committed insurance fraud by setting fire to the pub when he found out he was losing the lease.

Chapman pictured in the 1890s

By 1902 he was up to his old tricks and asked his new romantic interest, Florence Rayner, to move to America with him. He reassured her that he would dispose of Maud and there would *"be no more Mrs. Chapman"*. Unsurprisingly, Maud began suffering from vomiting and diarrhoea, and when her father called for a doctor, it became apparent that she had been poisoned with arsenic. It was too late to save her, and she died on 22 October 1902.

When the bodies of Mary Spink and Bessie Taylor were exhumed, it was discovered that they had been poisoned too, in their case with tartar-emetic. George Chapman's insidious murders had come to an end. When he was arrested, Inspector Abberline was alleged to have said, *"You've got Jack the Ripper at last."*

George Chapman, or Seweryn Klosowski, was convicted of murder and hanged at Wandsworth Prison on 7 April 1903. Abberline felt there were several coincidences to support his candidacy for The Ripper, telling the Pall Mall Gazette:

"There are a score of things which make one believe that Chapman is the man; and you must understand that we have never believed all those stories about Jack the Ripper being dead, or that he was a lunatic, or anything of that kind. For instance, the date of his arrival in England coincides with the beginning of the series of murders in Whitechapel; there is a coincidence also in the fact that the murders ceased in London when Chapman went to America, while similar murders began to be perpetrated in America after he landed there. The fact that he studied medicine and surgery before he came over here is well established, and it is curious to note that the first series of murders was the work of an expert surgeon, while the recent poisoning cases were proved to be done by a man with more than an elementary knowledge of medicine. The story told by Chapman's wife of the attempt to murder her with a long knife while in America is not to be ignored."

Abberline's instinct was that anyone who could have callously watched the slow, painful demise of his wives and girlfriends would have been capable of anything and that although the victims were of a different class, what mattered was that they were women. He mentioned that there were Ripper-like murders in America but there is little evidence for this. A prostitute called Carrie Brown was strangled and mutilated in New Jersey on 24 April 1891, but English census records confirm that Chapman was in Whitechapel on 5 April. This does not exonerate him completely, as it took nine or ten days to sail from London to America so he could feasibly have made it there in time to commit the murder, but we do not have any documented proof that he travelled there at that time.

The points in favour of Chapman as a suspect are that he had medical training, he had a track record of murdering women, and he was probably in the East End during the Autumn of Terror. On the other hand, he was younger than eyewitness descriptions imply and photographs of him show that he would almost certainly have been identified as a "foreigner" with his dark complexion, heavy eyebrows, and distinctive moustache.

All this aside, there are significant differences between the methods of a wife-poisoner and those of the sanguinary Whitechapel Jack. Although not unheard of for killers to evolve or fine-tune their MO over time to avoid detection, this is seen more in modern cases thanks to the extensive information available in documentaries, books, and online, allowing them to learn from historical precedent. Notable examples include Richard Ramirez, Israel Keyes and Tommy Lynn Sells who all switched between strangulation, stabbing and shooting. The Zodiac Killer also shot most of his victims but on one occasion used a knife. However, it would be highly unusual for a serial killer to de-escalate from the hideous mutilations seen in 1888, to a very hands-off, bloodless method like poisoning. Curiously, male serial poisoners are rare, and their motive is usually financial gain, which was evidently not the case for The Ripper.

If we were to concede that Chapman could have been the Whitechapel Murderer, we would have to take as axiomatic that he had not only switched from frenzied bloodbaths to slow and painful deaths, but from penurious to paramour in his victim selection. Although not impossible, it is in my opinion improbable.

Frederick Deeming

This diabolical lothario was born into a religious family in Leicestershire in 1853. As an adult he became a thief and a fraudster, and travelled around South Africa, England, Australia, and India under a multitude of aliases. In 1891 at his home in Merseyside, England, he murdered his first wife Marie and their four young children with an axe while they were sleeping. On Christmas Eve of the same year, he slit the throat of his second wife Emily Mather at a house they were renting in Melbourne, Australia. He fled the scene of the crime after burying Emily's body under the hearthstone of one of the bedrooms, covering it with cement.

His crime was not discovered until the following year, when a potential tenant went to view the house and complained of a sickening smell. Deeming was apprehended on 12 March 1892 in Western Australia, and not a moment too soon, as he had recently met another woman who he intended to marry. He confessed to his crimes and the newspapers leapt on the possibility that he was Jack the Ripper. Deeming spent his last hours alive reading the bible and sketching coffins, before walking calmly to the gallows and uttering his anticlimactic last words, *"Lord receive my spirit."*

There is no evidence to suggest he was in Whitechapel at the time of the murders, and his method of killing and his choice of victims were very different from those of the canonical five. In marked contrast with the Whitechapel murders, he did not mutilate his victims, and he preyed on his own family with money as the motive, entombing the bodies to hide his actions. He did not match any of the witness descriptions, as he had fair hair and a ginger moustache. Like George Chapman, it appears that his signature was killing the women in his life who had outlived their usefulness.

Frederick Deeming, Illustrated Police News

Dr Francis Tumblety

Dr Francis Tumblety was born in Ireland in 1830 and was the youngest of 11 children. He grew up in Rochester, New York and did well out of selling Indian herbal medicines. He was in trouble with the law at a young age for fraud, pickpocketing and perjury, and was even arrested for being an accomplice in Abraham Lincoln's assassination in 1865. Tumblety had spent time in Montreal, Canada, where he attracted the attention of the police for selling abortion-inducing pills to a prostitute, and a patient died after taking medicine he had prescribed. He fled to Boston where he became known for his grandiose, flamboyant style, wearing a military outfit and parading around on a white horse. He was known to be a fantasist, claiming at various times to have met Charles Dickens and to have provided medical treatment to Napoleon.

He traversed several other cities, and his hatred of women soon became apparent. He was arrested in Liverpool, England, on 7 November 1888 for "acts of gross indecency" with four separate men between July and November. Homosexual activity was illegal at the time and remained so until as late as 1967. He was bailed on 16 November and ran away to America, stopping in France en route, before arriving in New York on 3 December under the name Frank Townsend.

He allegedly collected women's uteri and was thus assumed to have anatomical knowledge, and there were rumours that he had violent tendencies. Detective Chief Inspector Littlechild believed he could have been The Ripper because of his criminal record and hatred of women, but New York Police Inspector Byrnes investigated him and found no cause for concern. Nothing was ever found to implicate him in the Ripper murders, the story of the collection of female organs comes from an unreliable source, and he did not remotely resemble the witness descriptions. He was also nearly 60 at the time of the murders. Someone like Tumblety with his huge moustache and flamboyant dress, not to mention his height of at least 5'10" would have made him stand out in the area.

Francis Tumblety

    The killer must have known the ins and outs of all the alleys and back streets in the area to have escaped so quickly after each murder. Tumblety was not a local, although the Chicago Tribune wrote in October 1888 that he owned a herb shop in Whitechapel, which has not been verified. It is also important to recognize that it is virtually unheard of for gay men to kill women. Typically, female victims are targeted by heterosexual male killers, while gay killers select male victims. Francis Tumblety died in New York in 1903 of heart disease. Whether or not he was in the area at the time of the murders, it is unlikely that he was the killer, for the reasons described above.

Thomas Cutbush

Thomas Haynes Cutbush first came to public attention as a potential Jack the Ripper suspect when the Sun newspaper released a series of articles about him in February 1894. About a week later, Melville Macnaghten wrote his internal memorandum, offering three suspects he considered more promising. More information about Cutbush was brought to light more recently by controversial author and researcher A.P. Wolf, who put him forward as a suspect in his book Jack the Myth. Wolf asserted that the Macnaghten memorandum was written to protect a police superintendent called Charles Cutbush, who was supposedly Thomas Cutbush's uncle.

Cutbush was investigated by the constabulary, but they found no evidence to detain him. He was unemployed at the time of the murders but had previously worked as a clerk and was known to study medical journals and perambulate the streets at night, returning home with clothes covered in mud, with some reports even claiming that they were bloodstained. He was sent to Lambeth Infirmary in March 1891, reportedly suffering from syphilis and paranoid delusions. He escaped for four days, during which time he stabbed a woman in the buttocks with a toy dagger and attempted to do the same to another.

Cutbush was admitted to Broadmoor a month later, where he was declared a "criminal lunatic". The Broadmoor records became available to the public in 2008 and his admission notes paint an interesting picture. Here is what was recorded:

Born: 29 June 1866
Age: 26

Height: 5ft 9 ½ inches
Weight: 9 stones 6 ½ lbs
Hair: Black
Whiskers: Black (very short)
Eyes: Dark blue (very sharp)
Complexion: Dark
Build: Slight
Features: Thin
Marks: Slight bruise on left knee. One tooth out in front upper jaw

His admission notes state: *"A man of average height and slight build; expression vacant, eyeballs protruding. Is restless, and incoherent in conversation. Stated this morning that he had often been drunk, though not a "drinker", afterwards that he had never been drunk through drink as he had been a total abstainer for years. That the charges brought against him were absolutely false and that he had no recollection of doing anything to cause such charges to be brought against him. He has more the appearance of an imbecile than any other kind of insane person. States that he feels sulphur rise into his throat from a cavity in the left lung, that he does not taste it or smell it or feel it but "knows" that it is so and that in consequence he has tuberculosis. That he suffered from palpitation of the heart some time ago but not lately. States he was at Peckham House Asylum "on a visit" for a few days after he was charged with his crime. He states that there is no insanity in his family although he thinks both his mother and aunt are "bad enough" to want care in the way of being eccentric. Says he has often suffered from fits of uncontrollable temper. His tongue is tremulous...complains of slight headache this morning which he states is unusual."*

Further notes over the next few years describe him as violent at times, on one occasion striking another patient without provocation, but also mention that he was *"dirty, dull and apathetic"*, which later progressed into *"demented, absurd and incoherent"*.

His ability to take care of himself seems to have deteriorated over time along with his speech, which is suggestive of paranoid schizophrenia and bears some similarities to the symptoms experienced by modern serial killer Richard Chase. Thomas Cutbush died of chronic kidney disease on 5 July 1903.

It has never been proven whether Superintendent Charles Cutbush really was Thomas's uncle. It is pertinent to be aware that some newspaper articles of the time confused Cutbush with another man named Colicott, who stabbed six young women with a sharp object a couple of months before. The Sun proclaimed that Cutbush had syphilis, but there is no mention of this in his Broadmoor records.

He lived in Kennington at the time of the murders, some three miles from Whitechapel, although this would not necessarily eliminate him from suspicion as he was known to wander for many hours at night. If he were a killer, he would almost certainly have been a disorganized one due to his mental illness and would have been unable to plan and execute the crimes so seamlessly, disappearing into the shadows without arousing suspicion. It would also be out of character for a serial killer to de-escalate from such brutal violence and plundering organs to being satisfied with stabbing women in the bottom with a harmless toy dagger. Leaving aside his occasional violent tendencies, Thomas Cutbush was probably not the Whitechapel Fiend.

Joseph Barnett

Joseph "Joe" Barnett, Mary Jane Kelly's boyfriend, has fallen under the finger of suspicion in recent years, first put forward by writers Mark Andrews in 1977, then Bruce Paley in 1995. Joe was born in Whitechapel in May 1858, to Irish immigrant parents. His father died when he was just three years old, and nothing is known about his mother. He was 30 at the time of the murders and was 5'7" with a medium build, fair complexion, a moustache, and blue eyes, so he closely resembled Joseph Lawende's eyewitness account of the man talking to Catherine Eddowes near Mitre Square shortly before her death.

Just a month before Polly Nichols was killed in Bucks Row, Barnett lost his fish porter's license for reasons unknown, which some people contend was a trigger for the violence. Bruce Paley researched this for his book on the subject and found that some of the infractions that could lead to a fish porter losing his license included swearing or stealing.

We only have Barnett's word for the fact that the key to 13 Miller's Court had recently gone missing. Could he have secretly kept it and used it to access the room, locking the door from the outside when he left after the bloody frenzy? On the other hand, if he was the murderer, he would not even have needed the key, as he would have known that all he had to do was reach in through the hole in the window to latch or unlatch the door. Anybody could have observed Mary Jane Kelly opening the door this way, including the clients she brought home.

Barnett and Kelly had an explosive argument shortly before her death because he was unhappy about her turning to sex work and allowing her fellow prostitutes to share her room. Could this have been a motive for murder?

Sketch of Joe Barnett

He visited her just a few hours before her death, although according to him, the visit ended on friendly terms. Due to his relationship with Kelly, it is conceivable that he knew some of the other Ripper victims as he had previously lived in some of the same roads as they did. Catherine Eddowes is alleged to have known who the killer was, and that shortly before her death she said she intended to collect the reward money. Could Barnett have been this man? Credible as this may be, it cannot be proven. The fact that he had been in a relationship with Kelly stands in his defense as he would have been known in Miller's Court, having lived there for a time and continuing to be a regular visitor. Had he been the killer, he would have been at significant risk of being spotted and recognized as he entered or exited the court. Catherine Eddowes and Mary Jane Kelly were the only victims to have suffered facial mutilations after death, which tends to happen when a killer has an emotional connection to the victim, according to forensic psychologists.

Even so, there were no doubt countless others in Whitechapel who knew both women. The Ripper might also have escalated his butchery to the point where facial mutilations were the next logical step, so it does not necessarily mean that they were known to him.

If it was a crime of passion by Barnett, it is hard to credit that he would have been capable of butchering his girlfriend's body to such an extent. Even if we imagine that he cut her throat in a fit of rage and then decided to make it look like a Ripper killing to detract police attention away from himself, it would be a horrific, nauseating experience to slice a human body beyond recognition and remove organs, particularly for someone who has never previously shown any violent urges.

Those who favour Barnett as a suspect argue that his job as a fish porter would have meant he was well practiced in using a knife and gave him an outlet for any suppressed rage, which led to a breakdown and a burning need to express this aggression after his license was revoked. In fact, it is not known whether his job would have involved gutting fish at all, as the role of a fish porter was primarily to unload and carry crates of fish from one place to another. Lots of men in the East End were fishmongers, butchers, and horse slaughterers, and it is a stretch to suppose that even if he did cut up fish, that he would by extension know how to carve a human body. In any case, police surgeon Dr Thomas Bond and some other experts concluded that the killer did not have any knowledge of anatomy or experience with a knife, although this is not universally agreed upon.

The letters received by the press also contain clues which could point towards Joe Barnett. For example, the Dear Boss letter contained the line, *"I saved some of the proper red stuff in a ginger beer bottle over the last job to write with but it went thick like glue and I cant use it."* Interestingly, ginger beer bottles were found at 13 Miller's Court. Linguists have observed that the From Hell letter which accompanied the kidney sent to George Lusk, read as though it had been penned by someone Irish, and Barnett had Irish ancestry. None of the letters have been proven to be genuine, but out of all of them, the From Hell letter is the best candidate.

Major Henry Smith wrote in his memoirs that he believed the killer had washed his bloody hands in a sink *"up a close in Dorset Street"*, referring to Miller's Court, on the night of the "Double Event". If his memories were correct and he really did find a trough full of bloodied water there, this points towards Barnett. Perhaps he hurriedly cleaned himself up after committing the heinous acts of mutilation on Catherine Eddowes, before retreating inside number 13 as if nothing had happened.

Finally, Barnett's pipe was found in Mary Jane Kelly's room. Proponents of Barnett as the best suspect consider it strange that he did not take it with him when he moved out, maintaining that he left it there by mistake when he killed Kelly. This can easily be counterargued, as he visited her regularly and he freely admitted to having been there on the eve of her murder.

It cannot be denied that the FBI profile created in 1988, one hundred years after the murders, describes Barnett well. The profile was of a white male aged between 28 and 36 who lived or worked locally, but was employed below his intellectual ability, and a stressor of some kind triggered the murders. They believed he would have had an absent father and a disability of some kind, whether a physical one or something like a speech impediment. Records indicate that

Barnett had echolalia, which caused him to repeat the last words spoken to him.

Barnett lived an uneventful life after the murders and was awarded his fish porter's license again in 1906. His echolalia could have been the result of temporary stress caused by the brutal death of Mary Jane Kelly, or even a sign of autism. While profiling sometimes hits the mark, there are those within the criminal justice system who consider it a pseudoscience. Either way, profiling should only ever be used as a guide, and in conjunction with solid evidence.

Joseph Barnett later married but had no children, and he died of bronchitis at the age of 68. Although he is a fascinating suspect who has more in common with the FBI profile than most of the other known characters of interest, the arguments for his being The Ripper are based on speculation. He also had an alibi for the night of the murder and Inspector Abberline interrogated him for four hours, even examining his clothing for bloodstains, but nothing was found to cause law enforcement any concern. He is a strong candidate, but the jury is out.

Jacob Levy

Jacob Levy was born in 1856 into a Jewish family in Aldgate. He became a butcher like his father, and married Sarah Abrahams in 1879 with whom he had nine children. He was described as 5'3" tall and weighing 9 stones. His first brush with the law was in April 1886, when he was convicted along with another man for receiving 14lbs of beef stolen from the butcher's shop next door, owned by Hyam Sampson, for which he was sentenced to one year's hard labour. About a month later, he was certified insane and transferred to Essex County Asylum, as he was hearing strange noises and was thought to be suicidal. There was also a history of insanity in his family.

Levy was discharged as "cured" in January 1887. At the time of the murders, he lived with his family at 36 Middlesex Street, a predominantly Jewish neighbourhood very close to Goulston Street, where the scrap of Catherine Eddowes' apron and the cryptic graffito were found.

He did not remain a free man for long. On 15 August 1890 he was admitted to Stone Asylum near Dartford in Kent, with the reason given as "mania". His wife Sarah complained that he had nearly ruined their business, and that he did not sleep at night and wandered around aimlessly for hours. Levy's mother had died in 1888, so this tragic event could have triggered a descent into madness. Stone Asylum no longer exists and has long since been bulldozed to make way for apartment blocks.

Levy died in the asylum on 29 July 1891 from syphilis, which he had contracted through visiting prostitutes. This is one of the reasons why some criminologists consider him a strong suspect, with revenge as a possible motive. He had lived in the heart of Ripper territory since birth and indisputably knew the area well. He was 32 at the time of the murders and he was three inches taller than Catherine Eddowes, like the man described by witness Joseph Hyam Levy near Mitre Square. His height also matches Elizabeth Long's testimony, who thought that the man she saw with Annie Chapman near Hanbury Street was a little taller than the deceased, and Chapman was five feet tall. However, Joseph Lawende contradicted this by estimating the man's height as 5'7". Jacob Levy may have known Joseph Hyam Levy, because their butchers' shops were within 100 yards of each other. Whether or not Joseph would have been able to recognize Jacob in the dim light of Church Passage, had Jacob been the killer, we cannot say with certainty.

George Hutchinson, the witness who was standing outside Miller's Court on the night of Mary Jane Kelly's murder, reported that he had seen "astrakhan man" with the victim, and that he was of Jewish appearance. He said he saw the man again in Middlesex Street (where Jacob Levy lived and worked) in the days following the murder, but police were never able to find him.

Coincidentally, according to the 1891 census, Jacob's brother Isaac Levy lived at the five-storey high Wentworth Buildings on Goulston Street where the apron and graffito were found. The Wentworth Dwellings had been constructed on land that had been cleared of slums just a couple of years before the Ripper murders. Could Jacob, being familiar with the dwellings, have gone there to hide or drop off the piece of apron? The census records only prove that Isaac lived there in 1891, so we do not know how long he had been there. At the time, people tended to move around regularly.

It is not uncommon for serial killers to have an existing criminal record, no matter how small and seemingly insignificant, and Jacob Levy had one thanks to the stolen meat incident. On the subject of meat, many believe that as he was a butcher, he would have been used to wielding a knife and had a basic knowledge of anatomy. Conversely, a butcher would have little use for a long, thin knife of the kind favoured by The Ripper, and would be more likely to have a cleaver. Some argue that a person with homicidal inclinations would benefit from the outlet that working as a butcher would provide, and that it would thus be more probable that the killer had a non-manual job, such as a clerk, with no way to express his rage and bloodlust other than to kill human beings.

In Paul Begg and Martin Fido's 1996 edition of The Complete Jack The Ripper A-Z: The Ultimate Guide To The Ripper Mystery, it states that Steward Hicks, a researcher from Norfolk, England, alleged that Lady Anderson, the wife of Sir Robert Anderson, once remarked that *"The Ripper was interned in an asylum near Stone,"* but the source could not be recalled. This implies that the information was third hand, as if the source had been Lady Anderson herself, Hicks would have said so. There is no way to confirm or deny the statement, and Hicks died in 1993.

As referenced earlier in the section about Aaron Kosminski, Detective Inspector Robert Sagar of the City of London Police, in whose territory Catherine Eddowes was killed, wrote in his memoirs that:

"We had good reason to suspect a man who worked in Butcher's Row, Aldgate. We watched him carefully. There was no doubt that this man was insane, and after a time, his friends thought it advisable to have him removed to a private asylum. After he was removed, there were no more Ripper atrocities."

The problem is that Sagar's memoirs were unpublished and have never been traced. This extract was published in the Reynolds News in September 1946, more than 50 years after the murders, and more than 20 years after Sagar's death. On the other hand, there is some evidence that Sagar's words were true, being partly corroborated by Detective Inspector Harry Cox, also of the City of London Police, who wrote in 1906 that he had been involved in a three-month surveillance of a Jewish suspect after the murder of Mary Jane Kelly. He mentioned that the suspect ran a business in the East End and that the motive was revenge, as the man had been *"wronged by a woman of the lower classes"*. He went on to say that the suspect spent time in an asylum in Surrey and was known to take nightly walks, and that while no evidence was found to connect their suspect to the murders, he believed that the reason there were no further atrocities was that the suspect knew he was being watched. Cox described this man as being 5'6" with black curly hair.

Some have championed the idea that the suspect both Sagar and Cox were referring to was Jacob Levy. Unfortunately, not all the facts fit as he was never in an asylum in Surrey, and the one that he was in was not private, besides which he was shorter than the man described by Cox. Even with these disparities, it remains a possibility that the suspect being pursued was indeed Levy or Kosminski, or neither of them.

Jacob Levy is not mentioned by name in any of the surviving police documentation on The Ripper, but strangely, the official case files were closed in 1891, the year of his death. Only three years had passed since Whitechapel had been terrorized by the faceless killer who managed to evade capture with uncanny good fortune, so why close the case so soon? As with all the suspects, there is no physical evidence linking him to the crime scenes and all we can go on is circumstance and conjecture. Levy is a good suspect in many ways, and one who would benefit from further research, if there is anything more to be dug up about him.

Charles Lechmere/Cross

Charles Lechmere, alias Charles Cross, the carman who first found the body of Polly Nichols in Bucks Row on 31 August 1888, could have been Whitechapel Jack himself. On hearing the approaching footsteps of fellow carman Robert Paul, he might have cut short his fiendish work and pretended to have innocently stumbled across the corpse moments before. The lack of more severe mutilations than those seen in later murders implies that the killer was disturbed before he had a chance to complete them. Equally, it could have been someone else, the unknown killer, who was disturbed by the approaching footsteps of Charles Lechmere.

Lechmere only came forward at the inquest after Robert Paul revealed there was another man present at the discovery of the body. He gave his name as Charles Cross at the inquest, which police accepted without question. He may have provided this name because his late stepfather, Thomas Cross, was a police constable, which he may have felt gave him credibility. The deception over his name went unnoticed until some keen-eyed modern researchers spotted this inconsistency in the census records, but it is important to acknowledge that it was not uncommon at the time for people to go by different names.

Charles Lechmere was born on 5 October 1849, making him 39 at the time of the murders. He had been working at Pickford's at Broad Street Station for many years. He never knew his real father and had two stepfathers (presumably not at the same time.) He married in 1870 and had 12 children. It would have taken him only seven or eight minutes to walk to Bucks Row from his home, but this is not reason enough to suspect him, as all the murders were committed within an area of half a mile, so anyone living in the vicinity could have passed the murder sites on a daily basis. Lechmere usually left for work at about 3:30 a.m. but he was running late on the day of Polly Nichols' murder. Robert Paul told the Lloyds Weekly News that he entered

Bucks Row at exactly 3:45 a.m. but did not mention this at the inquest, only testifying that he left home *"just before 3:45 a.m."*. We do not know how accurate these timings were and whether Paul and Lechmere were basing their timings on a pocket watch, a clock at home, or a nearby church clock they had heard, so we cannot know for sure how long Lechmere had been in Bucks Row before Paul came along; it could have been minutes or moments. Some accounts speculate that Lechmere heard Paul's footsteps and rapidly pulled down the victim's clothing to hide the wounds, but this is misleading, as Paul asserted at the inquest that he had been the one to pull Polly Nichols' clothes down to make her appear decent, not Lechmere.

In a documentary called The Missing Evidence, Lechmere was put forward as a suspect and in the reconstruction of the scene, he was portrayed leaning over the body. This has been distorted, and according to original source material from the time, he was in fact standing in the middle of the road when Robert Paul appeared. This documentary has been criticized by students of the case and by Steve Blomer, an expert on the Polly Nichols murder. Blomer has written an extremely detailed book, Inside Bucks Row, which at 575 pages long serves to remind us that the case is incredibly complex, and an in-depth discussion of each crime scene could easily fill an entire volume alone.

It is repeatedly questioned why neither Paul nor Lechmere saw any blood on Polly Nichols and were unsure if she was even alive or dead. Forensic physician Dr Payne-James has asserted that if the victim was asphyxiated first before the carotid artery was cut, this would lower the blood pressure and cause blood to leak out gradually rather than spurt. This would not only have made it harder for the carmen to see any blood in the dark, but the killer's clothing might have been reasonably free from bloodstains too.

It is opined that there were no easy escape routes from Bucks Row, which might have led Lechmere to pretend to have stumbled on the body, rather than attempt to get away before Robert Paul approached. A brief examination of a map of the area proves this false. The killer would have been able to leave the scene and arrive at the western corner of the Board School without hurrying. He could then have walked into Whites Row or turned north in either Queen Ann Street or Thomas Street.

Charles Lechmere in 1912

He could have doubled back down Winthrop Street, passing nightwatchman Alfred Mulshaw, although Mulshaw said he had not seen anyone. Alternatively, the killer could have walked to the end of the Board School then turned into Whitechapel Road via Woods Building or Court Street. This could have been done in under a minute, easily removing the killer from the scene before Paul reached the position of the body.

Charles Lechmere died in 1920 aged 71. The points in favour of his being Jack the Ripper are that he was in the area at the time of the murders, he was discovered at one of the murder sites very close to the victim's time of death, he was tardy in attending the inquest, only coming when he knew Robert Paul had mentioned him, and it has been propounded that all five canonical murder sites were on his way to work. It is questionable that he gave a different name at the inquest, but he gave the correct address, so he may not have had any nefarious intent. It is curious that Robert Paul and Charles Lechmere had, as far as we know, never met prior to the night of the murder. They left for work at a very similar time, and it might have been sensible for them to travel together for protection in such an unsafe area. But we do not know how long Paul had been working for his employer, or whether he had recently changed his shift patterns, which could explain it. This is one of those little oddities to which we are unlikely to find an answer.

Lechmere started work at 4:00 a.m. which would not have fitted with the timing of Annie Chapman's murder, as she was killed at approximately 5:30 a.m. Liz Stride and Catherine Eddowes died at 12:45 a.m. and 1:45 a.m. respectively, but one would wonder when Lechmere had any chance to sleep if he walked about all night looking for victims, while keeping an eye on the nearest church clock to ensure he got to work on time. Mary Jane Kelly's time of death is disputed, but in all likelihood, it was around 4:00 a.m., when Lechmere would have been due at work. It also seems strange that someone would choose to commit a murder en route to their job, risking turning up in disarray and sporting bloodstains. Some would argue that as a carman, he may have transported meat and would thus have had an explanation for any visible blood, but this remains supposition in the absence of firm evidence; for all we know, he could have transported fruit and vegetables.

From our modern insight into the minds of serial killers, we can contemplate that Jack the Ripper would have wanted to mentally relive the murder and luxuriate in his memories of the brutality, so to immediately be forced to spend the rest of the day doing something as mundane as carrying items around London in a horse and cart would have been frustrating beyond measure.

As with many suspects, the evidence against Charles Lechmere is purely circumstantial, but the fact that he was indisputably at one of the crime scenes very near to the victim's time of death means that we cannot dismiss him out of hand. He remains an interesting character who will no doubt continue to be listed as a suspect for many years to come.

George Hutchinson

In recent years, George Hutchinson, one of the key witnesses in the Mary Jane Kelly murder, has made it onto the suspect list. After all, he was at the scene very close to the time of Kelly's death, and his extraordinarily detailed description of the flamboyant astrakhan man raised red flags. Nobody knows for sure who Hutchinson was, or if that was even his real name, and his birth, life and death are even more cloudy than Mary Kelly's origins and the circumstances of her murder. He was described by different sources as being between 22 and 33 years old, and he said he was a groom by trade, but that he had been working recently as a labourer.

A groom's status in Victorian England was higher than that of a typical labourer or dock worker, and someone seeking work as a groom might have been asked for a letter of recommendation from a gentleman. According to job advertisements from newspapers of the time, the ideal groom was respectable, good tempered, and able to ride horses. They were usually hired by people accustomed to riding for pleasure, and who wished to present their animals well, so it was not a role that would have been in demand in Whitechapel. There were 50,000 horses in London, but those in the East End would have been owned by folk like Louis Diemschutz, the man who discovered Liz Stride's body at Dutfield's Yard. He would have had neither the money nor the inclination to hire a full-time groom to look after his horse, and would either have brushed it himself, not brushed it at all, or hired a young boy to do it on occasion for a coin or two. Sadly, horses were treated as disposable, hence the need for so many horse slaughterers, who killed them and used them for cats' meat when they outlived their usefulness. The fact that Hutchinson was described by Sarah Lewis as wearing a wideawake hat backs up his story of being a groom, as this sort of headwear was typically worn by people in the countryside and would not have been terribly common in the East End.

A search of old newspaper archives confirms there were barely any vacancies for grooms in the East End, whereas papers in the more rural neighbouring county of Essex had multiple advertisements, which explains why Hutchinson had walked eleven miles to Romford to look for work on the day of Mary Jane Kelly's murder. His profession may be one of the few things about which he told the truth. Given the lack of country houses and stables in Whitechapel, it is strange that he was there at all. If he really had worked as a groom in the past, it would indicate that he was of smart appearance and was articulate enough to convince a relatively wealthy family of his trustworthiness to look after their horses; some vacancies even came with the perk of being allowed to live in the family home. Hutchinson easily convinced the police that he was just a witness on the night of Kelly's death, and they did not appear to have any misgivings about him whatsoever, despite his having been lurking outside Miller's Court for so long, with rather a thin explanation for it.

The fact Hutchinson took so long to come forward as a witness raises doubts. He first appeared three days after the murder, on the evening of Monday 12 November 1888, conveniently just after the inquest had been completed. He told the newspapers that he informed a policeman on the Sunday morning of what he had seen, but he did not go to the station and there is no evidence that he spoke to a policeman at all. Hutchinson avouched that the next day, he discussed the matter with a fellow lodger at the Victoria Home for Working Men in Commercial Street, who urged him to report what he had seen. This does not ring true, as he had apparently already told a police officer, so there was no need for him to seek further advice. It is also peculiar that the policeman had not asked Hutchinson to accompany him to the station to give an official statement. As the Victoria Home was so close to the Commercial Street police station, it would have made more sense for Hutchinson to go there immediately, rather than approaching a Bobby in the street, from which we could infer that he was using smoke and mirrors to distort the truth for his own ends.

It could be that he was prompted into coming forward by Sarah Lewis's testimony at the inquest. She had seen a man looking up at the court, which could well have been Hutchinson. She stated:

"I live at 24 Great Powell Street, Spitalfields. I am a laundress. I know Mrs. Keyler in Miller's Court. I was at her house at half past two on Friday morning. She lives at number two in the court on the left on the first floor. I know the time by having looked at Spitalfields Church clock as I passed it. When I went in the court I saw a man opposite the court in Dorset Street standing alone by the lodging house. He was not tall - but stout - had on a black wideawake hat - I did not notice his clothes - another young man with a woman passed along - the man standing in the street was looking up the court as if waiting for someone to come out. I went to Mrs. Keyler's. I was awake all night in a chair, I dozed. I heard no noise. I woke up about half-past three - I sat awake until nearly five - a little before four I heard a female voice shout loudly once, "Murder!" The sound seemed to come from the direction of the deceased's room. There was only one scream - I took no notice of it - I left Mrs. Keyler's at about half past five in the afternoon as the police would not let us out before."

We could argue that Hutchinson chose to make himself known to the police after discovering that Sarah Lewis had spotted him that night, as he feared being identified and suspected as being Jack the Ripper, whether he was or not. This could also explain the extraordinary appearance of the astrakhan man he swore to have seen; could he have created a vivid, overtly Jewish character to detract attention away from himself and in a direction that he thought would be readily believed?

Hutchinson spoke to the Pall Mall Gazette on 13 November 1888, just a day after giving Inspector Abberline his original description of the man he saw.

Artist's impression of George Hutchinson

In the space of a day, he somehow generated additional memories, as the slight moustache he initially reported had now become a dark one, the pale complexion had changed to dark, and the small parcel the man carried was given a more detailed description (eight inches long with a strap around it, clasped tightly in his left hand, and covered with dark American cloth). The mysterious astrakhan man had also gained a gold chain with a big seal and a red stone hanging from it, and a pair of brown kid gloves carried in his right hand. These details conveniently reinforced the idea of a "foreign looking" man, like the one spotted by Elizabeth Long at Hanbury Street. Let's not forget the red handkerchief that appeared in Hutchinson's original description; an intriguing inclusion, as Joseph Lawende had described the man he saw with Catherine Eddowes near Church Passage as having worn a "reddish handkerchief" around his neck. It sounds as though Hutchinson was cobbling together pieces of different witness descriptions and mixing them with his own imagination to create an elaborate picture.

On the matter of the red handkerchief, it is noteworthy that this detail was concealed at the inquest of Catherine Eddowes, and it never appeared in the newspapers – although a note was printed in the article stating that certain information had deliberately been withheld. Could Hutchinson have been the man wearing the red neckerchief on the night of 30 September 1888? Was he concerned that this detail had been spotted and was being deliberately held back, so he made a point of mentioning astrakhan man's red handkerchief and wove it into his account? Wearing something like this around the neck would also have been common attire for someone working in a stable, although this would not be peculiar to that trade and could apply to many others.

Some may hold that George Hutchinson really did see astrakhan man, but he said that he did not think the man was a murderer, so it is strange that he paid such close attention to him. It was dark, so it would have been difficult to make out such intricate details when he only glimpsed the man for a moment. When you add this to the consideration that witness descriptions are notoriously unreliable, and that Hutchinson did not come forward for three days after the sighting, it begins to sound very fishy. It is also dubious that a man dressed in such finery would dare to go down Dorset Street and into Miller's Court, known as one of the worst parts of Whitechapel. He would have been lucky to emerge with his life, let alone his valuables, and chances are that other witnesses would have noticed him and been able to corroborate Hutchinson's story. It is very telling that Sarah Lewis spotted George Hutchinson, as well as a "young man and a woman" walking past, but she saw nothing that would support Hutchinson's account of astrakhan man. The mention of a horseshoe pin, spats, and gaiters are intriguing additions which may give us a look into his mind. A horseshoe pin is something that might spring easily to the thoughts of someone who has worked as a groom, and the idea of spats and gaiters could have come from the memory of a landowner, rector, or middle-class gentleman for whom he had worked in the past in Essex. It is coincidental that such details were present in the unidentified man's dress; details which could reasonably have sprung to Hutchinson's mind had he been asked to invent a person based on his past encounters. His own choice of hat is also a potential clue. The wideawake hat, typical of the countryside, would have stood out in Whitechapel.

Hutchinson announced in an interview with the Pall Mall Gazette that he saw astrakhan man again on Sunday 11 November in Petticoat Lane, the day before he offered his statement to the police. Yet this apparent sighting was not recorded in the police report of Monday 12 November. He also remarked that the man he saw lived in the neighbourhood, but this is paradoxical, as he maintained that he did not know the man and that he stood out because his attire was too rich for the area. He cannot have it both ways. If the man did indeed live in the area, it is odd that he had never been seen before or since by anyone else.

Another aspect of Hutchinson's story that cannot be verified is his relationship with Mary Jane Kelly. He disclosed that he had known her for about three years and that he sometimes gave her a shilling, which was a lot of money to give a casual acquaintance. If he genuinely did give her such sums of money, it would hint at a closer relationship, but as far as we know, none of Kelly's other friends or neighbours ever mentioned him. This has led some people to surmise that Hutchinson was in fact Joseph Fleming, Kelly's ex-boyfriend, but although this would be a neat explanation, there is zero evidence for it.

George Hutchinson mentioned he saw no policemen in Dorset Street on the morning of the murder, which confirms what we already know about the force's reluctance to traverse such a perilous place. The very fact he noticed the absence of the law is thought-provoking. Jack the Ripper must have known it too, hence his choice of Miller's Court for his final bloodbath; after all, life was becoming very difficult for him with the increased police presence on the streets. Could George Hutchinson and Jack the Ripper have been one and the same? If so, it was a risky strategy to wait outside the court for so long, taking the chance of being seen, but perhaps his desire to kill inside a private room outweighed his caution. The main problem with Hutchinson as the Ripper is that it would have been virtually unthinkable for his comings and goings to have gone unnoticed at the Victoria Home. How could he have washed blood from his clothes without attracting attention, and what did he do with the organs he plundered? As far as we know, the police never checked up on his story as they believed he was just a witness, so we only have Hutchinson's word for it that he was living in a lodging house. It is apposite to remember at this point that Major Henry Smith had found a bloody trough of water in Miller's Court after the murder of Catherine Eddowes, so it is conceivable that the killer found ways and means of cleaning himself up sufficiently to evade notice.

Hutchinson's reasons for loitering outside Miller's Court in the rain have been debated by theorists over the years, and the arguments go round in circles. Some propose that his original story was plausible, and that he was simply unable to access the Victoria Working Men's Home because he had returned late from Essex after the doors closed for the night. He could genuinely have known Kelly, albeit casually, and was waiting in the hope she would let him sleep on her floor after her clients had left. He told Inspector Abberline that he was keeping watch because the man he saw looked too well dressed for the area, but what exactly he was keeping watch for was not explained and this contradicts his later statement that he saw the man in Petticoat Lane and that he lived locally. It has been speculated that he was waiting for astrakhan man to emerge from Mary Jane Kelly's room with the intent to rob him, but this theory is predicated on astrakhan man existing in the first place.

It is worth remarking on Hutchinson's intrepid nature. He seemed happy enough to skulk around Dorset Street in the early hours of the morning, but Charles Booth's poverty map graded the area as "vicious, semi-criminal" and we have heard many times that even law enforcement were too scared to intervene. From his own statement we know he was dawdling there for at least 45 minutes, and he boldly stooped down to stare into the face of astrakhan man. His actions do not sound like those of a cautious or nervous person, when compared to Robert Paul, who admitted that when he had seen Charles Lechmere in Bucks Row, he immediately feared being set upon and robbed. Bucks Row, although dangerous enough, was not considered as bad as Dorset Street. This provides us with a striking insight into Hutchinson's character, if we combine it with the fact that more than one newspaper described him as having a "military bearing". Whether or not he really had been in the military, this indicates that he was probably standing up straight and proud, rather than shrinking away into a corner. Having been in the army is a common trait of modern organized serial killers, and studies have shown that as many as two thirds of organized killers had military training. Clearly this does not apply to every murderer, but there are many notable examples including Charles Whitman, Dean Corll, and Gary Ridgeway. Could Hutchinson have worked as a groom in the army, looking after cavalry men's horses? This is of course conjecture.

Whether or not George Hutchinson had military experience, what we know of his behaviour paints a picture of a man who felt at home in the most threatening parts of the East End, who was clearly unafraid of gangs, pickpockets, and drunks. Could this be because he was the one everyone should have feared, and *he* was the apex predator at the top of the food chain: Jack the Ripper himself? One could argue that Cox and Lewis were also running a risk in going out, but we must remember that they lived in Miller's Court and had no choice; they also did not stay outside for as long as Hutchinson did.

By Thursday 15 November, the Star newspaper had discredited Hutchinson's statement about astrakhan man, explaining that the blotchy faced man seen by Mrs. Cox was more critical to the investigation. The following day, the Evening News reported that a clerk named Mr. Galloway had seen someone resembling the blotchy faced, carroty-moustached man, whom he had followed up Whitechapel Road and Commercial Street. The man seemed to be aware that he was being tracked, and when they entered Thrawl Street, the blotchy faced man was startled by the appearance of a policeman. Galloway pointed the man out to the constable, who declined to arrest him, saying that he was looking for somebody of a very different appearance. If this tale is true, it is a great shame that the policeman did not at least question the blotchy faced man, as even if he was not the killer, he could have helped clear up the uncertainty around the timings, confirming when he had left Mary Jane Kelly's company. Whether he really was up to no good, or whether he was frightened of being accused of her murder, we will never know.

Within days of Hutchinson making his statement to Inspector Abberline, he faded into obscurity and was never mentioned in the records again. We can only assume that the police eventually realised that he had embroidered his story and had thoroughly wasted their time. Ironically, the police may have had Jack the Ripper right under their noses. It is not unusual for killers to insert themselves into an investigation, for example John Christie of 10 Rillington Place fame, Stephen Young, who shot a husband and wife in East Sussex in 1993, the serial arsonist John Leonard Orr in California, and Ian Huntley, who shocked the country with the double murder of schoolgirls Holly Wells and Jessica Chapman in Suffolk in 2002.

It is the sort of thing that would have made the Ripper chuckle quietly to himself as he recalled how he outwitted the police, telling lies to their face and getting away with it, while distracting and derailing the investigation. In the Victorian era, without the benefit of all the knowledge and criminal precedent that we now have, it would never have occurred to the police that a guilty party would dream of boldly offering themselves up as a witness.

There are enough questions about Hutchinson and his statement to fill a book on its own, and Ripper theorists still hammer away at his story, trying to work out what he was doing there that night. There have been unsubstantiated assertions that he was a plumber called George William Topping Hutchinson, but nobody knows for sure. He is my personal favourite suspect as not only did he admit to being at Miller's Court very near to the time of the murder, but there are enough inconsistencies in his story to raise more than a few eyebrows.

I try never to get too attached to a suspect, as more than 130 years have passed, and we lack any physical evidence that could prove it one way or another. It is entirely possible that it is someone of whom we have never heard, who doesn't even appear on a suspect list or witness list at all. Major Henry Smith, Acting Commissioner of the City of London Police at the time of the murders, later summed it up in his memoirs: *"He completely beat me and every police officer in London; and I have no more idea now where he lived than I had twenty years ago."*

Why did he stop?

Much discussion has ensued over the years as to why Jack the Ripper stopped killing. It is generally believed that killers only stop if they are dead, incarcerated, suffering from ill health, or find a healthier outlet for their desires. With the benefit of over 100 years of crime history since the Ripper murders, we can now consider this with a more discerning eye based on other cases. I propose that The Ripper stopped because he was close to being discovered.

Let's take the example of the Zodiac killer, who I have already referenced in this book, as he was like Jack the Ripper in many ways; he wrote letters, he left graffiti, the murders attributed to him eventually stopped, and he faded away without ever being unmasked.

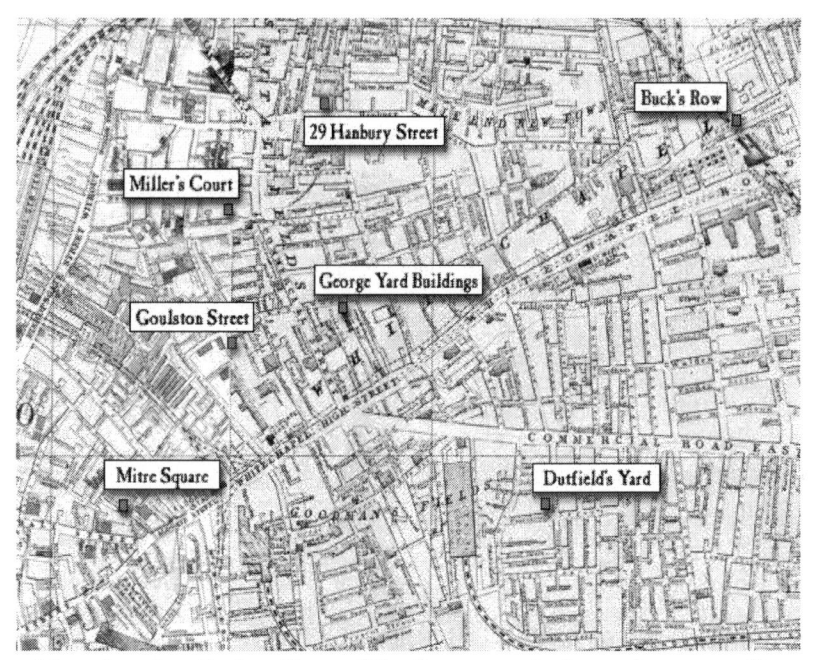

Map showing the locations of the five canonical murders, as well as the murder of Martha Tabram (casebook.org)

After the murder of taxi driver Paul Stine, the last confirmed Zodiac killing, he wrote a letter to the San Francisco Chronicle stating that he was no longer going to announce his murders. This was a strange volte-face considering his previous communications which showed that he was thrilled by telling people about his crimes and revelled in being a faceless, nameless threat. The night of that final murder was the time that Zodiac came closest to being captured, as he was not only spotted by some teenagers who gave an eyewitness description, but he also came face to face with two police officers who failed to apprehend him due to a communication mishap, as the radio dispatcher told them to look for a black man. Zodiac was highly intelligent and organized, and self-preservation was more important to him than killing. Although many people believe, mainly thanks to popular media and films, that the Zodiac has been named as Arthur Leigh Allen, much of what has been written about this suspect is born out of misinformation courtesy of San Francisco Chronicle cartoonist Robert Graysmith, and the case remains very much unsolved.

Dennis Rader, a.k.a. BTK (Bind, Torture, Kill) murdered ten people over the span of three decades, so he had sufficient control to wait as many as eight years in between victims. Forensic psychologist Katherine Ramsland, who interviewed Rader, has explained that this was due to changes in his life circumstances and demands as a husband, father or employee.

Serial killer Lonnie Franklin, a.k.a. The Grim Sleeper, is another example. He murdered more than ten prostitutes and earned his sepulchral nickname because he went completely quiet for over a decade after his last murder in 1988. The reason for this was his close call with his final victim, who survived being shot in the chest and left for dead in an alleyway. The subsequent investigation took police to within a few houses of where Franklin lived, and this close shave may have led him to cease killing. He eventually murdered again 14 years later and was caught in 2010 when familial DNA testing tied him to the crimes.

Applying this to Jack the Ripper, we could posit that he came close to being caught on the night of Mary Jane Kelly's murder and decided to stop. If this is true, it could point towards George Hutchinson. Had he been the killer, the fact that he was spotted by Sarah Cox, and was subsequently escorted around Whitechapel by police for two days to look for the elusive astrakhan man, could have been more than enough to make him lie low for a while.

It may be that he only planned to stop temporarily until things died down and the police presence reduced, but for some reason he never got the opportunity to try again, either due to ill health or a change in family circumstances. Nowadays, the idea of a serial killer succumbing to an illness like tuberculosis or rolling over and dying prematurely in his armchair seems unbelievable but given that the average life expectancy in London during the latter part of the 19th century was just 41 years of age, this should not be too surprising.

Alternatively, he could have been incarcerated for another crime and lived out the rest of his years behind bars, or moved to another continent, got married, or found another outlet for his desire to kill. Of course, all of this could be applicable to Jack the Ripper regardless of who he was. All discussion of suspects in this case is purely circumstantial, and I won't claim that the case is solved and that Hutchinson is indisputably the best suspect. There is no physical evidence tying him to the murders, nobody knows where he was on the nights of the other killings, and I cannot explain where he stored his knife or washed his hands.

It is a possibility that he did not make up his description of astrakhan man for any nefarious reasons, but embellished his account after having seen *someone*, or to make himself the centre of attention in the hope of making some money out of it, as the police did reimburse him for his time. Psychologists have proven that eyewitness descriptions can be influenced by newspaper accounts, being questioned by someone with their own hypothesis who asks leading questions, or by the person's own biases and experiences.

It is peculiar that given how little we know about George Hutchinson and who he really was, the tidbits we *do* have about him are extremely suspicious and hint that he was lying about some things at least. He remains my personal favourite suspect, but everyone is entitled to their own preferred theories and I am ready to be proven wrong. All we can do for now is continue to research, build on existing information, theorize, speculate, and theorize some more. We might never solve the case, but we can at least learn something from the experience and keep the victims' stories alive, remembering that they were all someone's mother, daughter, sister, partner, or friend, trying to survive in the unforgiving environs of the poverty and crime stricken East End.

Final Words

Jack the Ripper has been immortalized in film, books, and theatre throughout the decades. There are far too many to mention but I do recommend the 1988 TV series starring Michael Caine as Inspector Abberline. Although the royal conspiracy it favours has long since been debunked, it is an entertaining watch and visually captures the spirit of the time, with a particularly atmospheric representation of Hanbury Street. We will not examine that theory here but suffice it to say that a royal coach would not have gone unnoticed splashing through the narrow muddy alleyways of Whitechapel. Meanwhile, From Hell, the 2001 film starring Johnny Depp and Heather Graham, portrays the inhabitants of the East End as unrealistically glamorous and with more teeth than they really had.

Going back in time to 1944, The Lodger, starring Laird Cregar in the title role, alongside legend of film Merle Oberon, imagines a respectable, well-spoken man in a dark coat, carrying a sinister looking bag, lodging in a family home. When horrific murders begin to take place nearby, the household becomes suspicious, albeit far more slowly than the audience. Cregar died shortly after the making of the film, aged just 31, as the intensive weight loss he undertook for the role had put a strain on his body.

1979 movie Time After Time is well worth a watch, starring David Warner and a youthful Malcolm McDowell. Horror meets science fiction when The Ripper steals H.G. Wells' time machine to escape justice in his own time. For those who like gaming, Sherlock Holmes versus Jack the Ripper is an atmospheric, immersive foray into the world of Victorian London. The writers based it on their own number one suspect, who is revealed in the finale, but I won't give it away here.

Will there ever be an end to all the appearances of the Whitechapel Fiend in literature, media, and film? I doubt it. The case is over a century old, but it shows no signs of disappearing into the shadows the way The Ripper himself did. Just like many unsolved mysteries, the human mind refuses to let go of it, always wondering, and hoping that one day there will be an answer. We are fascinated by the enigma of it, the sheer impossibility of the killer's escapes from right under the noses of police and passers-by. Every year it seems a new story emerges; someone finds a letter in their attic or a great-grandfather's artefact, and each one believes whole-heartedly that *their* relative was The Ripper or knew him. Unlike the suspects and even the murderer himself, interest in the case will never die.

Controversially, a shawl was acquired by a Ripper enthusiast in 2007, which was purportedly found next to Catherine Eddowes' body. It was tested in a lab and the results showed that mitochondrial DNA matched a descendant of Eddowes, confirming the item of clothing really had belonged to her. Shockingly, DNA obtained from a semen stain on the shawl was also said to match a descendant of Aaron Kosminski. This might sound like it is all neatly wrapped up, but the provenance of the shawl has been questioned, the garment has been dated to more than one different time, and it could have come from anywhere in Europe. According to historians, there is inadequate documentation linking the shawl to Eddowes, and it did not appear in the police inventory of the clothes found on her when she died. Scientists have explained that mitochondrial DNA can only exclude a suspect and could potentially have come from many other people. It is unfortunate that the bloody piece of Eddowes' apron discarded in Goulston Street is no longer in the evidence locker, having been lost or destroyed sometime after the inquest. Back then, police were not to know that DNA testing would one day become a reality.

This is not the first occasion a forensic test on a supposed Ripper artefact has been attempted. US crime author Patricia Cornwell asked scientists to look for DNA in samples taken from the letters supposedly sent by the killer. Based on the findings, she concluded that painter Walter Sickert was guilty. Another analysis of the same letters found that the murderer could have been a woman. All this tells us is that the case remains well and truly open.

Something about the unholy reign of the most infamous murderer in history still sends a shiver down our spines as we draw our blankets tighter around us, safe indoors as autumn and winter arrive to cut short the days and lengthen the nights. We continue to imagine fog and streetlamps, Gladstone bags and black flapping cloaks, images which persist even though we know the difference between fact and fiction.

No matter how compelling the idea of this unnamed, unknown murderer might be, we must never forget that the story belongs to the victims, the women who were trying to navigate their stark and dreary existence, making money any way they could just to have a bed for the night. Those who had no choice but to put their trust in the men willing to pay for their bodies. Those who might even have recognized and greeted a familiar face with a smile, ushering him into a dark corner before realising they had made a terrible mistake. Those are the ones we should remember. The Canonical Five: Polly Nichols, Annie Chapman, Liz Stride, Catherine Eddowes, and Mary Jane Kelly, as well as those who came before and after. They are the ones this story is truly about. Gruelling, frustrating, fascinating, and heart-breaking, this case will certainly be with us for another century and more.

ABOUT THE AUTHOR

Prash Ganendran is a writer, podcaster, and voice actor known for the immersive true crime podcast 'Prash's Murder Map'. From the time he first stumbled across a book on Jack the Ripper in his local library aged eight, he has been fascinated with mysteries - and not just the morbid kind! His work history and hobbies are varied and have included equine biology, fraud investigation and photography. His IT experience as a Cisco Certified Network Engineer gave him the methodical approach to troubleshooting and evidence assessment that he uses in his true crime analysis, and he leaves no stone unturned to get to the bottom of a case. He is passionate about the psychological aspects of crime and understanding what factors create a killer.

He has worked with his wife, writer M. Ganendran, on several joint projects including The Porcelain Cat; a Victorian murder mystery, and No Albatrosses Allowed; a book of fiendish lateral thinking puzzles.

Prash will return with more true crime books in the near future.

You can find his work here, including video productions on YouTube and his immersive Jack the Ripper audio series: https://linktr.ee/prashsmurdermap

OTHER BOOKS BY THIS AUTHOR

I Just Wanted To Kill: 15 True Crime Cases

From the creator of the immersive Prash's Murder Map podcast comes this informative yet accessible volume, brimming with 15 sinister true crime cases from around the globe. Discover the stories behind some of the most horrifying murders, past and present, solved and unsolved, and dig deep into the psyche of the world's most notorious killers. *I Just Wanted To Kill* is a fascinating collection of true crime cases which take the reader on a challenging journey around the world, from the Californian coast terrorized by the Zodiac, to the Frankston Killer who shocked everyone Down Under, and many others in between.

The Porcelain Cat: A Detective Amarnath Mystery

As October of 1900 draws to a close, London's foggy, lamplit streets are hit by a string of burglaries which puzzle Scotland Yard. When they culminate in a gruesome murder, Sherlock Holmes is called in to investigate. But has he put the wrong man behind bars? In this atmospheric mystery, an Indian Detective seeks answers with the help of his assistant Madeleine Carmichael. With a touch of humour and a great deal of determination, the unconventional duo must use the most modern techniques to unravel the depths of human cunning.

Praise for the book:
"*Very much enjoyed this husband and wife creation. I would love to see this (and subsequent stories) as BBC productions. The writing put me right into the characters' world and was wonderfully and strikingly visual.*" – Taylor Ridgeway

Can I Ask A Favour?

If you enjoyed this book, I would really appreciate it if you could rate and review it on Amazon. As an independent author, it means a lot to receive feedback from readers.

Thanks for your support!

Prash checking out a historical crime scene

Sources

Adam, David, March 2019, "Does a new genetic analysis finally reveal the identity of Jack the Ripper?", Science Mag, https://www.sciencemag.org/news/2019/03/does-new-genetic-analysis-finally-reveal-identity-jack-ripper

Ackroyd, P & other contributors, 2008, "Jack the Ripper and the East End", Chatto & Windus, in association with the Museum in Docklands & Museum of London

"Another Supposed Murder at the East End", Evening News, 13 November 1888, Casebook.org, https://www.casebook.org/press_reports/evening_news/18881113.html

Author Interviews, 2015, "Dirty Old London", NPR, https://www.npr.org/2015/03/12/392332431/dirty-old-london-a-history-of-the-victorians-infamous-filth?t=1594571339515&t=1594657184121

"A Victorian Mental Asylum", June 2018, Science Museum London, https://www.sciencemuseum.org.uk/objects-and-stories/medicine/victorian-mental-asylum

Barnardo's, "Our History", https://www.barnardos.org.uk/who-we-are/our-history

Begg, P, Fido, M, & Skinner, K, 2015, "The Complete Jack the Ripper A-Z – The Ultimate Guide to the Ripper Mystery", John Blake

Blomer, Steve E, 2019, "Inside Bucks Row – Mary Ann Nichols: An Anatomy of Murder, The Whitechapel Murders Project Book 1"

British Newspaper Archive, Essex Herald, 27 August 1888

British Newspaper Archive, Lloyds Weekly Newspaper, 2 September 1888

British Newspaper Archive, Daily News, 4 September 1888

British Newspaper Archive, St James's Gazette, 10 September 1888,

British Newspaper Archive, St James's Gazette, 14 September 1888

British Newspaper Archive, Warwick and Warwickshire Advertiser, 15 September 1888

British Newspaper Archive, St James's Gazette, 6 October 1888

British Newspaper Archive, Lloyd's Weekly, 7 October 1888

British Newspaper Archive, Reynolds Newspaper, 7 October 1888

British Newspaper Archive, Morning Post, 16 October 1888

British Newspaper Archive, Reynolds Newspaper, 21 October 1888

British Newspaper Archive, London Evening Standard, 17 October 1888

British Newspaper Archive, Tamworth Herald, 10 November 1888

British Newspaper Archive, Pall Mall Gazette, 14 November 1888

British Newspaper Archive, Huddersfield Chronicle, 29 December 1888

British Newspaper Archive, Reynolds Newspaper, 22 February 1891

British Newspaper Archive, Cork Constitution, 19 May 1892

British Newspaper Archive, Reynolds Newspaper, 15 September 1946

"Bucks Row, Now Durward Street", Jack The Ripper 1888, Jack The Ripper.org, https://www.jack-the-ripper.org/bucks-row-then-and-now.htm

"Bucks Row", Casebook.org, https://www.casebook.org/victorian_london/sitepics.w-bucks.html

Chew, Stephen L., "Myth: Eyewitness Testimony is the Best Kind of Evidence", Samford University, August 20 2018, Association for Psychological Science, https://www.psychologicalscience.org/teaching/myth-eyewitness-testimony-is-the-best-kind-of-evidence.html

Clack, Robert & Hutchinson, Philip, 2009, "The London of Jack the Ripper Then and Now", The Breedon Books Publishing Company Limited, Derby

Cagliostro, Dina, PhD "Paranoid Schizophrenia", September 30 2020, https://www.psycom.net/paranoid-schizophrenia

Conrad Stoppler, Melissa, MD "Echolalia: Symptoms & Signs", 9 October 2019, MedicineNet, https://www.medicinenet.com/echolalia/symptoms.htm

Daley, Jason, March 2019, "No, We Still Cannot Confirm the Identity of Jack the Ripper", Smithsonian Mag, https://www.smithsonianmag.com/smart-news/jack-rippers-dna-collected-shawl-though-doubts-linger-180971726/

"Dr Bond's Post Mortem on Mary Kelly", Casebook.org, https://www.casebook.org/official_documents/pm-kelly.html

Evans, Stewart P., & Rumbelow, D, 2006, "Jack the Ripper – Scotland Yard Investigates", Sutton Publishing Ltd, Gloucestershire

"Dr Francis Tumblety", Jack The Ripper Tour, https://www.jack-the-ripper-tour.com/francis-tumblety/

"Dutfield's Yard", Casebook.org, https://wiki.casebook.org/dutfield's_yard.html

Evans, Stewart P., & Skinner, K, 2001, "The Ultimate Jack the Ripper Sourcebook An Illustrated Encyclopedia", Robinson London

Evans, Stewart P., "Ex-Detective Inspector Edmund Reid and Jack the Ripper", Casebook.org, https://www.casebook.org/dissertations/spe3.html

Evening News, 12th November 1888, Casebook.org, https://www.casebook.org/press_reports/evening_news/18881112.html

"George Chapman", Casebook.org, https://www.casebook.org/suspects/gchapman.html

Godl, John, "The Life and Crimes of Frederick Bailey Deeming", Casebook.org, https://www.casebook.org/dissertations/dst-deeming.html

Griffiths, Arthur, "Mysteries of Police and Crime", Casebook.org, https://www.casebook.org/ripper_media/rps.griffiths.html

Hannaford, Scott, "Anderson and the Swanson Marginalia", Casebook.org, https://www.casebook.org/dissertations/dst-andr.html

Higginbotham, Peter, "Common Lodging Houses," Workhouses.org, http://www.workhouses.org.uk/lodging/

Impact of the DSM-IV to DSM-5 Changes on the National Survey on Drug Use and Health, Substance Abuse and Mental Health Services Administration (US), Table 3.22, DSM-IV to DSM-5 Schizophrenia Comparison, June 2016, https://www.ncbi.nlm.nih.gov/books/NBK519704/table/ch3.t22/

"Inquest: Annie Chapman", Casebook.org, https://www.casebook.org/official_documents/inquests/inquest_chapman.html

"Jack the Ripper", FBI Records: The Vault, July 6 1988, https://vault.fbi.gov/Jack%20the%20Ripper/Jack%20the%20Ripper%20Part%201%20of%201/view

"Jack the Ripper Murder Sites Then and Now - Buck's Row", Jack the Ripper Tour, Feb 2015, https://www.youtube.com/watch?v=buQ_c1JlBZU

"Jacob Levy", JTR Forums, https://www.jtrforums.com/forum/persons-of-interest-or-actual-suspects/jacob-levy/10445-jacob-levy/page8

"John Pizer", Casebook.org, https://www.casebook.org/ripper_media/book_reviews/non-fiction/cjmorley/149.html

Johnson, Ben, "The Great Horse Manure Crisis of 1894", History Magazine, https://www.historic-uk.com/HistoryUK/HistoryofBritain/Great-Horse-Manure-Crisis-of-1894/

Jones, Richard, January 2019, "Drinking in the East End", Drinking and Drunkenness in the Victorian East End, Jack The Ripper Tour, https://www.jack-the-ripper-tour.com/generalnews/drinking-in-the-east-end/

Jones, Richard, "The East End Common Lodging Houses", Jack The Ripper.org, https://www.jack-the-ripper.org/common-lodging-houses.htm

Jones, Richard, July 2020, "The View from Liverpool", The High Rip Gangs and the Jack the Ripper Murders, Jack The Ripper Tour, https://www.jack-the-ripper-tour.com/generalnews/the-view-from-liverpool/

Jones, Richard, "The Jewish East End", Jack The Ripper.org, https://www.jack-the-ripper.org/jewish-east-end.htm

Jones, Richard, "The Whitechapel Murders and the Jewish Community", Jack The Ripper.org, https://www.jack-the-ripper.org/jewish-history.htm

Jones, Richard, "The Dear Boss Letter", Jack the Ripper.org, https://www.jack-the-ripper.org/dear-boss.htm

Jones, Richard, "The Goulston Street Graffito – The Juwes Are The Men", Jack The Ripper.org, https://www.jack-the-ripper.org/goulston-street-graffito.htm

Jones, Richard, July 2016, "The Suicide of Dr Thomas Bond", Jack The Ripper Tour, https://www.jack-the-ripper-tour.com/generalnews/the-suicide-of-dr-thomas-bond/

Jones, Richard, "Aaron Kosminski", JacktheRipper.org, https://www.jack-the-ripper.org/kosminski.htm

Jones, Richard, "Aaron Kosminski – Jack the Ripper Prime Suspect?" 29 July 2021, YouTube, https://www.youtube.com/watch?v=wSlBZPCEn9M

Jones, Richard, "Donald Sutherland Swanson", JacktheRipper.org, https://www.jack-the-ripper.org/swanson.htm

Jones, Richard, "Frances Coles – Murdered 13th February 1891", JacktheRipper.org, https://www.jack-the-ripper.org/frances-coles.htm

Jones, Richard, "Montague John Druitt", JacktheRipper.org, https://www.jack-the-ripper.org/druitt.htm

Jones, Richard, "The Pinchin Street Torso", JacktheRipper.org, https://www.jack-the-ripper.org/pinchin-street-torso.htm

Jones, Richard, "Sir Melville Leslie Macnaghten", JacktheRipper.org, https://www.jack-the-ripper.org/macnaghten.htm

"Joseph Barnett", Casebook.org, https://www.casebook.org/suspects/barnett.html

Khazan, Olga, July 2017, "Nearly Half of All Murdered Women are Killed by Romantic Partners", The Atlantic, https://www.theatlantic.com/health/archive/2017/07/homicides-women/534306/

Knight, A & Watson, K, 2017, "Was Jack the Ripper a Slaughterman? Human-Animal violence and the world's most infamous serial killer", https://www.ncbi.nlm.nih.gov/pmc/articles/PMC5406675/

Leighton, DJ, 2006, "The Secret Lives of Montague Druitt", Sutton

Leisinger, Claudia, "The Last of the Billingsgate Fish Porters", https://www.claudialeisinger.com/the-last-of-the-billigsgate-fish-porters

Lester, David, & White, John, "Which Serial Killers commit suicide? An exploratory study", Forensic Science International, November 2012, Researchgate, https://www.researchgate.net/publication/232962840_Which_serial_killers_commit_suicide_An_exploratory_study

London's Royal Docks, "Forgotten Stories: Hop-Picking in the fields of Kent", https://londonsroyaldocks.com/forgotten-stories-hop-picking-fields-kent/

"Lonnie Franklin," Murderpedia, https://murderpedia.org/male.F/f/franklin-lonnie.htm

LSE, "Charles Booth's London Poverty Maps and Police Notebooks", https://booth.lse.ac.uk/

McBean, Brett, "Jacob Levy", 7 November 2010, Saucy Jacky Blog, https://saucyjacky.wordpress.com/suspects/my-top-3-suspects/1-jacob-levy/

Messori, Leryn R., "Frequencies Between Serial Killer Typology and Theorized Etiological Factors", Antioch University , 2016, https://aura.antioch.edu/cgi/viewcontent.cgi?article=1322&context=etds

Mooney, Graham, "Overall life expectancy at birth years London 1730 to 1910", Table 1, ResearchGate, https://www.researchgate.net/figure/Overall-life-expectancy-at-birth-years-London-1730-to-1910_tbl1_229937211

New York Herald resources, Casebook.org, https://www.casebook.org/press_reports/new_york_herald/881111.html

Osborne, Derek F., "The Man Who Shielded Jack the Ripper – George Hutchinson and his Statement: An Analysis", Casebook.org, https://www.casebook.org/dissertations/ripperoo-hutch.html

Paley, Bruce, 1996, "Jack the Ripper: The Simple Truth", Headline

Pall Mall Gazette, 15 September 1888, "The Pensioner's Statement – Another Futile Arrest – Funeral of the Latest Victim", Casebook.org, https://www.casebook.org/press_reports/pall_mall_gazette/18880915.html

Pall Mall Gazette, 24 March 1903, Casebook.org, https://www.casebook.org/press_reports/pall_mall_gazette/19030324.html

"Richard Chase", Murderpedia, https://murderpedia.org/male.C/c/chase-richard.htm

Rippervision, "To Catch A Killer: The Hunt for the Ripper", JackTheRipperTour.com, https://thejacktherippertour.com/blog/to-catch-a-killer-the-hunt-for-jack-the-ripper/

Roland, Paul, 2006, "The Crimes of Jack the Ripper", Arcturus Foulsham

Sederstrom, Jill, "Why did Dennis Rader, the BTK Killer, wait so long between his murders?", August 29 2018, Oxygen True Crime, https://www.oxygen.com/martinis-murder/dennis-rader-btk-killer-wait-so-long-between-his-murder-victims

Schram, Jamie, "Why I Killed Jeffrey Dahmer", New York Post, April 28 2015 https://nypost.com/2015/04/28/meet-the-prisoner-who-murdered-killer-cannibal-jeffrey-dahmer/

Slade, Paul, 2013, "Broadside Ballads Songs, Murder Ballads", PlanetSlade.com, http://www.planetslade.com/broadside-ballads-mary-arnold.html

Smith, Sir Henry, 1910, "From Constable to Commissioner", Chatto & Windus [facsimile reprint 2015]

Spallek, Andrew, "The 'West of England MP' Identified", Casebook.org, https://www.casebook.org/dissertations/rip-west-of-england.html

"Suspects", Casebook.org, https://www.casebook.org/suspects/

"The East End Trouble", East London Observer, 15 September 1888, Casebook.org, https://www.casebook.org/press_reports/east_london_observer/elo880915.html

"The East End Murders", Evening News, 15 November 1888, Casebook.org, https://www.casebook.org/press_reports/evening_news/18881115.html

"The Latest Horror", Evening News, 12 November 1888, Casebook.org, https://www.casebook.org/press_reports/evening_news/18881112.html

"The Reign of Terror in Whitechapel", Evening News, 1 October 1888, Casebook.org, https://www.casebook.org/press_reports/evening_news/18881001.html

"The Ten Bells Pub", Casebook.org, https://www.casebook.org/victorian_london/tenbells.html

"The Macnaghten Memoranda", Casebook.org, https://www.casebook.org/official_documents/memo.html

Uren, Amanda, "Hop Pickers c. 1900 – 1949", Mashable.com, https://mashable.com/2017/06/03/hop-pickers/?europe=true

"Victoria Working Men's Home", Casebook.org, https://wiki.casebook.org/victoria_working_men's_home.html

"Walter Purkis", July 2009, https://kpoulin1.wordpress.com/2009/07/14/walter-purkis/ from Lloyds Weekly Newspaper, 9th September 1888

"Wentworth Dwellings", Casebook.org, https://wiki.casebook.org/wentworth_dwellings.html

Whittington-Egan, Richard, 1975, "A Casebook on Jack the Ripper", Wildy & Sons Ltd

Williams, Paul, 2020, "Jack the Ripper Suspects: The Definitive Guide and Encyclopaedia"

Zuppello, Suzanne, "Grim Sleeper Serial Killer: Everything you need to know", August 18 2016, Rolling Stone, https://www.rollingstone.com/culture/culture-features/grim-sleeper-serial-killer-everything-you-need-to-know-252246/

Index

A

Abberline, Inspector Frederick   46, 66, 91, 178, 189, 219, 234, 235, 248, 260, 265, 267, 272
Aberconway, Lady Christabel   216
Albrook, Lizzie   161, 163
Anderson, Robert   92, 182, 189, 225, 251
Arnold, Superintendent   91, 153
Astrakhan Man   168, 171, 172, 230, 250, 257, 260, 261, 262, 263, 265, 266, 271
Asylums   223

B

Bagster Phillips, George   55, 56, 64, 90, 103, 105, 183, 184, 186, 191, 194
Barnaby and Burgho   142, 152, 190
Barnardo, Thomas   96, 279
Barnett, Joseph   154, 159, 161, 162, 163, 173, 174, 244, 245, 246, 248, 286
Barnett, Reverend Samuel   12, 13, 76
Batty Street   146
Baxter, Wynne   48, 65, 66, 67, 176, 182, 192
Beck, Inspector   100, 151, 152, 191
Berner Street   84, 85, 89, 91, 97, 98, 99, 102, 194, 229
Billingsgate Fish Market   43, 159
Blackwell, Dr   90
Blenkinsop, James   138
Bond, Dr Thomas   155, 182, 189, 206, 207, 246
Booth, Charles   60, 265, 287
Bowyer, Thomas   150, 173
Brady Street   48, 50
Britannia Public House   61
Brown, Dr Gordon   117
Brown, James   99, 101
Brown's Stable Yard   32, 45, 50, 193
Bryant & May   10

Bucks Row   30, 32, 34, 35, 36, 37, 38, 42, 44, 45, 46, 47, 48, 49, 51, 52, 55, 176, 193, 197, 244, 252, 253, 254, 255, 265, 280, 281

C

Cadosch, Albert	64, 124
Central News Agency	79, 84
Chandler, Inspector	52, 55
Chapman, Annie	6, 52, 57, 58, 63, 66, 69, 78, 84, 103, 122, 144, 145, 172, 177, 193, 218, 230, 233, 249, 256, 275
Chapman, George	232, 233, 234, 235, 237, 283
Christ Church	148, 168
Coldwell, Charlotte	48
Coles, Frances	185, 186, 191, 197, 286
Colney Hatch	75, 223, 224, 226, 227, 228
Commercial Road	20, 25, 61, 97, 102, 182, 184
Conway, Thomas	108, 109, 142
Cooney's Lodging House	110, 112, 114, 159
Cooper, Eliza	61
Coram, Thomas	105
Cox, Mary Ann	163, 164, 172
Criminal Profiling	189, 203, 206, 207, 209, 247, 248
Cross, Charles	See Lechmere, Charles
Crossingham's Lodging House	61, 168
Cutbush, Thomas	210, 241, 243

D

Davis, John	52
Dear Boss	80, 81, 82, 84, 134, 137, 176, 246, 285
Deeming, Frederick	237, 238
Dew, Detective Constable	152
Diemschutz, Louis	86, 87, 88, 103, 258
Donovan, Timothy	61
Dorset Street 10, 60, 61, 62, 67, 130, 146, 147, 149, 150, 167, 170, 174, 177, 178, 195, 247, 260, 262, 264, 265	
Druitt, Montague John	211, 212, 213, 286
Durward Street	42, 50, 281
Dutfield's Yard 83, 84, 85, 86, 89, 98, 99, 104, 107, 194, 200, 258, 282	

E

Eagle, Morris 88, 99
Eddowes, Catherine 6, 107, 108, 112, 113, 114, 115, 117, 120, 121, 123, 127, 129, 134, 138, 140, 142, 145, 159, 175, 194, 208, 229, 244, 245, 247, 249, 251, 256, 262, 264, 274, 275
Essex Wharf 45, 46, 50

F

Farquharson, Henry 216
Fiddymont, Mrs 75
Fleming, Joseph 158, 163, 264
Flower and Dean Street 10, 76, 95, 96, 110, 112, 159, 166
From Hell 134, 135, 247, 272

G

Gardner and Best 97, 100
George Yard Buildings 20, 21, 27
Goulston Street 125, 127, 129, 131, 218, 249, 250, 274, 285
Graffito 125, 285
Greenwood, James 10

H

Halse, Detective Constable 127, 128, 129, 130, 131
Hanbury Street 32, 52, 53, 54, 55, 62, 63, 67, 73, 76, 78, 79, 84, 124, 172, 193, 230, 249, 261, 272
Hardiman, Harriet 52
Harris, Harry 138, 229
Harvey, Maria 154, 162, 163
Harvey, PC James 116
Hewitt, Francis Fisher 27
Holland, Emily 39, 41, 44, 142
Hutchinson, George 165, 167, 173, 174, 178, 230, 250, 257, 261, 262, 263, 264, 266, 270, 272

I

Isenschmid, Jacob 75
Itchy Park *See* Christ Church

J

Jews 8, 70, 72, 73, 86, 87, 125, 127, 128, 195, 223, 229, 230, 231

K

Kaminski, Nathan 228
Kelly, John 109, 110, 112, 113, 114, 140, 143, 158
Kelly, Mary Jane 6, 114, 144, 145, 154, 156, 158, 160, 166, 167, 176, 177, 179, 181, 183, 190, 194, 197, 200, 207, 215, 216, 227, 244, 245, 247, 248, 250, 251, 256, 257, 258, 263, 265, 267, 270, 275
Kidney, Michael 94, 95, 96, 104, 229
Killeen, Dr Timothy 22
King's Bench Walk 213, 218
Kosminski, Aaron 222, 224, 226, 228, 230, 274, 285
Kozebrodsky, Isaac 88

L

Lamb, Constable 88, 89, 91
Lane, Catherine 96
Lawende, Joseph 138, 172, 208, 229, 244, 249, 261
Lechmere, Charles 32, 34, 36, 38, 43, 44, 49, 252, 253, 254, 255, 256, 257, 265
Levy, Jacob 248, 249, 250, 252, 284, 287
Levy, Joseph Hyam 138, 229, 249
Lewis, Maurice 173
Lewis, Sarah 170, 172, 174, 258, 259, 260, 263
Lilley, Harriet 49
Lipski 73, 86, 229
Llewellyn, Dr 34, 35, 36
Lodging houses 18, 19, 39, 41, 42, 60, 62, 67, 95, 96, 101, 104, 112, 163, 165, 170, 172, 174, 179, 181, 183, 184, 186, 260, 264
Long, Elizabeth 63, 64, 172, 230, 249, 261
Long, PC Alfred 125, 127
Lusk, George 67, 68, 133, 135, 247

M

Marginalia 225, 226, 228, 230
Marshall, William 97, 98, 100, 101
Maxwell, Caroline 172

McCarthy, John 150, 152, 173, 174, 178
McKenzie, Alice 183, 191
Metropolitan Police 19, 33, 125, 127, 128, 130, 135, 152, 157, 181, 189, 191, 210
Middlesex Street 8, 131, 132, 249, 250
Miller's Court 130, 145, 146, 147, 149, 150, 152, 153, 154, 159, 162, 163, 164, 165, 168, 170, 173, 174, 177, 178, 197, 200, 244, 245, 247, 250, 259, 262, 264, 265, 266, 268
Mitre Square 105, 107, 115, 116, 117, 118, 122, 123, 124, 129, 130, 131, 138, 140, 194, 218, 229, 244, 249
Mizen, Constable 32, 33, 34, 36, 38, 197
Morris, George 117, 122
Morrison, Arthur G. 47
Mortimer, Fanny 98
Mulshaw, Patrick 48
Mylett, Catherine 182

N

Neil, Constable 34
Nichols, Mary Ann 6, 30, 38, 39, 40, 41, 43, 44, 45, 50, 51, 52, 55, 66, 69, 145, 156, 189, 193, 218, 244, 252, 253, 254, 275

O

Ostrog, Michael 211, 221, 222

P

Packer, Matthew 98
Palmer, Amelia 60, 62
Paranoid Schizophrenia 203, 206, 243
Paul, Robert 32, 34, 36, 38, 43, 253, 254, 255, 256, 265
Paumier, Mrs 173
Pearly Poll 22, 26, 27
Peel Act 14
Petticoat Lane 10, 132, 263, 265
Phillips, Watts 10
Phossy Jaw 11
Pickett, Catherine 164, 172
Pinchin Street 85, 184, 185, 191, 197, 286

Pizer, John	70, 102
Prater, Elizabeth	165, 172
Purkiss	45, 46

R

Reid, Edmund	19, 20, 25, 26, 27, 45, 66, 91, 92, 179, 187, 188, 208, 231, 232, 283
Richardson, Amelia	53, 62
Richardson, John	62, 63, 70
Robinson, Detective Sergeant	141, 142

S

Sagar, Inspector Robert	227, 228, 251, 252
Saucy Jacky	136, 137, 138, 287
Schwartz, Israel	84, 93, 101, 104, 229
Seaside home	225, 228, 229, 230
Sequeira, Dr George	117, 122
Smith, Emma	6, 17, 18, 20, 41, 145
Smith, Major Henry	127, 129, 131, 247, 264, 268
Smith, PC William	89, 98, 99, 100
Spratling, Inspector	35
St Botolph's Church	114, 115
St Mary's Church	18
Stanley, Ted	61, 67
Stride, Elizabeth	6, 83, 90, 93, 94, 96, 97, 98, 100, 101, 102, 103, 104, 105, 107, 136, 137, 145, 156, 172, 185, 194, 208, 229, 256, 258, 275
Swanson, Donald	99, 127, 191, 225, 226

T

Tabram, Martha	6, 22, 24, 28, 45, 65, 105, 145
Tanner, Mrs	96
Thain, Constable	34, 47, 49
Thames Torso Murders	185
Thrawl Street	9, 10, 41, 159, 266
Tumblety, Dr Francis	238, 239, 240, 282

V

Valentine's School	213

Venturney, Julia	163
Victoria Working Men's Home	165, 265, 290

W

Warren, Sir Charles	14, 78, 127, 141, 142, 153, 177, 190, 191
Watkins, PC Edward	117
Wentworth Dwellings	19, 125, 126, 127, 131, 132, 250, 291
Wentworth Street	19, 132, 263
White's Row	186
Whitechapel Vigilance Committee	67, 68, 133, 180
Winthrop Street	48, 193, 255
Workhouse	11, 39, 40, 62, 75, 94, 112, 200

Printed in Poland
by Amazon Fulfillment
Poland Sp. z o.o., Wrocław
15 December 2022

355bab5d-0061-4ebd-aa87-5bf82ef310ecR01